Dead Countries of the Nineteenth and Twentieth Centuries

Aden to Zululand

by
Les Harding

The Scarecrow Press, Inc.
Lanham, Md., & London
1998

SCARECROW PRESS, INC.

Published in the United States of America
by Scarecrow Press, Inc.
4720 Boston Way
Lanham, Maryland 20706

British Library Cataloguing in Publication Information Available

Library of Congress Cataloging-in-Publication Data

Harding, Les. 1950–
    Dead countries of the nineteenth and the twentieth centuries :
Aden to Zululand / by Les Harding.
        p. cm.
    Includes bibliographical references.
    ISBN: 978-0-8108-3445-3
    ISBN: 0-8108-3445-6
    1. Postage stamps—History. 2. Stamp collecting. I. Title.
  HE6182.H34   1998
909—dc21   97-39850
                                             CIP

Contents

Contents

List of Maps

Preface

In better philatelic circles a dead country is the term used for a place, not necessarily a sovereign country, that once issued postage stamps but now no longer does so, usually because it has ceased to exist. Although I do collect stamps, my interest in dead countries has probably arisen from the fact that I was born in a dead country — Newfoundland.

One day I was leafing through a book on postage stamps of the world and noticed how many dead countries there were. Becoming curious to know something about these dead countries it did not take long to discover that there was no handy place to find the basic information I sought. What I have attempted to do here is to provide that handy place. I have gone beyond philately and identified all the countries, colonies, protectorates, princely states, etc. that I could find that have existed since 1800 but now do not and to provide some basic statistics and a short almanac-type entry for each, explaining how it came into existence, what happened to it while it did exist and why it does not exist now. For illustrations I have used stamps as well as quotations from the vast world of travel literature. I admit that on a few occasions I had to fudge my quotations. Try as I might I could not find a traveler who visited the Duchy of Reuss-Schleitz and wrote about it in English. However I did find a quote about the general area it is in. The quotations were chosen to be as varied as possible. Some are laudatory, while others are definitely not. With *Dead Countries of the Nineteenth and Twentieth Centuries: Aden to Zululand* I have attempted to combine the usefulness of a reference book with the stimulus of a book that is fun and interesting to read. Whether or not I have succeeded is for the reader to decide.

My primary criterion for dead country status was political. The place in question had to have had some sort of political independence, semi-independence, or distinctiveness that it no longer has. Thus Czechoslovakia is included because it was born in 1918 out of the ruins of the Austro-Hungarian Empire (a dead country in its own right) and ceased to exist on January 1, 1993, when it was divided into the Czech Republic and Slovakia. Puerto Rico is not included because it went from being a Spanish to an American territory and to my way of thinking has never been a dead country or lost its semi-independent status.

My other criterion for inclusion was name change. Even though Siam, Abyssinia and Persia exist today as Thailand, Ethiopia and Iran I have included them as dead countries up until the adoption of their modern names.

Inevitably there are gray areas. St. Pierre and Miquelon, a French-owned archipelago off the Newfoundland coast, has been included as a dead country because it seems to me to have abandoned colonial status and been fully integrated into the French republic. Others might disagree. St. Pierre and Miquelon continues to issue its own stamps, for instance. I have endeavoured to be as inclusive and accurate as possible with my dead countries but any deficiencies or omissions are entirely my fault.

Acknowledgments

A thank you to the staff of the Queen Elizabeth II Library at the Memorial University of Newfoundland who put up with my presence for many hours in the reference room and to Dianne Taylor-Harding and Kathryn Collins, Fisheries and Marine Institute for proofreading and text processing assistance. A thank you to the staff of the Map and Design Library, Memorial University for help with maps.

Thank you to the following for permission to use material under copyright:
— John Murray (Publishers) Ltd. for quotations from Arthur Grimble's *A Pattern of Islands*, Freya Stark's *Coast of Incense*, Patrick Leigh Fermor's *Time of Gifts* and *Traveller's Tree*, and Dervla Murphy's *In Ethiopia with a Mule.*
— A quote from *Brazilian Adventure* by Peter Fleming, used by permission of Jonathan Cape, publisher.
— A quote from *The Middle Passage* (Penguin Books 1969, first published by André Deutsch, London) copyright (c) V.S. Naipaul, 1962. Reproduced by permission of Penguin Books Ltd.
— A quote from *Much Sounding of Bugles* reproduced by permission of Curtis Brown Ltd., London on behalf of Betty Harris. Copyright (c) John Harris 1975.
— The National Geographic Society for quotes from the following *National Geographic* magazine articles: "Sailing Forbidden Coasts," by Ida Treat, September 1931; "What is the Saar?" by Frederick Simpich, February 1935; "Flying around the Baltic," by Douglas Chandler, June

1938; "Rhodes, and Italy's Aegean Islands," by Dorothy Hosmer, April 1941; "A Visit to Three Arab Kingdoms," by Junius B. Wood, May 1923.

— A quote from S.J. Perelman's *Westward Ha!* (c) 1948, Random House.

— HarperCollins Publishers for a quote from *Inside Africa* by John Gunther. Copyright (c) 1955.

— Malyn Newit for permission to quote from his book *The Comoro Islands*.

— Excerpt from *HANOI*, copyright (c) 1968 by Mary McCarthy, reprinted by permission of Harcourt Brace & Company.

— A quote from Osbert Sitwell's *Escape with Me*, published by Macmillan in 1939. Reprinted by permission of David Higham Associates.

— A quote from George Woodcock's *Asia, Gods & Cities* copyright (c) 1966. Used by permission of Sheil Land Associates Ltd.

— A quote from an article in the *Observer*, 22 July 1979. Copyright (c) 1979 by Conor Cruise O'Brien. Reproduced by permission of Greene & Heaton Ltd.

— A quote from John Gunther's *Inside Asia*. Used by permission of Jane Gunther.

— Quotes from *Through the Labyrinth* (c) 1979 by Jonathan Raban. Reprinted with the permission of Aitken & Stone Ltd.

— A quote from the *Gulf Emirates* by Philippe Lanois, reprinted with permission of Les Éditions Nagel.

— A quote from *Biafra* (c) Frederick Forsyth, 1969. Reprinted by permission of Curtis Brown on behalf of Frederick Forsyth.

— A quote from *Destinations: Essays From Rolling Stone* by Jan Morris copyright (c) by Rolling Stone Press and Jan Morris, and a quote from Arnold Toynbee's *East to West*. Both used by permission of Oxford University Press.

— An extract from *White Tribes of Africa* by Richard West. Reprinted by permission of the Peters Fraser & Dunlop Group Ltd.

— A quote from Arthur J. Knoll's *Togo Under Imperial Germany, 1884-1914*. Used by permission of the Hoover Institution.

— A quote from "Fiasco in Addis Ababa," by Patrick Balfour, that appeared in *Abyssinian Stop Press*, edited by Ladislas Farago. Used by permission of Robert Hale Ltd.

— A quote from *Guinea: the Mobilization of a People* by Claude Rivière. Used by permission of Cornell University Press.
— An extract from Hugh A Stayt's *Bavenda* used by permission of Frank Cass & Company Ltd.

I have attempted to contact all copyright holders of quoted material. Some have proven elusive. Omissions will be corrected in any future edition.

CHAPTER 1

North America

America was too big to have been discovered all at one time. It would have been better for the graces if it had been discovered in pieces about the size of France and Germany at a time.
— Samuel Butler, 1934.

BRITISH COLUMBIA / NEW CALEDONIA

If I had known what it was like I wouldn't have been content with a mere visit. I'd have been born here.
— Stephen Leacock, 1937.

Area: 366,253 sq. miles (948,596 sq. km); Capital: Victoria
Population: 36,247 (est. 1871)

A mountainous colony on the Pacific coast of Canada. Before gold was discovered along the lower Fraser River in 1857 the Indians of British Columbia had been visited by few Europeans other than explorers and fur traders. With the gold came the gold rush and an influx of settlers, miners and speculators. The Colony of British Columbia was established in 1858 in order to bring some control over the gold seekers. The name of the territory had been New Caledonia, after its alleged resemblance to the Highlands of Scotland, but it was changed to British Columbia to avoid confusion with the French island of New Caledonia in the South Pacific. Vancouver Island was not originally part of British Columbia but a separate colony. However, the governor of Vancouver Island was also governor of the new colony on the mainland. In order to reduce the cost of administration the British merged Vancouver Island and British Columbia in 1866, under the name of the latter. For the first two years the capital was in New Westminster but in 1868 it was removed to Victoria, on the island, the largest settlement. In 1871 British Columbia decided to join the Dominion of Canada as a province on the understanding that the Government of Canada would build a railway to the Pacific coast. The Canadian Pacific Railway was constructed but the people of British Columbia had to wait fifteen years to see it.

Miner panning gold

Readings: Johnston, 1996; Ormsby, 1958.

CALIFORNIA REPUBLIC

California is an Italy without its art.
— Oscar Wilde, 1882.

Area: 158,693 sq. miles (411,000 sq. km); Capital: Sonoma
Population: 65,000 (est. 1848)

A large territory on the Pacific coast of what became the United States. California was in the Spanish sphere of influence for about 250 years before the first European settlement was established in 1769, at San Diego. Los Angeles was founded in 1781. When Mexico achieved its independence from Spain in 1821 California was included as its sparsely populated northwestern province. Mexico secularized most of the Spanish missions in California and encouraged settlers to immigrate. Most of the newcomers were Americans who soon began to agitate for annexation to the United States. The United States offered to buy California in 1845 but the offer was rejected by Mexico. In

1846 American settlers took matters into their own hands and proclaimed the Republic of California. Their flag, depicting a lone red star and a crudely drawn grizzly bear surmounting the words "California Republic," became the basis for the state flag of California. Within the year war broke out between Mexico and the United States. In 1848 a defeated Mexico was compelled to cede California to the United States nine days before gold was discovered at Sutter's Mill. A wild gold rush ensued which swelled California's population overnight. California bypassed the customary period of being a territory and was admitted to the United States as the 31st state in 1850.

Sutter's Mill

Readings: Bean, 1968; Lavender, 1976.

CAPE BRETON ISLAND

> North America is a large island to the west of the continent of Cape Breton.
> - Ray Smith, 1967.

Area: 3,981 sq. miles (10,311 sq. km); Capital: Sydney
Population: 27,580 (est. 1851)

A rugged island separated from the mainland of Nova Scotia by the narrow Strait of Canso. Cape Breton Island, the name is derived from Cap Breton in the Basque region of France, was probably visited by Basque fishermen in the 15th century. The French claimed the island as part of Acadia but basically ignored it for many years. It was only after the rest of Acadia was ceded to the British in 1713 that the French began to take an interest in the island that remained to them. Recognizing Cape Breton's strategic importance, guarding the entrance to the Gulf of St. Lawrence and New France (Québec), the French constructed the immense Fortress of Louisbourg, the largest

NORTH AMERICA
and the WEST INDIES

1 Vancouver Island	11 St. Pierre and Miquelon	22 Mosquito Coast
2 British Columbia	12 Newfoundland	23 Free State of the Isthmus
3 Rupert's Land	13 California Republic	24 Canal Zone
4 Red River Colony	14 Texas	25 Turks Islands
5 Upper Canada	15 Republic of the Rio Grande	26 Danish West Indies
6 Lower Canada	16 Spanish Florida	27 St. Christopher—Nevis—Anguilla
5 + 6 Province of Canada	17 Confederate States of America	28 Guadeloupe
7 New Brunswick	18 Yucatán	29 Martinique
8 Prince Edward Island	19 Chiapas	30 Tobago
9 Nova Scotia	20 British Honduras	31 Trinidad
10 Cape Breton Island	21 Central American Federation	

fortification in North America. Despite its massive walls the fort was destroyed in the Seven Year's War and Cape Breton Island was ceded to the British in 1763 and made part of Nova Scotia. In 1784 Cape Breton Island became a separate colony as United Empire Loyalists, waves of Scottish immigrants and returning Acadians settled the island. Since 1820 Cape Breton Island has again been part of Nova Scotia.

Margaree River, Cape Breton Island

Readings: Donovan, 1990; Hornsby, 1992.

CHIAPAS

A scene of wild and surpassing beauty, with banks shaded by some of the noblest trees of the tropical forests, water as clear as crystal, and fish a foot long playing in it as gently as if there were no fishhooks.
— John L. Stephens, 1841.

Area: 28,732 sq. miles (74,416 sq. km); Capital: Tuxtla Gutiérrez
Population: 150,000 (est. 1869)

A state in southeastern Mexico bordered by Guatemala and the Pacific ocean. From the 1520s to 1821 Chiapas was part of the Spanish Captaincy-General of Guatemala. With the breakup of the Spanish empire Chiapas achieved a measure of independence until it was incorporated into Mexico in 1824.

Mayan bas-relief

Readings: Greene, 1979; Stephens, 1841.

CONFEDERATE STATES OF AMERICA

> In the South, the war is what A.D. is elsewhere: they date from it.
> — Mark Twain, 1883.

Area: 756,000 sq. miles (1,950,000 sq. km); Capital: Richmond
Population: 9,000,000 (est. 1860)

The Confederate States of America comprised the southern states of Virginia, North Carolina, South Carolina, Georgia, Florida, Tennessee, Alabama, Mississippi, Louisiana, Arkansas and Texas which seceded from the United States (1860-1861). Rump confederate governments were also formed for Kentucky and Missouri. Southerners felt themselves subject to economic and political domination by the rising power of the industrializing North and many believed that their way of life depended upon the continuation of slavery and its expansion to new states. Abraham Lincoln and the Republican Party were opposed to slavery and the southern states, fearing that their rights were in danger, seceded and created their own republic. Northerners were not willing to dissolve the Union and war broke out in 1861. The American Civil War, the bloodiest war in American history, was fought almost entirely on Confederate soil. When the conflict ended in 1865 the South had been defeated and its territory devastated. In all, about 750,000 men served in the army of the Confederacy. Though their cause was probably hopeless from the start, the Confederate States, with their smaller population and much smaller industrial base, put up a remarkable fight.

With the end of the Civil War came the period known as Reconstruction. The last federal troops were withdrawn from the South in 1877 and the rebellious states re-admitted to the Union.

Jefferson Davis

Readings: Eaton, 1975; McPherson, 1982.

LOWER CANADA / CANADA EAST

> You may perhaps *Americanise*, but depend upon it . . . you will never *Anglicise* the French inhabitants of the Province.
> — Lord Elgin, 1848.

Area: 210,000 sq. miles (544,000 sq. km); Capital: Québec
Population: 890,261 (est. 1851)

Lower Canada, which grew out of the British conquest of New France in 1760, occupied the southern portion of the present-day Canadian province of Québec. Lower Canada was created in 1791 when the British decided to split in two the territory they called the Province of Québec. The land west of the Ottawa River became Upper Canada (Ontario). In order to guarantee the cooperation of the majority French-speaking Catholic population in Lower Canada the British did not interfere in matters of language and religion. The policy was successful as Lower Canada remained under British control despite an American invasion during the War of 1812 and rebellions in 1837 and 1838. The British were reluctant, however, to share economic and political power. Throughout the existence of Lower Canada there was an uneasy relationship between the French majority and the English-speaking minority who dominated business, commerce and government.

As a means to save money and counterbalance what they perceived to be an unreliable population, the British merged Lower Canada with Upper Canada in 1841 to create the Province of Canada. Although officially renamed Canada East the earlier name continued in use and Lower Canada remained a distinct entity. In 1867 Lower Canada, once again Québec, became one of the four provinces that formed the Dominion of Canada.

Cornelius Krieghoff,
painter of Lower Canada

Canada CORNELIUS KRIEGHOFF painter·peintre 1815-1872 8

Readings: Dickinson, 1993; Ouellet, 1979.

NEW BRUNSWICK

Where the deep Mississippi meanders, or the distant Saskatchewan rolls? Ah, no! in New Brunswick we'll find it — A sweetly sequestered nook — Where the swift gliding Skoodoowabskooksis unites with the Skoodoowabskook.
— James de Mille, 1870.

Area: 28,354 sq miles (73,437 sq. km); Capital: Fredericton
Population: 285,394 (est. 1871)

In eastern Canada bordered by the Gulf of St. Lawrence and the Bay of Fundy. New Brunswick was visited by Jacques Cartier in 1534 and explored by Samuel de Champlain in 1604. When New Brunswick was transferred to British rule in 1713, and annexed to Nova Scotia, its European inhabitants were primarily French-speaking Acadians, large numbers of whom were deported during the Seven Year's War (1756-1763). In 1784 the British divided Nova Scotia. The western portion became the Colony of New Brunswick, named after a duchy in Germany, Brunswick-Lunenburg, ruled by King George III of Great Britain. Returning Acadians and immigrants from Québec made New Brunswick's population about one-third French-speaking. The rest of the European population were United Empire Loyalists and immigrants from Britain and Ireland. New Brunswick was one of the four provinces that confederated in 1867 to form the Dominion of Canada.

Queen Victoria

Readings: Hannay, 1909; MacNutt, 1963.

NEWFOUNDLAND (Terra Nova)

We'll rant and we'll roar like true Newfoundlanders.
— H.W. Lemessurier, c. 1880.

Area: 143,501 sq. miles (371,665 sq. km); Capital: St. John's
Population: 321,177 (est. 1945)

Newfoundland is the name of an island on the Atlantic coast of Canada, as well as the name of a self-governing dominion that included both the island and the territory of Labrador (two-thirds of the total area) on the North American mainland.

Newfoundland was visited and briefly settled by the Norse about A.D. 1000. By the 15th century the island was regularly visited by fleets from the Basque Country, France, Spain and England to exploit the Grand Banks fishery, the richest in the world. Newfoundland's indigenous people, the Beothuk, became extinct in the 19th century. Sir Humphrey Gilbert, under a charter from Elizabeth I, took possession of Newfoundland in 1583. Settlement was discouraged however, as it was feared that a resident population would compete with European fishermen. Even so, over the next three centuries, settlers, mostly English and Irish did occupy the coast.

Political development in Newfoundland was slow. No governor was appointed until 1817 and responsible government was not achieved until 1855. Newfoundlanders, who were proud of their independence and unique way of life, rejected invitations to federate with the mainland provinces of Canada. In the 20th century Newfoundland was a dominion equal in status to Canada, until 1934.

The Great Depression dealt Newfoundland an especially hard blow. The country sank into poverty and the government into bankruptcy. In an unprecedented step the Newfoundland government voted itself out of existence and a commission government composed of Newfoundland and British civil servants ruled the Dominion by decree. The commission government was always intended as a temporary measure. After World War II, rising prosperity, made the restoration of self-government inevitable. Discussions were held as to Newfoundland's future and after two hard-fought referenda Newfoundland, by a narrow margin, chose not to return to dominion status but became a province of Canada. The union was enacted at 11:59 P.M. on March 31, 1949. The time was carefully chosen to ensure that Newfoundland would not become Canada's tenth province on April Fool's Day.

John Cabot's Discovery of Newfoundland, 1497

Readings: Rowe, 1980; Smallwood, 1981-1994.

NOVA SCOTIA (New Scotland)

> When I am abroad I brag of everything that Nova Scotia is, has, or
> can produce; and when they beat me at everything else, I turn round
> on them and say, 'How high does your tide rise?'
> — Joseph Howe, 1906.

Area: 21,425 sq. miles (55,490 sq. km); Capital: Halifax
Population: 387,800 (est. 1871)

A heavily indented peninsula in eastern Canada surrounded by the
Atlantic Ocean, the Gulf of St. Lawrence and the Bay of Fundy.
Almost an island, Nova Scotia is connected to the Canadian mainland
by the narrow Isthmus of Chignecto. At various times New Brunswick
and Prince Edward Island have been part of Nova Scotia.

The earliest permanent agricultural settlement in Nova Scotia (and
Canada) was made by the French at Port Royal in 1605. Between 1613
and 1710 Nova Scotia passed between the French and British ten times.
When Nova Scotia was ceded to the British for the last time, in 1713,
its European inhabitants were almost exclusively French-speaking
Acadians. The British decided to offset the undesirable French
influence by founding Halifax in 1749 and forcibly deporting many of
the Acadians. In later years some of the Acadians returned even as
Nova Scotia became the home of large numbers of Scots and United
Empire Loyalists.

When Nova Scotia achieved responsible government in 1848 it was
the first overseas jurisdiction in the British Empire to do so. In the face
of much bitter opposition Nova Scotia became one of the four original

provinces of the Dominion of Canada in 1867. Tides of forty-seven feet (14 m), the highest in the world, have been recorded in the Bay of Fundy.

Queen Victoria

Readings: Brebner, 1969; Campbell, 1948.

PRINCE EDWARD ISLAND

Spud Island. The Garden of the Gulf. The Million Acre Farm.
— Anon. Popular sayings.

Area: 2,185 sq. miles (5,660 sq. km); Capital: Charlottetown
Population: 94,021 (est. 1871)

A crescent-shaped island in eastern Canada separated from New Brunswick and Nova Scotia by the Strait of Northumberland. In 1534, although not realizing that it was an island, Jacques Cartier was probably the first European to sight the coast of Prince Edward Island. Naming it Ile St. Jean, the French settled the island in 1719. The British took the island in 1758, expelled most of the Acadian settlers, and annexed it to Nova Scotia in 1763. The island was renamed Prince Edward Island in 1799 in honor of Queen Victoria's father, Prince Edward, Duke of Kent, who was commander of British forces in North America at the time. From 1769 to 1873 Prince Edward Island was a separate colony. When the Dominion of Canada came into being in 1867 Prince Edward Island remained aloof. But massive public debt, British pressure and Canadian enticements convinced Prince Edward Island to join Canada as a province in 1873. The island is famous for its potatoes and Lucy Maud Montgomery's fictional character, Anne of Green Gables.

Lucy Maud Montgomery's Anne of Green Gables

Readings: Bolger, 1991; Bumsted, 1987.

PROVINCE OF CANADA

Advancing quietly; old differences settling down, and being fast
forgotten; public feeling and private enterprise alike in a sound
and wholesome state; nothing of flush or fever in its system,
but health and vigour throbbing in its steady pulse: it is full of
hope and promise.
— Charles Dickens, 1842.

Area: 331,280 sq. miles (858,000 sq. km); Capital: Ottawa
Population: 2,507,657 (est. 1861)

A union (1841-1867) of predominantly English-speaking Upper
Canada (Ontario) with predominantly French-speaking Lower Canada
(Québec). The union arose as a result of a report issued by Lord
Durham in 1839. The British government had appointed Lord Durham
to investigate the causes of the Canadian rebellions of 1837 and to
make recommendations for the future. The Durham Report urged the
creation of a united colony with a single government, legislature and
commercial system. The united colony would have an English-speaking
majority representation by population and would therefore, in Durham's
opinion, be a good candidate for responsible government. Responsible
government was implemented in 1848 but when the British Government
created the province they gave the two parts equal representation rather
than proportional. In effect a dual state was created rather than a
unitary one, with an inherent tendency toward political deadlock. The

two parts of the Province of Canada were officially renamed Canada West and Canada East (although the earlier names of Upper and Lower Canada continued in popular use). The capital of the province was shunted between Toronto, Kingston, Montréal and Québec until Queen Victoria selected the small lumbering town of Ottawa, on the border between Canada West and Canada East, in 1858. The Province of Canada was dissolved in 1867 becoming the provinces of Ontario and Québec in the Dominion of Canada. The confederation of Canada was approved by both English and French majorities in the Province of Canada's Parliament.

Three penny beaver stamp of 1851

Readings: Careless, 1967; Morton, 1964.

RED RIVER COLONY / DISTRICT OF ASSINIBOIA

Out and in the river is winding
The links of its long red chain
Through belts of dusky pine land
And gusty leagues of plain.
— John G. Whittier, 1860.

Area: 116,000 sq. miles (300,000 sq. km); Capital: Fort Garry
Population: 25,228 (est. 1871)

A colony centred around the Red and Assiniboine Rivers in what was to become southern Manitoba and parts of North Dakota and Minnesota. It was the first agricultural settlement in western Canada. Beginning in 1801 the Earl of Selkirk wanted to establish a colony in the southern portion of Rupert's Land, a vast territory over which the Hudson's Bay Company enjoyed a monopoly. After Selkirk and his family gained control of the Company in 1810 the settlement scheme became feasible. Selkirk obtained a grant in 1811 of a tract of land in the Winnipeg Basin that was called the District of Assiniboia. Settlers were recruited in the Highlands of Scotland and they began arriving in

1812. The colonists were hardy people and they needed to be. They faced a catastrophic flood, clouds of grasshoppers, crop failure and severe weather. Not the least of their troubles was conflict with the Métis (people of mixed race) and agents of the rival North West Company. The settlement on the Red River was twice destroyed. The colony was reestablished but trouble and violence continued until the Hudson's Bay Company and the North West Company merged in 1821. Population growth came mostly from discharged fur traders moving to the colony with their native families. When, without the consent of its inhabitants, the Red River Colony was transferred from the Hudson's Bay Company to Canada a rebellion erupted and a provisional government under Métis leader, Louis Riel, was declared. After a short military campaign the District of Assiniboia was reluctantly incorporated into Canada in 1870 as the Province of Manitoba.

The Earl of Selkirk, founder of the Red River Settlement

Readings: MacEwan, 1977; Wood, 1964.

REPUBLIC OF THE RIO GRANDE

> . . . the Republic of the Rio Grande with its spacious notions,— its constitution, its president, its commander-in-chief, its army, its two-room adobe and stone capitol building on the high bank of the river at Laredo.
> — Paul Horgan, 1954.

A short-lived republic (1839-1841) centered around the town of Laredo, Texas. Laredo was founded by the Spanish in 1755 as a ferry crossing and was named for the city of Laredo in Spain. For more than 200 years the Rio Grande country was the site of Indian wars, border violence and banditry. After the Texas revolt against Mexico in 1836 the area became a no-man's-land. Mexicans who opposed their country's centralist government, with the help of Texans, set up a republic comprising the Mexican states of Tamaulipas, Nuevo Léon, Coahuila and Texas west of the Nueces River. A mixed force of Mexicans and Texans then attempted to liberate northern Mexico. The attempt failed, as did the Republic of the Rio Grande itself, when Texas government support was not forthcoming. The territory north of the Rio Grande became part of Texas and that to the south, part of Mexico.

Readings: Horgan, 1954; Richardson, 1981.

RUPERT'S LAND / PRINCE RUPERT'S LAND

> Colonization and the fur trade could not exist together.
> — Sir George Cartier and William McDougall, 1869.

Area: 1,400,000 sq. miles (3,600,000 sq. km)
Population: 48,000 (est. 1871)

In 1670 King Charles II of England granted an enormous tract of land in what became Québec, Ontario, northern and western Canada to the Hudson's Bay Company. The territory comprised the drainage basin of Hudson Bay and extended into what is now the United States. Rupert's Land was named after Prince Rupert of the Rhine, the director of the Hudson's Bay Company and cousin of the King. The Company established trading posts throughout Rupert's Land to exploit the fur trade. Except in the Red River Colony, settlement was discouraged and the territory was left unincorporated. Upon payment of £300,000 Rupert's Land was transferred to Canada in 1870.

Wood bison

Readings: Newman, 1985; Traill, 1970.

SAINT-PIERRE AND MIQUELON (St.-Pierre et Miquelon)

> I understand "bottle fishing" has done more for St. Pierre than
> codfishing ever did.
> — George Allan England, 1929.

Area: 93 sq. miles (241 sq. km); Capital: St. Pierre
Population: 5,450 (est. 1974)

Two islands, 12 miles (20 km) southwest of Newfoundland.
Discovered in 1520 by the Portuguese. St. Pierre and Miquelon was
claimed by France and settled by Normans and Basques in 1604.
When the British claimed the islands, under terms of the Treaty of
Utrecht in 1713, they were uninhabited. St. Pierre and Miquelon was
returned to France in 1763 and resettled. The British captured the
islands twice more but since 1814 Saint-Pierre and Miquelon has been
French.

The islands are barren and have few resources, however they have
provided France with a base for the exploitation of the Grand Banks,
the richest fishing grounds in the world. During Prohibition in the
1920s St. Pierre and Miquelon became a major center for rum runners
smuggling Canadian liquor into the United States. In World War II the
islands were in Vichy hands until they were liberated by a daring
landing of Free French forces. France is determined to hold St. Pierre
and Miquelon and supports the islands with generous subsidies.

St. Pierre and Miquelon became an overseas départment of France
in 1976 with the same status of a départment in metropolitan France.
Since 1985 St. Pierre and Miquelon has been a collectivité territorial.
The population are citizens of France and have elected representation
in the French National Assembly and Senate.

Lighthouse and fishing boats

Readings: Andrieux, 1983; Rannie, 1977.

SPANISH FLORIDA

If we push them strongly with one hand, holding out a price in the other, we shall certainly obtain the Floridas, and all in good time.
— Thomas Jefferson

Area: 60,000 sq. miles (155,000 sq. km); Capital: St. Augustine
Population: 5,000 (est. 1821)

Spanish navigators reached the Florida coast by 1500. When Juan Ponce de Leon went ashore in 1513 searching for the Fountain of Youth he named the land Pasqua de Flores, after the Feast of Flowers. The Spanish established their first permanent settlement in Florida at St. Augustine in 1565, which became the oldest permanent European settlement in the United States. Florida was ceded to Great Britain in 1763 and given back to Spain in 1783. The Spanish hold on Florida however, was steadily weakened by American expansionism. By 1810 the settlers of west Florida, most of whom were Americans, demanded annexation by the United States. The Spanish were unable to stop west Florida being added to Louisiana and Mississippi in 1812. American pressure on the rest of Florida continued. Realizing that they had no hope of retaining Florida, Spain sold it to the United States for $5,000,000 in 1819. The transfer took place in 1821 and Florida became an American state in 1845.

Ponce de Leon

Readings: Gannon, 1996; Weeks, 1992.

TEXAS

We saw the land lying idle; we took it. This to other nations is all we can say.
— Frederick Law Olmsted, 1857.

Area: 261,914 sq. miles (678,358 sq. km); Capital: Austin
Population: 135,000 (est. 1845)

North of the Rio Grande, Texas became the second largest state in the United States. The Spanish reached Texas as early in 1519 but did not begin to establish missions and settlements for another 150 years. Texas was a remote northern province of Mexico when that country won its independence from Spain in 1821. In 1812-1813 a Mexican rebel set up a so-called Republic of Texas until ousted by Spanish soldiers. Mexico, eager to develop Texas, threw open large tracts of land for settlement. Most of the settlers were Americans from Tennessee, Alabama, Mississippi, Arkansas and Louisiana. Before long Texas had a majority American population. The Mexicans became alarmed at this development and the settlers, chafing under increasingly restrictive Mexican rule, began to demand annexation to the United States. A rebellion began in 1835. The settlers formed the Republic of Texas, the independence of which was confirmed by the defeat of a Mexican army. Politicians in the southern United States were in favor of speedy annexation of Texas, but the presence of large numbers of slaves made abolitionists oppose the idea. It was 1845 before the Texas Republic was finally annexed to the United States and offered statehood. A war between Mexico and the United States soon broke out. Upon the defeat of the Mexicans the boundaries of Texas, and its possession by the United States, were confirmed.

Texas statehood, 1845

Readings: Fehrenbach, 1988; Richardson, 1981.

UPPER CANADA / CANADA WEST

Toronto, soul of Canada, is wealthy, busy, commercial, Scotch, absorbent of whisky.
— Rupert Brooke, 1916.

Area: 121,000 sq. miles (313,000 sq. km); Capital: York
Population: 455,688 (est. 1841)

Upper Canada was the predecessor of the Canadian province of Ontario. In the 17th century Upper Canada was visited by Samuel de Champlain and other French explorers, missionaries and fur traders. It was an unorganized appendage of New France (Québec) until the British defeated the French in 1760. Upper Canada then became part of the Province of Québec. At the time, the permanent French-speaking European population were clustered along the Detroit River. After the American Revolution Upper Canada was transformed by a stream of Loyalist refugees from the United States. It was largely due to their lobbying that the British Government created Upper Canada as a separate entity in 1791.

During its fifty-year existence Upper Canada survived an American invasion during the War of 1812 and a rebellion in 1837. The population grew steadily in size, prosperity and sophistication. In 1841 the British, to save money and to counterbalance French-speaking Lower Canada, amalgamated Upper and Lower Canada into the Province of Canada with a single government and legislature. Upper Canada was officially known as Canada West, although the earlier name continued in common use. Upper Canada became the Province of Ontario in 1867 and joined Québec, New Brunswick and Nova Scotia to form the Dominion of Canada.

Niagara-on-the-Lake, early capital of Upper Canada

Readings: Bothwell, 1986; Craig, 1968.

VANCOUVER ISLAND (Vancouver's Island)

> In Victoria the people turn over in the morning to read the daily
> obituary column. Those who did not find their names there, fall back
> and go to sleep again.
> — Stephen Leacock, c. 1936.

Area: 12,079 sq. miles (31,284 sq. km); Capital: Victoria
Population: 6,000 (est. 1871)

The largest island on the Pacific coast of North America. In the
18th century Spanish, Russian, French, British and American fur
traders and explorers were active in Vancouver Island. The activities
of British trading companies, the voyage of Captain James Cook, the
circumnavigation of the island by George Vancouver and negotiations
in Europe gradually allowed the British to become paramount. In 1843
the Hudson's Bay Company built a fort at the southern tip of
Vancouver Island which developed into the town of Victoria. The
Colony of Vancouver Island was established in 1849 but as a cost-
saving measure the British government merged Vancouver Island with
British Columbia in 1866. The united colony became a province of the
Dominion of Canada in 1871.

Vancouver Island marmot

Readings: Forward, 1979; Ormsby, 1958.

YUCATÁN

Yucatan received the name from . . . the first discoverers asking the place, the Indian answering tectetan, tectetan, that is, I understand you not.
— Garcilasso de la Vega, c. 1580.

Area: 55,400 sq. miles (140,000 sq. km); Capital: Mérida
Population: 422,365 (est. 1871)

Home of the Maya civilization, Yucatán is a peninsula in southern Mexico dividing the Gulf of Mexico from the Caribbean Sea. The peninsula was discovered by the Spanish in 1517 who began its conquest in 1557. The Spanish faced determined resistance from the Mayas and never controlled more than half of Yucatán. After gaining independence from Spain in 1821 Yucatán voluntarily federated with Mexico three years later. But Yucatán would not accept the increasingly centralized government of Mexico and a revolution erupted in 1839, followed by a declaration of independence in 1840. Yucatán maintained its independence until 1843. It seceded from Mexico again in 1847 but was readmitted as a state in 1848, when it needed assistance to suppress an Indian revolt.

Readings: Baudez, 1992; Stephens, 1841.

CHAPTER 2

West Indies

Oh, what stars they are, those in that western tropical world! How beautiful a woman looks by their light, how sweet the air smells, how gloriously legible are the constellations of the heavens!
— Anthony Trollope, 1860.

DANISH WEST INDIES (Dansk Vestindien)

The Danish influence is felt everywhere. It is especially noticeable in the gabled and shingled houses and the clean white cobbles, the massive and brightly painted buildings, the statues, and coats of arms, and the names of streets and towns. The capital has a childish and Scandinavian aspect which is very strange indeed.
— Patrick Leigh Fermor, 1951.

Area: 133 sq. miles (344 sq. km); Capital: Charlotte Amalie
Population: 26,051 (est. 1917)

A group of islands (St. Thomas, St. John, St. Croix) east of Puerto Rico which were visited by Columbus in 1493. The islands, which were named after St. Ursula and the Eleven Thousand Virgins, became a favorite pirate lair in the 17th century.

St. Thomas, the largest island, was colonized by the Dutch and British before the Danish West India Company established a colony in 1671. The neighboring island of St. Croix was colonized by the Dutch, British, Spanish, French and the Knights of Malta before being purchased by the Danish in 1733. The Danes established an economy based on sugar, cotton and slavery. Before slavery was abolished in 1848 the Danes had to contend with several slave revolts. In 1835 the capital of the islands, Charlotte Amalie, was the third largest city under the Danish monarchy. By 1917 the Danish West Indies had gone into a steep decline and were sold to the United States for $25,000,000. The Americans wanted the islands because the Danish West Indies controlled the main passage through the Caribbean to the Panama Canal. The islands are now known as the U.S. Virgin Islands.

King Frederick VIII of Denmark

Readings: Farr, 1978; Trollope, 1860.

GUADELOUPE

These green slopes, hemmed in by their Garden of Eden forests, have an almost miraculous beauty. In the extending shadows of the late-afternoon sunlight they appeared as idyllic and eternal as the clearings in a rather sad heaven.
— Patrick Leigh Fermor, 1951.

Area: 687 sq. miles (1,780 sq. km); Capital: Basse-Terre
Population: 271,262 (est. 1946)

A former French colony between Dominica and Antigua. The main area of Guadeloupe consists of the islands of Basse-Terre and Grande-Terre separated by a saltwater channel a mere 100-400 feet (30-120 metres) wide. There are several dependencies: Marie-Galante, La Désirade, Iles des Saintes, St. Barthélemy and the northern half of St. Martin (the southern half being part of the Netherlands Antilles). The population of Guadeloupe is mostly mulatto.

The Spanish were driven out of Guadeloupe by the French in 1635, who exterminated the Carib Indians and established a settlement. Between 1664 and 1816 Guadeloupe passed between Great Britain and

France eight times. Since 1816 the islands have remained French. Sugar cane plantations worked by African slaves formed the basis of the economy until slavery was abolished during the French Revolution. When Napoleon restored slavery in 1802 a bloody revolt was the result. Slavery was finally abolished in 1848. Between 1940 and 1943 Guadeloupe supported the Vichy regime in France. In 1946 Guadeloupe ceased to be a colony and became, in theory, a part of France. Its population are full French citizens and the islands are politically and administratively integrated with France. Since 1974 Guadeloupe has been a région of France.

Woman and Basse-Terre harbour

Readings: Gastmann, 1978; *Encylopædia Britannica*, 1926.

LEEWARD ISLANDS FEDERATION / TERRITORY OF THE LEEWARD ISLANDS

I was altogether unprepared for their beauty and grandeur. For hundreds of miles, day after day, the steamer carried us past a shifting diorama of scenery which may be likened to Vesuvius and the Bay of Naples, repeated again and again with every possible variation of the same type of delicate loveliness.
— Charles Kingsley, 1871.

Area: 422 sq. miles (1,093 sq. km); Capital: St. John's (on Antigua); Population: 131,644 (est. 1956)

A British federal colony established in 1871. The Leeward Islands were divided into the presidencies of Antigua (with Barbuda and Redonda), Montserrat, St. Christopher (St. Kitts) with Nevis and Anguilla, and the British Virgin Islands. Each presidency had local autonomy. The island of Dominica was a presidency between 1883 and 1940. The Leeward Islands were discovered by Christopher Columbus in 1493 and settled by the British in the early 17th century. Frequently fought over, the Treaty of Versailles restored them to British rule in 1783. The Leeward Islands were defederated in 1956 becoming the Territory of the Leeward Islands which itself was incorporated in the West Indies Federation in 1958. The Leeward Islands were so named because they were to the lee of the northeast trade winds. The British Virgin Islands, Montserrat and Anguilla remain British dependencies. The other islands have all proceeded toward independence.

King George VI

Readings: *Encyclopædia Britannica*, 1926; Lux, 1975.

MARTINIQUE

> Imagine old New Orleans, the dear quaint part of it, young and idealized as a master-artist might idealize it, - made all tropical, with narrower and brighter streets, all climbing up the side of a volcanic peak to a tropical forest, or descending in terraces of steps to the sea.
> – Lafcadio Hearn, 1887.

Area: 421 sq. miles (1,090 sq. km); Capital: Fort-de-France
Population: 261,595 (est. 1946)

A volcanic island between St. Lucia and Dominica. Discovered by Columbus in 1502 a French colony was established on Martinique in the 1650s. Wars with the Carib Indians, British and Dutch followed. Slavery was introduced as sugar, cocoa and coffee became the economic mainstays. Before slavery was abolished in 1848 there were three serious slave revolts.

In 1902 the volcano Mont Pelée exploded in a violent eruption which wiped out the town of Saint-Pierre, killing 30 to 40,000 people, and devastating 10 percent of the island.

Martinique supported Vichy in World War II but after an economic blockade changed sides in 1943. The island became a French département in 1946 and a région of France in 1974. The islanders are

French citizens. Martinique is politically and administratively integrated with France.

The empress Joséphine, consort of Napoleon, was born on Martinique in 1763. The mother of Sultan Mahmud II of Turkey was also from Martinique.

Women of Martinique

Readings: *Encyclopædia Britannica*, 1926; Gastmann, 1978.

ST. KITTS-NEVIS-ANGUILLA / ST. CHRISTOPHER-NEVIS-ANGUILLA

> The ruggedness of this central cluster only renders the contrast of the cultivated lands below more striking, and the entire prospect is so charming, that I could not help agreeing with the captain's clerk, who said he wondered that Colon, who was so delighted with this island as to give it his own name, should not have made a full stop upon its shores.
> — H.N. Coleridge, 1826.

Area: 136 sq. miles (352 sq. km); Capital: Basseterre (on St. Kitts)
Population: 57,617 (est. 1966)

Three of the Leeward Islands discovered by Christopher Columbus in 1493. St. Kitts was the first West Indian island to be colonized by the British, in 1623. Nevis and St. Kitts, only 2 miles (3 km) apart, have long had a close association. They and Anguilla were administered by the British as presidencies of the Leeward Islands Colony until 1956, and as part of the West Indies Federation from 1958 to 1962. In 1967 their status as a colony was changed to that of a self-governing state in association with the United Kingdom.

Anguilla, smallest of the islands, some 60 miles (100 km) northwest of St. Kitts, became linked to St. Kitts in 1882, against its will. Opposition to this federation simmered until 1967 when Anguilla expelled St. Kitts's police and unilaterally seceded. British troops landed to restore order and end what was probably the world's only pro-colonial rebellion. In effect Anguilla became a separate British dependency although officially it remained part of the state of St. Kitts-Nevis-Anguilla until 1980. Anguilla remains a British dependency whereas the other two islands became independent in 1983 as the Federation of St. Kitts and Nevis.

Salt Pond, Anguilla

Readings: Lux, 1975; *New Encyclopædia Britannica*, 1991.

TOBAGO

> I am somewhat consoled by the thought that there is not a great deal to be seen at Tobago, where the legendary Old Man lived on rice, sugar and sago.
> — Lady Brassey, 1885.

Area: 115 sq. miles (298 sq. km); Capital: Scarborough
Population: 17,054 (est. 1871)

An island between Trinidad and Grenada, originally inhabited by Carib Indians. Visited by Columbus in 1498 Tobago was virtually ignored until the 18th century when the Dutch attempted to settle it. The island then passed between French, Dutch and British hands before the British acquired it for the last time in 1814. Tobago became a major producer of sugar and a crown colony in 1877. A calamitous drop in sugar prices forced Tobago to amalgamate with Trinidad in 1889. Legal and fiscal arrangements kept Tobago distinct until 1899 when it became a ward of Trinidad. The island is now part of the Republic of Trinidad and Tobago. Tobago was named after tobacco which was cultivated there.

Tobago thinks of itself as the setting for Daniel Defoe's story of Robinson Crusoe. Defoe based his tale on the true story of Alexander Selkirk, a sailor marooned for four years in the Juan Fernandez Islands off Chile. With poetic license Defoe made good use of printed accounts of Tobago for his descriptive passages.

In 1909, forty-four greater birds of paradise were brought from New Guinea and released on an islet near Tobago. Their descendants are still there, the only free ranging birds of paradise to be found outside New Guinea.

Queen Victoria

Readings: Brassey, 1885; Lux, 1975.

TRINIDAD

Port of Spain possesses a forcefulness and a vulgarity that are almost pleasing. It is a large and startlingly cosmopolitan town. The streets blaze with milk-bars, drug stores, joints and picture-palaces, and almost everybody on the pavement chews gum.
— Patrick Leigh Fermor, 1951.

Area: 1,864 sq. miles (4,828 sq. km); Capital: Port-of-Spain
Population: 109,638 (est. 1871)

Off the coast of Venezuela; the most southerly island in the West Indies. Trinidad was discovered by Columbus in 1498 and named after three mountains that he thought he saw there. The island was a neglected Spanish possession until 1797 when a British expedition captured it. The island had an excellent harbour at Port-of-Spain, and rich agricultural land. It also produced pitch, which was essential for caulking wooden ships. The only thing Trinidad lacked was a supply of labor. The original Arawak Indians had died out and were replaced by African slaves and indentured labourers from India. In 1889

Trinidad was amalgamated with the neighboring island of Tobago to form the colony of Trinidad and Tobago. Since 1962 Trinidad and Tobago has been an independent nation.

Britannia

Readings: Lux, 1975; *New Encyclopædia Britannica*, 1991.

TURKS ISLANDS (Turques Islands)

> Turks Islands derive their name from a beautiful scarlet cactus, in shape like a fez or tarbouch, which covered the islands in profusion when they were first discovered.
> — Lady Brassey, 1885.

Area: 166 sq. miles (430 sq. km); Capital: Grand Turk
Population: 4,723 (est. 1871)

A group of coral islands and rocks south of the Bahamas. Sighted by Juan Ponce de Leon in 1512 the Turks Islands were left alone until they were visited by Bermudian salt collectors beginning in 1678. There was no permanent settlement until the arrival of United Empire Loyalists at the end of the American Revolution. The Turks Islands were associated with the Bahamas from 1799 until 1848 when, together with the nearby Caicos group, they became part of the Colony of the Turks and Caicos Islands. Since 1917 there have been unofficial attempts to have the islands join Canada.

Queen Victoria

Readings: *New Encyclopædia Britannica*, 1991; *Worldmark Encyclopedia of the Nations*, 1976.

WEST INDIES FEDERATION

. . . like a statue, each island is compact and complete in itself, an isolated and self-dependent organism; and therefore, like every beautiful statue it looks much smaller than it is.
— Charles Kingsley, 1871.

Area: 8,029 sq. miles (20,795 sq. km); Capital: Port-of-Spain (on Trinidad); Population: 3,117,370 (est. 1960)

A federation, established in 1958, of the British West Indian island colonies of Antigua, Barbados, Dominica, Grenada, Jamaica, Montserrat, St. Kitts-Nevis-Anguilla, St. Lucia, St. Vincent, Trinidad and Tobago. The British wanted the Federation to proceed toward independence but when the big islands of Jamaica and Trinidad withdrew in 1961 that ambition was no longer realistic. The West Indies Federation was dissolved in 1962. All the islands, except Montserrat and Anguilla, have since become independent.

Queen Elizabeth II and
map of the federation

Readings: Lux 1975; *New Encyclopædia Britannica*, 1991.

WINDWARD ISLANDS FEDERATION / TERRITORY OF THE WINDWARD ISLANDS

The head-quarters of the world for fruit.
— Anthony Trollope, 1860.

Area: 821 sq. miles (2,126 sq. km); Capital: St. George's (on Grenada); Population: 326,168 (est. 1957)

In 1833 the British West Indian colonies of Barbados, St. Vincent,

Grenada and Tobago were placed under a single government. The governor of Barbados was also the governor of the other islands. St. Lucia was added to the federation in 1838. Barbados was removed in 1885 as was Tobago in 1889. Dominica, which had been in the Leeward Islands Federation, was transferred to the Windward Islands in 1940. The islands of Dominica, St. Lucia, Grenada and St. Vincent were incorporated as the Territory of the Windward Islands in 1956, prior to their becoming part of the West Indies Federation in 1958.

Readings: Lux, 1975; Trollope, 1860.

CHAPTER 3

Central and South America

South America is bounded at its northern end by an isthmus and at its
southern by a strait. . . . An isthmus and a strait are, to the historical
geographer and to the geographical historian, the most interesting
things with which geographical science has to deal.
— James Bryce, 1912.

ACRE (República de Acre; Aquiry)

Night in these jungles had a curious rhythm to it. It was as though one
was in some nightmare engine-room, a vast place working quietly to
some predestined purpose.
— Peter Fleming, 1933.

Area: 58,915 sq. miles (152,589 sq. km); Capital: Rio Branco
Population: 92,379 (est. 1920)

A rubber-producing area in the Amazon region of Brazil, bordered
by Bolivia and Peru, Acre had been visited by only a few Portuguese
and Brazilian explorers before being ceded by Brazil to Bolivia in
1867. Encouraged by a rubber boom, settlers, mostly Brazilian, arrived
between 1870 and 1878. Taking advantage of a civil war in Bolivia the
settlers proclaimed the Republic of Acre in 1899. Brazil's covert
support of the settlers and Bolivia's inability to reassert its authority
persuaded Bolivia to sell its rights in Acre to Brazil for $10,000,000.

Acre was annexed by Brazil as a territory in 1903 and elevated to statehood in 1962.

Readings: *Encyclopædia Britannica*, 1926; Heath, 1972.

BERBICE

> At present life certainly stagnates at New Amsterdam. Three persons in the street constitute a crowd, and five collected for any purpose would form a goodly club.
> — Anthony Trollope, 1860.

Area: 21,000 sq. miles (54,000 sq. km); Capital: Nieuw Amsterdam
Population: 50,000 (est. 1883)

A Dutch colony in what became eastern British Guiana (Guyana), named after the Berbice River. The Dutch had trading posts in the area of Berbice as long ago as 1580 but were driven out by the Spanish. The Dutch West India company returned to Berbice in 1626 and stayed until the colony was purchased by the British in 1814. A massive revolt of slaves, the most serious uprising in the Caribbean, nearly destroyed Berbice in 1763. In 1831 Berbice was merged with the ex-Dutch colonies of Demerara and Essequibo to create British Guiana.

Readings: *Encyclopædia Britannica*, 1926; Trollope, 1860.

BRITISH GUIANA

> The form of government is a mild despotism, tempered by sugar.
> — Anthony Trollope, 1859.

Area: 83,000 sq miles (215,000 sq. km); Capital: Georgetown
Population: 653,000 (est. 1965)

On the northeast coast of South America between Venezuela and Dutch Guiana (Surinam). Although the Spanish explorer Christopher Columbus sailed along the coast of British Guiana in 1498 the first European outposts were established by the Dutch in 1580. Adventurers, among them Sir Walter Raleigh, were drawn to the country in search of the legendary city of gold, El Dorado. Beginning in the 17th century large numbers of African slaves were imported to harvest sugar cane.

The British captured the territory from the Dutch in 1781 and it then passed back and forth between Great Britain, France and Holland until the British captured it for the last time in 1803. The three Dutch colonies of Berbice, Demerara and Essequibo were purchased by the British in 1814 and consolidated in 1831 as the Colony of British Guiana. Unique in the British Empire the colony's law and administration were based on a Dutch model. After slavery was abolished in 1838 indentured laborers from India were imported. About one-half the population of British Guiana were East Indians and one third Black. The rest were Indians and people of mixed race. The first elected government in British Guiana was deposed by British troops in 1953 for being too friendly with communism. British Guiana became independent as Guyana in 1966.

King George VI and map of the colony

Readings: Lux, 1975; Trollope, 1860.

BRITISH HONDURAS / HIS MAJESTY'S SETTLEMENTS IN THE BAY OF HONDURAS

> I had noticed the judges and jurors, but I missed an important part of an English court. Where were the gentlemen of the bar? . . . there was not a single lawyer in the place, and never had been.
> — John L. Stephens, 1841.

Area: 8,867 sq. miles (22,965 sq. km); Capital: Belmopan
Population: 119,645 (est. 1970)

The northernmost territory in Central America, bordered by the Caribbean Sea, Guatemala and Mexico. If there ever was a colony which came into being without being planned British Honduras was the

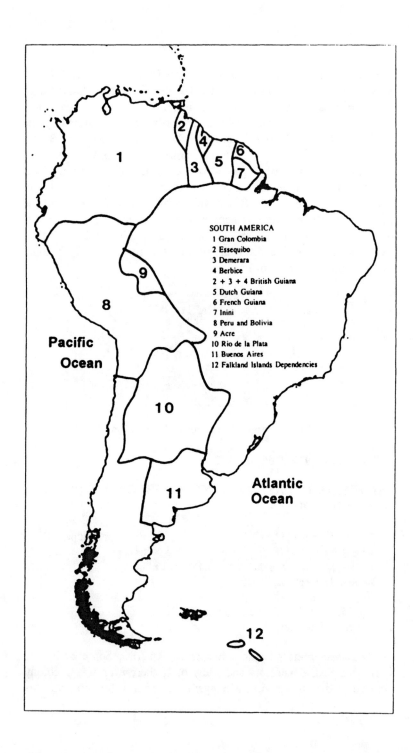

SOUTH AMERICA
1 Gran Colombia
2 Essequibo
3 Demerara
4 Berbice
2 + 3 + 4 British Guiana
5 Dutch Guiana
6 French Guiana
7 Inini
8 Peru and Bolivia
9 Acre
10 Rio de la Plata
11 Buenos Aires
12 Falkland Islands Dependencies

Pacific
Ocean

Atlantic
Ocean

one. When a party of British woodcutters and buccaneers was shipwrecked there in 1638 they stayed to exploit the country's mahogany forests. The coast was claimed by Spain and the presence of British settlers was not officially recognized by anyone, including Great Britain. The Spanish made several efforts to remove the interlopers by force, the last in 1798. The colony was self-governing until it was given a British superintendent in 1786. Even though the colony, grudgingly referred to as His Majesty's Settlements in the Bay of Honduras, had an executive council and a partially elected legislative assembly, it had no legal status. Great Britain did not officially recognize its existence until 1862, at which date it became a dependency of Jamaica. British Honduras finally became an colony in its own right in 1884. The name was changed to Belize in 1973 and it was under that name that the country became independent in 1981. The name Belize, or Belice, in use since at least 1840, is said to be derived from the Spanish pronunciation of Wallace, a Scottish buccaneer who was active on the coast in the 17th century. Guatemala has inherited the Spanish claim to the territory of Belize.

Queen Elizabeth II and great curassow

Readings: *Encyclopædia Britannica*, 1926; Lux, 1975.

BUENOS AIRES (Buenos Ayres)

> Nowhere in the world does one get a stronger impression of exuberant wealth and extravagance.
> — James Bryce, 1912.

Area: 63,000 sq. miles (163,000 sq. km); Capital: Buenos Aires
Population: 343,866 (est. 1869)

A province and city in eastern Argentina, southeast of the Rio de la Plata. After Argentina gained its independence from Spain in 1816, as the United Provinces of Rio de la Plata, it was anything but united. The interior provinces resented domination by Buenos Aires and the country was in a state of continual turmoil. In 1853 a new federal structure creating equal provinces was introduced in Argentina. Now it was Buenos Aires which was unhappy. Buenos Aires refused to accept this arrangement and set itself up as a separate country. It took armed force to bring it back into the Argentine confederation in 1859. Over the next two decades Buenos Aires continued to be involved in revolts and civil wars until its status within Argentina was finally resolved. In 1880 the city of Buenos Aires became a federal territory and the national capital. The province of Buenos Aires was separated from the city and given its own provincial capital.

Steamship

Readings: Delpar, 1974; Martin, 1968.

CANAL ZONE / PANAMA CANAL ZONE

> I took the Canal Zone and . . . while the debate goes on, the canal does also.
> — Theodore Roosevelt, attrib.

Area: 647 sq. miles (1,676 sq. km); Capital: Balboa Heights
Population: 39,000 (est. 1978)

When the Colombian government rejected an American proposal to build a canal across the Isthmus of Panama (then a state of Colombia), Panama declared its independence on November 3, 1903. With unseemly haste the United States recognized the new republic three days later. Only twelve days after that a treaty was signed between Panama and the United States making it possible for a canal to be built linking the Atlantic and Pacific Oceans. The treaty, apart from guaranteeing the independence of the Republic of Panama, created the

Canal Zone, a 10-mile (16 km)-wide zone straddling the canal and bisecting Panama. Upon payment of $10,000,000 and a yearly rental the United States was awarded powers in the Zone "as if they were sovereign," in perpetuity. The Americans, taking over from a bankrupt French company, began construction in 1904 and the canal was opened in 1914. The 51-mile (82 km) voyage through the canal reduced sailing distance between New York and San Francisco by 9,000 nautical miles (16,000 km). The president of the United States appointed a governor of the Zone who was also ex-officio director of the Panama Canal Company, the agency of the U.S. Defense Department responsible for the operation of the Canal. The Panama Canal Zone was abolished in 1979 and its territory returned to Panama. A joint American-Panamanian commission now operates the canal. Full Panamanian control is scheduled to come into effect in 2000. The United States maintains a strong military presence in the region.

Girl Scout badge and camp at Gatun Lake

Readings: Delpar, 1974; Hedrick, 1970.

CENTRAL AMERICAN FEDERATION / UNITED PROVINCES OF CENTRAL AMERICA (Provincias Unidas de Centro-América)

These Central American Republics are queer concerns. I do not, of course precisely know what a last year's calf's ideas of immortal glory might be, but probably they are about as lucid as those of a Central American, in regard to a republican form of government.
— Charles F. Browne, 1865.

Area: 175,000 sq. miles (453,000 sq. km); Capital: San Salvador; Population: 1,500,000 (est. 1869)

A union of Guatemala, Honduras, El Salvador, Nicaragua and Costa Rica in a federal republic. The Spanish provinces in Central America achieved independence in 1821 and then, for a short time,

were part of Mexico. In 1823 Central America declared its
independence from Mexico and established a loose federation. The
history of the Federation was one of chaos. It was beset by factional
and sectarian rivalries and endured two civil wars before collapsing in
1838. The Federation was the second country in the world (after Haiti)
to abolish black slavery. There have been numerous unsuccessful
attempts to revive the Central American Federation.

Readings: Delpar, 1974; Martin, 1968.

CONFEDERATION OF PERU AND BOLIVIA (Confederacion Perú-Boliviana)

> Just as on no side has it anything that can be called a natural frontier,
> neither have its inhabitants any distinctive quality or character to
> distinguish them sharply from other peoples.
> — James Bryce, 1912.

Area: 920,000 sq. miles (2,380,000 sq. km); Capital: Lima
Population: 5,000,000 (est. 1870)

In the time of the Spanish empire Peru and Bolivia were united, the
latter being known as Upper Peru. Bolivia's second president, Andres
Santa Cruz, who had been a general in the fight for independence, and
administrator of Peru, dreamed of restoring the union. His chance came
in 1836 when Peru was divided by factional war. Bolivian troops
entered Peru, in aid of one of the factions, and created the
Confederation of Peru and Bolivia. Santa Cruz styled himself Supreme
Protector. Chile, alarmed at the change in the region's balance of
power, sent its army into Peru, on behalf of the other faction.
Argentina became involved in 1837. After three years of fighting the
Bolivians and their Peruvian allies were defeated and the Confederation
came to an end.

Readings: Martin, 1968; Heath, 1972.

DEMERARA

> If there were but a snug secretaryship vacant there — and these things
> in Demerara are very snug — how I would invoke the goddess of
> patronage; how I would nibble around the officials of the Colonial

Office; how I would stir up my friends' friends to write little notes to their friends! For Demerara is the Elysium of the tropics.
— Anthony Trollope, 1860.

Area: 4,800 sq. miles (12,400 sq. km); Capital: Georgetown
Population: 148,026 (est. 1861)

One of three Dutch colonies in what became British Guiana (Guyana). Demerara, located on the central coast of British Guiana, was settled by the Dutch West India Company about 1613 and named after the Demerara River. Until 1773 it was a dependency of the adjacent colony of Essequibo. A railway was built in Demerara in 1848, the oldest in South America. The colony became British in 1814 and was united with Essequibo and Berbice in 1831 to form British Guiana

Stabroek Market, Georgetown

Readings: *Encyclopædia Britannica*, 1926; Trollope, 1860.

DUTCH GUIANA / NETHERLANDS GUIANA (Nederlandsch Guyana) / SURINAM

In Surinam Holland is Europe; Holland is the centre of the world.
. . . Surinam feels like a tropical, tulipless extension of Holland; some Surinamers call it Holland's twelfth province.
— V.S. Naipaul, 1962.

Area: 63,251 sq. miles (163,820 sq. km); Capital: Paramaribo
Population: 450,000 (est. 1977)

In northern South America bordered by British Guiana (Guyana) and French Guiana. The Spanish, British, French and Dutch were all interested in the area that became Dutch Guiana. The Dutch received it from the British in 1667 in exchange for Manhattan Island. Apart from British occupation during the Napoleonic Wars Guiana remained in Dutch hands until 1975 when it became independent as the Republic of Suriname.

During the 18th and 19th centuries the Dutch imported slaves from Africa to work their plantations. Slavery in Dutch Guiana was especially harsh resulting in large numbers of runaways. These people, "Bush Negroes" or Maroons, escaped to the rain forest where they retained their languages and re-created African village life. Despite the efforts of Dutch colonial troops to eradicate them these settlements have survived to the present. When slavery was abolished in 1863 there was a labor shortage, which was alleviated by contract workers from India, China and the Dutch East Indies (Indonesia). The descendants of all these peoples make up the melting pot that Dutch Guiana became. Of the small Dutch population about one-third were Jewish.

Between 1828 and 1845 Dutch Guiana was united with the Dutch islands of the West Indies under a single government with a governor residing in Guiana. From 1954 until independence Dutch Guiana was an autonomous unit of the Kingdom of the Netherlands.

Citrus fruit

Readings: *Collier's Encyclopedia*, 1994; *Encyclopædia Britannica*, 1926.

ESSEQUIBO

This delightful scenery of the Essequibo made the soul overflow with joy, and caused you to rove in fancy through fairyland.
— Charles Waterton, 1825.

Area: 67,500 sq. miles (174,800 sq. km); Capital: Suddie
Population: 24,925 (est. 1861)

A Dutch colony in what became British Guiana (Guyana) named after the largest river in British Guiana. The Dutch had established outposts in Essequibo by 1613 but a recognizable colony did not exist until about 1740 when settlers were attracted by free land and a ten-year tax holiday. The British purchased Essequibo in 1814 and merged it with Berbice and Demerara to create the colony of British Guiana in 1831.

King George V and Kaieteur Falls

Readings: *Encyclopædia Britannica*, 1926; Trollope, 1860.

FALKLAND ISLANDS DEPENDENCIES

The wild rocks raised their lofty summits till they were lost in the Clouds and the Vallies lay buried in everlasting snow. Not a tree or shrub was to be seen, no not even big enough to make a tooth-pick. . . . Our Botanists found here only three plants.
— Captain James Cook, 1775.

Area: 660,000 sq. miles (1,700,000 sq. km)

A collection of extremely remote islands (South Georgia, South Orkneys, South Sandwich, South Shetlands) under British control about 1,000 miles (1,600 km) southeast of the Falklands in the south Atlantic Ocean, and Graham Land on the Antarctic mainland. The islands were visited by Captain James Cook in 1775 and were long frequented by sealers and whalers. In response to the signing of the Antarctic Treaty in 1962, which placed in abeyance decisions regarding international claims in Antarctica, the United Kingdom created the British Antarctic

Territory. That portion of the Falkland Islands Dependencies south of 60° south latitude became the new territory. The rest of the Falkland Islands Dependencies have since become the Territory of South Georgia and South Sandwich Islands. Argentine forces briefly occupied much of the area in 1982 until ousted by the British.

There have been no permanent residents since 1966 when the last whaling station on South Georgia was closed. Since then the population has consisted of a few hundred scientific and meteorological personnel as well as a small military garrison.

Queen Elizabeth II and the John Biscoe

Readings: *New Encyclopedia Britannica*, 1991; *Statesman's Yearbook*, 1962.

FREE STATE OF THE ISTHMUS / STATE OF THE ISTHMUS OF PANAMA

> The country through which we pass is very beautiful. But it will not do to trust it much, because it breeds fevers and other unpleasant disorders at all seasons of the year. Like a girl we most all have known, the Isthmus is fair but false.
> — Charles F. Browne, 1865.

Area: 32,000 sq. miles (82,900 sq. km); Capital: Panama
Population: 220,542 (est. 1870)

A short-lived country in the Isthmus of Panama. Panama broke away from Spain in 1821 and joined Colombia as a state but a revolution in 1840 saw Panama secede and establish the Free State of the Isthmus. Neighboring Costa Rica quickly gave its recognition. During its thirteen months of existence the Free State developed a constitution and attempted to establish diplomatic relations with the United States. Following a period of negotiation the Free State of the Isthmus returned to the Colombian fold in 1841.

Readings: *Encyclopædia Britannica*, 1926; Hedrick, 1970.

FRENCH GUIANA (Guyane Française) / CAYENNE

> I looked around my cell. It was hard to believe that a country like mine, France, the cradle of liberty for the entire world, the land which gave birth to the Rights of Man, could maintain, even in French Guiana, on a tiny island lost in the Atlantic, an installation as barbarously repressive as the Réclusion of Saint-Joseph.
> — Henri "Papillon" Charrière, 1969.

Area: 32,252 sq. miles (83,533 sq. km); Capital: Cayenne
Population: 28,537 (est. 1946)

On the northeast coast of South America bordered by Brazil and Dutch Guiana (Surinam). Since 1946 French Guiana has been a French overseas department and an integral part of France.

After a French expedition failed to find El Dorado, the City of Gold, in 1604, a permanent settlement was established in 1640. In 1763, based on inflated promises of wealth, about 12,000 settlers from Alsace Lorraine were lured to French Guiana to their doom. Within two years more than 11,000 had died of fever and privation. Most of the survivors returned to France. At various times French Guiana has been captured by the Dutch and the Portuguese but since 1817 it has been in French hands.

For most of its history French Guiana was used as a penal settlement. The infamous Devil's Island (Ile du Diable), a low rocky island about 10 miles (16 km) off the coast, became notorious for its unhealthy climate and the harsh punishments meted out to its prisoners. The most famous prisoner sent to Devil's Island was Alfred Dreyfus, a French army officer unjustly convicted of treason in 1895. Unlike most he returned alive. Between 1852 and 1939, when transportation was abolished, more than 70,000 convicts were shipped to French Guiana. The last prisoners on Devil's Island were not repatriated until 1953. It was the custom that when a prisoner served his sentence he was freed but obliged to remain in the colony for an equal number of years.

Great anteater

Readings: Charrière, 1970; *Encyclopædia Britannica*, 1926.

GRAN COLOMBIA

> The ladies rarely go out. Domestic habits, joined to severe stomach-aches, caused by the garlic, tobacco, pork and chicha of which they partake very freely, cause them to be almost completely indisposed.
> — G. Mollien, 1824.

Area: 925,000 sq. miles (2,400,000 sq. km); Capital: Bogotá
Population: 6,500,000 (est. 1870)

A republic that included present-day Colombia, Venezuela, Ecuador and Panama. Beginning in 1810 Simón Bólivar led a struggle for the independence of what the Spanish called New Granada. The Spanish were defeated and the Republic of Gran Colombia was declared in 1819. From the outset the country was crippled by dissention and separatist movements. It was only the personal authority of Bólivar that kept it together at all. In 1830 Venezuela and Ecuador seceded and set up their own republics. Colombia and Panama stayed together under the name of New Granada.

Readings: Davis, 1977; Delpar, 1974.

ININI (Territoire de l'Inini)

> I listened to the night sounds of the bush and the constant chattering of the large-goitered monkeys with their powerful, raucous cry that you could hear miles away. This was very important, for as long as the cries were regular, the troop was eating and sleeping in peace. Therefore, we too were safe from man and beast.
> — Henri "Papillon" Charrière, 1969.

Area: 30,301 sq. miles (78,479 sq. km); Capital: St. Elie
Population: 5,024 (est. 1946)

A territory in the remote interior of French Guiana. Inini was split from French Guiana in 1930 and made a separate jurisdiction. It was restored in 1946 when French Guiana became an overseas department of France. Inini, used for penal settlements, was connected to French Guiana by rivers navigable only by small boats. Between 1951 and 1969 Inini was an arrondissement of French Guiana.

Maroni River rapids

Readings: Charrière 1970; *Statesman's Yearbook*, 1955.

MOSQUITO COAST / MOSQUITO SHORE

The boy was a shadow, and his flute no bigger than a twig, but the song was an invitation for us to stay a little longer on this Mosquito Coast. It had in it a promise and a plea, liquefied like the freshet of chirps from an oriole in a leafy tree.
— Paul Theroux, 1982.

Area: 9,000 sq. miles (23,000 sq. km); Capital: Bluefields
Population: 15,000 (est. 1905)

A vaguely defined geographical area along the Caribbean coast of Nicaragua named after its aboriginal inhabitants, the Miskito Indians. The British established a small settlement on the Mosquito Coast in 1630 and from 1655 to 1860 maintained a loose protectorate over the entire area. Various settlement attempts were made (mostly unsuccessful), which upset Spain, the republics of Central America and the United States. The United States, citing the Monroe Doctrine, was so annoyed with the British that it threatened war. The Americans were worried lest Great Britain establish a base in the area of the proposed interoceanic canal. The dispute was settled peacefully in 1850 when both countries agreed to withdraw from the Mosquito Coast. Even so it took a further ten years before the British transferred their protectorate to Nicaragua. The delay was caused by British insistence that the Miskito Indians be allowed to live on a self-governing reservation. The Indians enjoyed autonomy on the Mosquito Coast until the territory was officially merged with Nicaragua in 1894.

Readings: *Encyclopædia Britannica*, 1926; Lux, 1974.

NEW GRANADA (Nueva Granada) / UNITED STATES OF NEW GRANADA / GRANADINE CONFEDERATION / UNITED STATES OF COLOMBIA (Estados Unidos de Colombia)

"And why did you come to visit such a region as this?" asked Bolivar, when dying, of a Frenchman, to whom in his last days he was indebted for much. "For freedom," said the Frenchman. "For freedom!" said Bolivar. "Then let me tell you that you have missed your mark altogether; you could hardly have turned in a worse direction."
— Anthony Trollope, 1860.

Area: 518,000 sq. miles (1,340,000 sq. km); Capital: Bogotá
Population: 2,880,000 (est. 1870)

New Granada was the name of a Spanish viceroyalty centered around Colombia from 1538 until it was replaced by the Republic of Gran Colombia in 1819. Venezuela and Ecuador seceded from Gran Colombia in 1830 leaving Colombia and Panama to form the Republic of New Granada. New Granada was highly unstable and fragmented, racked by turmoil, dissentions, revolts and civil wars. The country has gone through a number of name changes but has been known as the Republic of Colombia since 1886. Panama seceded in 1903.

Readings: Delpar, 1974; Hedrick, 1970.

UNITED PROVINCES OF THE RIO DE LA PLATA

The absence of gentlemen by profession appears to an Englishman something strange.
— Charles Darwin, 1832-6.

Area: 452,700 sq. miles (1,172,000 sq. km); Capital: Buenos Aires
Population: 1,241,815 (est. 1869)

The forerunner of the present-day Republic of Argentina. In 1776 Spain detached its possessions in the basin of the Plata River (Argentina, Uruguay, Paraguay and parts of Bolivia) and created the Viceroyalty of the Rio de La Plata. With Spain under the control of Napoleon Buenos Aires inaugurated an administration to govern all of Rio de la Plata. Although independence from Spain was declared in 1816 it took years of hard fighting, led by José de San Martin, before the Spanish were defeated. The government in Buenos Aires wanted to maintain the boundaries of the Spanish viceroyalty but by 1828 Paraguay, Bolivia and Uruguay had broken away and created their own republics. The territory that remained constituted the Argentine Confederation. A conflict pitting centralists and federalists kept Argentina in turmoil for decades. The province of Buenos Aires seceded in 1853 but was forcibly reunited with Argentina in 1859.

José de San Martin

Readings: Delpar, 1974; Martin, 1968.

EUROPE — NAPOLEONIC PERIOD
1 United Kingdom of Great Britain and Ireland
2 Denmark and Norway
3 Batavian Republic
4 Confederation of the Rhine
5 Prussia
6 Grand Duchy of Warsaw
7 Austrian Empire
8 Neuchâtel
9 Geneva
10 Valais
11 Helvetian Republic
12 Cisalpine Republic
13 Ligurian Republic
14 Lucca
15 Ragusa
16 Montenegro
17 Ottoman Empire
18 Septinsular Republic

Atlantic
Ocean

North
Sea

Baltic Sea

Mediterranean
Sea

CHAPTER 4

Western Europe

I remember being much amused last year, when landing at Calais, at
the answer made by an old traveller to a novice who was making his
first voyage. "What a dreadful smell!" said the uninitiated stranger,
enveloping his nose in his pocket handkerchief. "It is the smell of the
continent, sir," replied the man of experience. And so it was.
— Frances Trollope, 1836.

BATAVIAN REPUBLIC (République Batave; Bataafse Republiek) / BATAVIAN COMMONWEALTH / KINGDOM OF HOLLAND

In no other country do the keels of the ships float above the chimneys,
and nowhere else does the frog, croaking from among the bulrushes,
look down upon the swallow on the house-top.
— Anon., q. by John W. Forney, 1867.

Area: 11,251 sq. miles (29,141 sq. km); Capital: Amsterdam
Population: 2,000,000 (est. 1810)

After the United Provinces (the Netherlands) was captured by the
forces of Revolutionary France in 1795 the Batavian Republic was
created by Napoleon as a buffer state. The republic, covering most of
what is now the Kingdom of the Netherlands, was closely monitored by
the French. Fearing that it was becoming too democratic, Napoleon
dissolved the Batavian Republic in 1805 and renamed it the Batavian

51

Commonwealth. This lasted little more than a year before emerging as the Kingdom of Holland, with Napoleon's brother Louis as its king. Unexpectedly, Louis Bonaparte proved to be a good and sympathetic ruler, who was reasonably popular with his subjects. King Louis exhibited a dangerous tendency to act for the benefit of Holland and not always for the Empire of France. As a result, Napoleon deposed him in 1810, abolished his kingdom and annexed it to France. The Netherlands reestablished its independence in 1813 as the United Netherlands, which included Belgium and Luxembourg.

Readings: Connelly, 1985; *New Encyclopædia Britannica*, 1991.

CISALPINE REPUBLIC (République Cisalpine; Repubblica Cisalpina)

> Milan was entered by us with anticipations the most gracious; which, contrary to ordinary experience, were surpassed by the events. The very name of this city as I write it, awakens feelings which the impartiality of veracious narrative should distrust.
> — Lady Morgan, 1820.

Area: 6,948 sq. miles (18,000 sq. km); Capital: Milan
Population: 5,000,000 (est. 1800)

A republic founded in northern Italy in 1797 by General Napoleon Bonaparte out of the Transpadane and Cispadane republics he had established earlier. Centered around the Po River valley the Cisalpine Republic comprised Lombardy, Emilia, Modena, Bologna and portions of the Venetian hinterland. The republic had a liberal constitution and, a government modeled on that of France, and it maintained an embassy in Paris. Independent in theory, the Cisalpine Republic was, in fact, propped up by French troops and money. In 1801 it was renamed the Italian Republic, with Napoleon as president, and in 1805 the Kingdom of Italy, with Napoleon as king. Under whatever name, the Cisalpine Republic perished with Napoleon.

Readings: Connelly, 1985; Coppa, 1985.

DENMARK-NORWAY

Norway is a hard country: hard to know, hard to shoot over, and hard — very hard — to fall down on: but hard to forsake and harder to forget.
— J.A. Lees, 1899.

Area: 131,000 sq. miles (340,000 sq. km); Capital: Copenhagen
Population: 2,815,000 (est. 1850)

Under the Kalmar Union of 1387 Norway and Sweden were united with Denmark. Sweden broke away after about two centuries but Norway remained under the Danish crown until 1814. Norway had become a mere Danish province in 1536. During the Napoleonic Wars Denmark-Norway sided with France, and Norway was blockaded by the British navy. At the end of the wars Denmark was forced to give up its claim to Norway. Norwegian desire for independence was thwarted by the great powers and the country was given to Sweden, which had joined the coalition against Napoleon. The Norwegians rebelled and declared their independence in 1814 but a Swedish invasion soon put an end to it. Norway did not achieve complete independence until 1905.

Readings: *Collier's Encyclopedia*, 1994; *Encyclopædia Britannica*, 1926.

REPUBLIC OF GENEVA (La République du Genève)

The Genevese are also much inclined to Puritanism. It is true that from habit they dance on a Sunday, but as soon as the French government was abolished in the town, the magistrates ordered the theatre to be closed, and measures were taken to pull down the building.
— Mary Shelley, 1816.

Area: 109 sq. miles (282 sq. km); Capital: Geneva
Population: 48,489 (est. 1815)

A canton in the southwestern corner of Switzerland, bordered on three sides by French territory. Although the second-smallest canton in Switzerland, Geneva has always been one of the most important. Inhabited for more than 2,000 years Geneva became an independent city-state in the 16th century. The city became the center of Calvinism and was known during the Reformation as the "Protestant Rome." Its acceptance of Calvinism alarmed the other cantons of Switzerland and delayed Geneva's admission into the Swiss confederation for generations. Geneva lost its independence in 1798 when it was annexed by Revolutionary France. The republic was restored in 1813 and it finally joined Switzerland as a canton in 1814. Geneva was the birthplace of Jean-Jacques Rousseau and a refuge for Voltaire. After World War I the city became the home of the League of Nations and is now the headquarters of many international agencies, such as the Red Cross.

Folk customs

Readings: *Collier's Encyclopedia*, 1994; *Encyclopædia Britannica*, 1926.

HELVETIC REPUBLIC (République Helvetique)

> Switzerland is simply a large, humpy, solid rock, with a thin skin of grass stretched over it.
> — Mark Twain, 1880.

Area: 13,541 sq. miles (35,071 sq. km); Capital: Rotated annually between Solothurn, Zürich, Basel, Lucerne, Fribourg and Berne
Population: 2,300,000 (est. 1850)

In 1798 France occupied Switzerland and converted most of it into a satellite state. Napoleon replaced a loose confederation of cantons, whose origins went back to 1291, with "The one and indivisible Helvetic Republic." At first the French were welcomed, particularly by those Swiss who wanted a unified state, but before long the French were seen as invaders and there were revolts that sparked brutal repression. Radical notions of democracy, individual liberty and strong central government were more than many Swiss were prepared to accept. Napoleon was inclined to make the Helvetic Republic neutral and then disengage but political chaos forced him to step in and impose order. Napoleon reestablished the semisovereign cantons but created a federal parliament and institutions. When French forces left the Helvetic Republic in 1813 the Swiss did not resist the advancing Allies. After protracted negotiations an independent, permanently neutral, Switzerland was organized in 1814, and the cantons of Geneva, Neuchâtel and Valais admitted.

The Swiss army fought the last foreign campaign in its history in 1815 during Napoleon's Hundred Days. The Helvetic Republic had served as an important recruiting ground for Napoleon. About 10,000 Swiss soldiers perished in the Russian campaign of 1812.

"Helvetia"

Readings: Connelly, 1985; *Encyclopædia Britannica*, 1926.

IRISH FREE STATE (Saorstát Eireann)

> Irish history is for Englishmen to remember and for Irishmen to forget.
> — Anon.

Area: 27,137 sq. miles (70,284 sq. km); Capital: Dublin
Population: 2,971,992 (est. 1926)

Ireland, which came under English control in 1691, was the scene of endemic revolt and sedition. On Easter Monday 1916 there was an uprising in Dublin. Although it was easily put down by the British the rising had serious political repercussions. Partly because of British over-reaction the moderate home rule faction in Irish politics was discredited and replaced by hard-line republicans. During the general election of 1918 Sinn Fein, the republican party, swept the polls in the 26, predominantly Roman Catholic, counties of southern Ireland. The voters of the northern six counties, mostly Protestant, indicated their continued desire to remain part of the United Kingdom. The south's proclamation of a republic in 1919 was not recognized and a bloody civil war broke out. The British, in 1920, passed the Government of Ireland Act, which allowed for the separation of Northern Ireland from the rest of the island and separate parliaments in the north and south. Only the northern parliament was established, as fighting continued in the south. Following a cease-fire in 1921 southern Ireland became the Irish Free State, a self-governing dominion within the British Empire. It was stated at the time that the Irish Free State was to have the same relationship to the imperial government as did Canada. But there were many in Ireland who wanted a republic with no ties to Britain whatsoever. The republicans gained power in the Irish Free State in 1932. By 1937, with a new constitution and a new name, Éire, the country, although still in the British Commonwealth, was a republic in everything but name. The last link with Britain was broken in 1948 with the establishment of the Republic of Ireland, which chose not to be a member of the Commonwealth.

Celtic cross

Readings: *Collier's Encyclopedia*, 1994; *New Encyclopædia Britannica*, 1991.

ITALIAN SOCIAL REPUBLIC (Repubblica Sociale Italiana) / SALO REPUBLIC

> It is not impossible to govern Italians. It is merely useless.
> — Benito Mussolini, attrib.

Area: 49,723 sq. miles (128,816 sq. km); Capital: Salò
Population: 20,082,541 (est. 1944)

A German client-state (September 1943 - April 1945) in the north of Italy, headed by Benito Mussolini. Early in World War II the Allies invaded Sicily and southern Italy. Soon after, Italian resistance crumbled. The liberated portion of Italy declared war on Germany and fascist dictator Mussolini was deposed and imprisoned. In a daring raid, Mussolini was rescued by German paratroopers and spirited away behind German lines, where he established the Italian Social Republic. Nominally an independent ally of Germany the Republic was, in practice, completely under German control and its leader a virtual prisoner guarded by the German SS. During its two-year existence the Republic had to contend with a strong antifascist resistance movement which resulted in the death of 36,000 resistance fighters and 10,000 civilians executed in acts of reprisal. Partisans finally caught up with Mussolini in April 1945 and executed him by hanging, thus bringing the Italian Social Republic to an ignominious end.

Basilica of San Lorenzo, Rome

Readings: Cannistraro, 1982; Coppa, 1985.

LIGURIAN REPUBLIC (République Ligurienne; Repubblica Ligure)

> The Genoese manner . . . is exceedingly animated and pantomimic; so that two friends of the lower class conversing pleasantly in the street, always seem on the eve of stabbing each other forthwith. And a stranger is immensely astonished at their not doing it.
> — Charles Dickens, 1844.

Area: 1,588 sq. miles (4,113 sq. km); Capital: Genoa
Population: 730,630 (est. 1861)

A republic consisting of the city of Genoa and its hinterland, in northwestern Italy. The Ligurian Republic was created in 1797 during General Napoleon Bonaparte's first Italian campaign and throughout its short existence was closely tied to France. Besieged and captured by the Austrians (1799-1800) the Ligurian Republic was reestablished in 1801, with Napoleon appointing its dodge, or chief executive. The republic ceased to exist in 1805 when it was annexed by the French empire. In 1814 Liguria was joined to the Kingdom of Sardinia and in 1861 became a province of the Kingdom of Italy.

Ligurian boat builder

Readings: Connelly, 1985; Coppa, 1985.

REPUBLIC OF LUCCA (République Lucquoise; Repubblica Lucchese)

> At Lucca, an enthusiastic sightseer once asked Mr. Ruskin, "What is the finest thing to see in Lucca?" The answer was: - "Oh, the clouds, you know."
> — Mrs. Henry Fawcett, 1885.

Area: 576 sq. miles (1,492 sq. km); Capital: Lucca
Population: 106,600 (est. 1774)

Lucca was a city-republic in northern Italy that maintained its independence, with a few interruptions, from 1118 until 1847. From medieval times the city was a major center of painting, sculpture, architecture and goldsmithing. Lucca was captured by Napoleon in 1799 and transformed into a republic, on the French model, in 1801. By 1805 Napoleon had changed his mind concerning Lucca and made it a principality under his sister Eliza. The city-state regained its independence in 1815 but as an absolutist duchy. When the royal house died out in 1847 Lucca was incorporated into Tuscany and became part of the Kingdom of Italy in 1860.

Readings: Connelly, 1985; Coppa, 1985.

MASSA-CARRARA (Massa e Carrara)

> This Towne . . . is famous for the marble, which is much preferred
> before other, as well for the exceeding whiteness of some stones, as
> for the length of pillars and tables digged thence.
> — Fynes Moryson, 1617.

Area: 680 sq. miles (1,760 sq. km); Capital: Massa
Population: 161,944 (est. 1871)

A tiny principality in north central Italy which became independent
in 1442. Carrara was added to Massa in 1473. Massa-Carrara became
a duchy in 1663 and maintained its independence until 1829 when it
passed, by marriage, to the Duchy of Modena. Massa-Carrara was
united with the Kingdom of Sardinia in 1859 and the Kingdom of Italy
in 1860. Sculptors from Michelangelo to Henry Moore have used the
famous marble from the quarries of Carrara.

Readings: *American Cyclopædia*, 1883; *Encyclopædia Britannica*, 1926.

MODENA

> An ill-built, melancholy place, all of brick . . .
> — Thomas Gray, 1739.

Area: 2,300 sq. miles (5,950 sq. km); Capital: Modena
Population: 273,231 (est. 1872)

A city-state in north central Italy. Originally an Etruscan town
Modena was captured by the Romans in 183 B.C., becoming a free
republic in 1135 and a duchy in 1452. Apart from short spans of
Austrian and Papal rule and a French occupation (1796-1814), during
which the city was included in Napoleon's Cisalpine Republic, Modena
maintained its independence until 1859. In that year its last duke was
overthrown and Modena was annexed by the Kingdom of Sardinia.
After a referendum in 1860 Modena voted overwhelmingly to join the
Kingdom of Italy.

Castle of Vignola

Readings: *American Cyclopædia*, 1883; *Encyclopædia Britannica*, 1926.

NEUCHATEL (Neuenburg)

. . . what was less than Switzerland was in some sort better, in its
meek sincerity and healthy purity.
— John Ruskin, 1885-9.

Area: 312 sq. miles (808 sq. km); Capital: Neuchâtel
Population: 48,000 (est. 1806)

Founded in 1648, an independent principality sandwiched between
Switzerland and France. After the extinction of its royal house in 1707
Neuchâtel passed to the King of Prussia until its occupation by France
in 1798. Between 1806 and 1814 Neuchâtel was again a principality,
but this time under Napoleon's chief of staff, Marshal Louis-Alexandre
Berthier. Although the prince never once visited his principality he took
its welfare seriously, reorganizing its finance and administration. A
detachment from Neuchâtel served in Napoleon's army and 977 of them
died.

After the final defeat of Napoleon in 1815 the Congress of Vienna
gave Neuchâtel a dual status. It would be a canton of Switzerland but
at the same time a hereditary principality and personal possession of the
King of Prussia. Neuchâtel was admitted as Switzerland's sole
monarchial canton but the arrangement pleased no one. An insurrection
in 1848 took advantage of Prussia's distraction elsewhere and
established a republican form of government in Neuchâtel.

In 1856 tiny Neuchâtel almost ignited a major European war. After
an unsuccessful coup d'état in the canton the plotters were arrested by

Swiss authorities and imprisoned. Prussia threatened Switzerland with war and France supported Switzerland. Fortunately, cooler heads prevailed. The leaders of the coup were released and Prussia renounced its sovereignty over Neuchatêl, although its king retained the princely title.

Centenary of the Neuchatêl Insurrection

Readings: Connelly, 1985; *Encyclopædia Britannica*, 1926.

PAPAL STATES (Stati Pontifici) / CHURCH STATES (Stati della Chiesa)

> Where the Pope is, there is Rome.
> — Italian proverb.

Area: 16,000 sq. miles (41,400 sq. km); Capital: Rome
Population: 3,124,758 (est. 1853)

The central Italian regions of Marche, Lazio, Umbria and Romagna awarded to Pope Stephen II in 756 by the Frankish king, Pepin the Short. The Church sought temporal power to provide itself with the revenues and political independence necessary to carry out its spiritual mission. Papal rule was loose until the middle of the 11th century when Pope Gregory VII, and his successors, began to assume more control. By the 15th century the popes ruled as absolute monarchs. The French occupied the Papal States during the Napoleonic Wars but the Congress of Vienna (1815) restored them to the papacy. The population of the Papal States, however, had become dissatisfied with what they considered to be a reactionary ecclesiastical regime and there were several uprisings that needed foreign intervention to suppress. Most of the Papal States were united with the Kingdom of Italy in 1860. Thanks to the presence of a French garrison the area around Rome remained

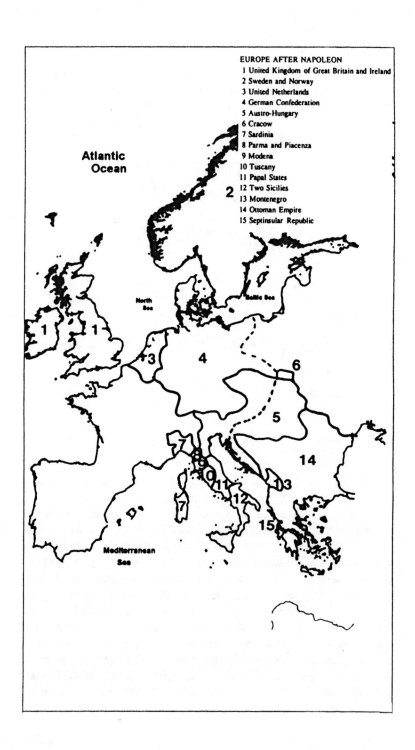

EUROPE AFTER NAPOLEON
1 United Kingdom of Great Britain and Ireland
2 Sweden and Norway
3 United Netherlands
4 German Confederation
5 Austro-Hungary
6 Cracow
7 Sardinia
8 Parma and Piacenza
9 Modena
10 Tuscany
11 Papal States
12 Two Sicilies
13 Montenegro
14 Ottoman Empire
15 Septinsular Republic

Atlantic
Ocean

North
Sea

Baltic Sea

Mediterranean
Sea

under papal rule. When the French went home Rome was annexed by Italy in 1870 and the Papal States ceased to exist. The papacy refused to accept the annexation and the popes withdrew into the Vatican in protest. This period, when the popes were "prisoners in the Vatican" lasted until the signing of the Lateran Pacts with Fascist Italy in 1929. Italy recognized the Vatican as a sovereign city-state with the pope as its head of state. Financial compensation was given for the loss of the Papal States and a guarantee that the Italian government would not interfere in ecclesiastical matters. In return the Church gave up its claim to the Papal States and recognized the existence of Italy with Rome as its capital. The Fascist government of Italy received a valuable boost in prestige and Catholic opposition was placated.

Papal arms

Readings: Cannistraro, 1982; Coppa, 1985.

DUCHY OF PARMA AND PIACENZA

A brown, decayed, old town, Piacenza is. A deserted, solitary, grass-grown place, with ruined ramparts; half-filled-up trenches, which afford a frowzy pasturage to the lean kine which wander about them: and streets of stern houses, moodily frowning at the other houses over the way.
— Charles Dickens, 1846.

Area: 2,376 sq. miles (6,154 sq. km); Capital: Parma
Population: 497,343 (est. 1851)

Parma and Piacenza was separated from the Papal States in 1545 by Pope Paul III who made it a duchy for his natural son, Luigi Farnese. The Farnese family ruled Parma and Piacenza until 1731 and were instrumental in making the duchy the most important center of art and culture in northern Italy. When the family died out Parma and Piacenza passed to the Spanish Bourbons, until annexed by France in 1808. Napoleon's second consort, Marie-Louise was given Parma and

Piacenza in 1815. When she died in 1847 the duchy was returned to the Bourbons, an unpopular move. After a period of rebellions, demands for Italian independence and the assassination of its duke Parma and Piacenza was annexed by Sardinia in 1860. Parma was the home of the celebrated Parmesan cheese and the equally celebrated conductor, Arturo Toscanini.

Readings: *American Cyclopædia*, 1883; *Encyclopædia Britannica*, 1926.

SARDINIA (Sardegna) / PIEDMONT (Piemonte) / PIEDMONT-SARDINIA

> A lady of a great house in Piedmont, having four sons, makes no scruple to declare, that the first shall represent the family, the second enter into the army, the third into the church, and that she will breed the fourth a gamester.
> — Tobias Smollett, 1766.

Area: 20,600 sq. miles (53,354 sq. km); Capital: Turin
Population: 3,312,000 (est. 1859)

Sardinia, the second-largest island in the Mediterranean Sea, lies off the west coast of Italy and south of Corsica. Piedmont is the northwestern portion of the Italian mainland and borders France and Switzerland. The Kingdom of Sardinia was founded in 1720 when the island, in exchange for the loss of Sicily, was added to the mainland territories of the House of Savoy - Piedmont. The Kingdom of Sardinia was expansionist and became the hotbed of the Risorgimento, the movement for Italian unification. Although the Piedmont portion of the kingdom was temporarily overrun by the forces of Napoleon Bonaparte Sardinia was unusual among Italian states in that it was otherwise strong enough to stay free of foreign domination. After Napoleon's downfall Sardinia and Piedmont were reunited. As a result of uprisings and war against Austria, Italian unification was achieved but at the cost of ceding Savoy and Nice to France. Sardinia-Piedmont was merged into the Kingdom of Italy in 1861. Victor Emmanuel II of Sardinia became the first king of unified Italy and Turin its first capital.

Sardinian shepherd

Readings: *American Cyclopædia*, 1883; *New Encyclopædia Britannica*, 1991.

SWEDEN-NORWAY

> The extraordinary sight of men employed in knitting stockings, so
> common in Sweden, is, perhaps, not to be seen elsewhere.
> — E. D. Clarke, 1824.

Area: 298,780 sq. miles (773,842 sq. km); Capital: Stockholm
Population: 7,900,000 (est. 1910)

Norway, which had been a Danish province for centuries, was
united with Sweden at the conclusion of the Napoleonic Wars in 1815.
The loss of Norway was Denmark's punishment for supporting
Napoleon. The gain of Norway was Sweden's reward for joining the
coalition against Napoleon and compensation for the loss of Finland to
Russia. During the horse trading that went on, the aspirations of
Norwegians were largely ignored. Norway declared itself independent
in 1814 but a Swedish army enforced the union of the two countries.
The union, from the Norwegian perspective was more irritating than
oppressive. Norway was a separate country under the Swedish king and
exercised considerable autonomy. Even so, Sweden was the dominant
partner and Norway often chafed under the restrictions placed upon it

by the union. In 1905, after a political crises, the union was dissolved and Norway became fully independent. War had threatened but the great powers pressured Sweden to accept the situation. The split was achieved peacefully.

Readings: *Collier's Encyclopedia*, 1994; *Encyclopædia Britannica*, 1926.

FREE TERRITORY OF TRIESTE (Triest; Trst)

"We are the furthest limit of Latinity," the Mayor of Trieste exclaimed to me one day, "the southern extremity of Germanness." Triestini love this sort of hyperbole.
— Jan Morris, 1980.

Area: 293 sq. miles (759 sq. km); Capital: Trieste
Population: 360,000 (est. 1953)

A city and region at the northwestern end of the Adriatic Sea, disputed by Italy and Yugoslavia after World War II. Trieste was Austrian territory from 1382 to 1918 and before World War I was Austria-Hungary's largest port. Desire to acquire the port, which had a majority Italian population, was one of the reasons Italy entered the war on the Allied side in 1915. The hinterland of Trieste was mostly Slav. Italy occupied Trieste in 1918 until replaced by the Germans in 1943. Under the peace treaty of 1947 Italy relinquished the Istrian Peninsula and the city of Trieste, which were then constituted as the Free Territory of Trieste. The territory was split into two zones: Zone A, comprising Trieste and its immediate environs, governed by a joint U.S.-U.K. military government; and Zone B, the Istrian Peninsula, which was placed under a Yugoslav military administration. In 1954 the city of Trieste went to Italy, all of Zone B and a small portion of Zone A, about two-thirds of the total area, became part of Yugoslavia. The Yugoslav portion has since become Slovenian.

Zone A. Italian stamp
overprinted AMG - FTT
(Allied Military Government
— Free Territory of Trieste)

Zone B. Yugoslavian stamp overprinted STT VUJNA "Slobodna
Teritorija Trsta Vojna Uprava Jugoslovenske Narodna Armije" (Free
Territory of Trieste Military Administration Yugoslav People's Army)

Readings: Coppa, 1985; *Statesman's Yearbook*, 1955.

TUSCANY (Toscana) / ETURIA

> To me, Italy had a certain hard taste in the mouth. Its mountains were
> too bare, its outlines too sharp, its lanes too stony, its voices too loud,
> its long summer too dusty.
> — Leigh Hunt, 1850.

Area: 8,890 sq. miles (23,025 sq. km); Capital: Florence
Population; 2,892,000 (est. 1859)

An ancient region of west central Italy on the Tyrrhenian Sea ruled, in turn, by Etruscans, Romans, Lombards and Franks. In the 11th century the Tuscan cities of Pisa, Lucca, Siena, Arezzo and Florence became important city-republics. Between the 14th and 16th centuries Florence rose to dominance and in 1569 the Medici ruler of Florence became the Grand Duke of Tuscany. The Medici family ruled until 1737 when Tuscany passed to the House of Habsburg-Lorraine. It remained in their possession, except for French rule (1799-1814), until the unification of Italy in 1860. In 1801 Napoleon created the Kingdom of Eturia out of the duchy but annexed it to the French Empire in 1808. Restored in 1814, Tuscany merged with Sardinia in 1860.

Tuscan potter

Readings: Connelly, 1985; *Encyclopædia Britannica*, 1926.

KINGDOM OF THE TWO SICILIES (Regno delle Due Sicilie) / KINGDOM OF NAPLES (Regno di Napoli)

> . . . Sicily was an excellent school of political economy; for, in any town there, it only needed to ask what the government enacted, and reverse that, to know what ought to be done; it was the most felicitously opposite legislation to anything good and wise.
> — Ralph Waldo Emerson, 1856.

Area: 43,146 sq. miles (111,776 sq. km); Capital: Naples
Population: 9,283,636 (est. 1865)

The Kingdom of Naples (comprising the southern half of the Italian Peninsula) and the Kingdom of Sicily (the largest island in the Mediterranean Sea) were united in 1442 by Alfonso V of Aragon, who referred to himself as the King of the Two Sicilies. The two kingdoms were later split apart but from 1504 to 1713, when Naples and Sicily were ruled by Spain, the name was again in use. In 1759 the name was used once more. Finally, in 1816, over Sicilian objections, Ferdinand IV of Naples amalgamated the kingdoms under himself as Ferdinand I of the Two Sicilies. Ferdinand's reactionary policies and a Sicilian desire for independence led to a revolt in 1820. Even so, the Two Sicilies endured until 1860 when Naples and Sicily were captured by the nationalist forces of Giuseppe Garibaldi. Since 1861 the Two Sicilies have been part of unified Italy.

Coat of arms of the Two Sicilies

Readings: Coppa, 1985; *Encyclopædia Britannica*, 1926.

UNITED KINGDOM OF GREAT BRITAIN AND IRELAND

England is not governed by logic, but by acts of Parliament.
— Anon.

Area: 121,385 sq. miles (314,386 sq. km); London
Population: 44,932,884 (est. 1931)

Great Britain (England, Scotland and Wales) and Ireland are two large islands off the northwest coast of Europe. Great Britain had dominated Ireland for hundreds of years before the British Prime Minister, William Pitt, amalgamated the Irish and English Parliaments. The union of the two countries came into effect on 1 January, 1801, creating the United Kingdom of Great Britain and Ireland. Ireland was guaranteed 20 percent of the members in the House of Commons. The union was not a happy one for Ireland and there was continual turmoil,

political dissent, and the threat of armed insurrection. As a result of the
Irish potato famine in the 1840s as many as 1,000,000 people died.
During the 19th century the United Kingdom, as a whole, went from
triumph to triumph. It became the superpower of its time and controlled
a vast worldwide empire. Yet its most intractable problem was not
found on the Northwest Frontier of India or even in the South African
veldt but close at hand — Ireland. Following a period of civil war, that
island was divided in 1921 between the Irish Free State and Northern
Ireland. The name of the entire country was now changed to the United
Kingdom of Great Britain and Northern Ireland to reflect the fact that
the Irish Free State had become a self-governing dominion. Northern
Ireland remains part of the United Kingdom, while the Irish Free State
has become the Republic of Ireland.

Queen Victoria

Readings: *Collier's Encyclopedia*, 1994; *Encyclopædia Britannica*, 1926.

UNITED NETHERLANDS (Verenigde Nederlands)

A country which art seems to have endeavoured to render picturesque
in proportion as it has been made otherwise by nature.
— Robert Southey, 1815.

Area: 27,806 sq. miles (72,017 sq. km); Capital: Amsterdam
Population: 5,500,000 (est. 1815)

Covering what is now Holland (the Netherlands), Belgium and
Luxembourg. Even before Napoleon's final defeat at Waterloo, in
1815, Holland had reestablished its independence as a kingdom. The
Allies, who did not want to give Belgium to France or any other great
power, decided to attach it to Holland as a part of a unitary state.
Belgium and Holland had been united until the 16th century but since
then had developed differently. Holland was Protestant, commercial and

Dutch-speaking. Belgium was Catholic, industrial and French- and Flemish-speaking. The Belgians, who were the majority of the population, resented Dutch domination and the imposition of Dutch as the official language. Even the Flemings, who spoke a Dutch dialect, were upset. A revolution in Belgium, in 1830, showed that the United Netherlands were united in name only. After some fighting the great powers imposed an armistice and recognized Belgium's independence. A German prince, Leopold of Saxe-Coburg, was installed as Belgium's first king. Meanwhile Luxembourg, which had sided with the revolutionaries in Belgium, was partitioned. The French-speaking west was united with Belgium and the remainder organized as an independent state in personal union with the Dutch king, a state of affairs which endured until 1890.

150th anniversary of the founding of the United Netherlands

Readings: *Collier's Encyclopedia*, 1994; *Encyclopædia Britannica*, 1926.

REPUBLIC OF VALAIS (République du Valais) / RHODANIC REPUBLIC (République Rhodanique)

> For a vision of the Valais with the coming of July,
> For the Oberland or Valais and the higher, purer air,
> And the true delight of living, as you taste it only there!
> — A. D. Godley, 1902.

Area: 2,018 sq. miles (5,227 sq. km); Capital: Sion
Population: 96,888 (est. 1870)

A canton in southern Switzerland, about two-thirds French-speaking and one third German-speaking, on the border of Italy and France. In 1798 Valais became part of the Napoleon-inspired Helvetic Republic.

However in 1802, in order to secure the strategic Simplon Pass through the Alps, Napoleon detached the canton and converted it into the separate Republic of Valais. It was also known as the Rhodanic Republic, from the Rhône River, which traversed it. Such independence as it enjoyed lasted only until 1810 when Valais was annexed outright by France. Since 1815 Valais has been part of Switzerland. The Matterhorn is located in Valais, on the Italian border.

Rhône glacier

Readings: *Encyclopædia Britannica*, 1926; *Grand Dictionnaire*, 1982.

VICHY FRANCE

> There's something Vichy about the French.
> — Ivor Novello, 1941, q. by Edward Marsh, 1964.

Area: 85,000 sq. miles (220,000 sq. km); Capital: Vichy
Population: 12,000,000 (est. 1945)

In World War II the world was stunned when France, possessor of the largest army in Europe, was totally defeated by Nazi Germany after a campaign lasting only six weeks. Following an armistice concluded on June 22, 1940, France was partitioned. The southeastern two-fifths of the country was to remain independent and sovereign while the remainder was placed under German military occupation. With Marshal Philippe Pétain, a hero of World War I, as premier and Pierre Laval as his deputy, a collaborationist government was set up, headquartered at the spa town of Vichy. Convinced that Germany had won the war the collaborators felt that France had no choice but to adapt to the new world order. In late 1942, when an Anglo-American force invaded Vichy-held North Africa, Vichy troops resisted only briefly before surrendering. In response, Germany occupied all of France. The government at Vichy continued to exist but in name only. It became a tool of the Germans useful for policing the country, combating the Resistance, and requisitioning food, raw materials and labor. Following the Allied liberation of France the Vichy government collapsed in September 1944. A Vichy government-in-exile survived until war's end in a German castle. At least 10,000 Vichy supporters were summarily executed by the Resistance. After the war Laval was tried and executed while Pétain died in prison.

Marshal Pétain

Readings: *Collier's Encyclopedia*, 1994; *New Encyclopædia Britannica*, 1991.

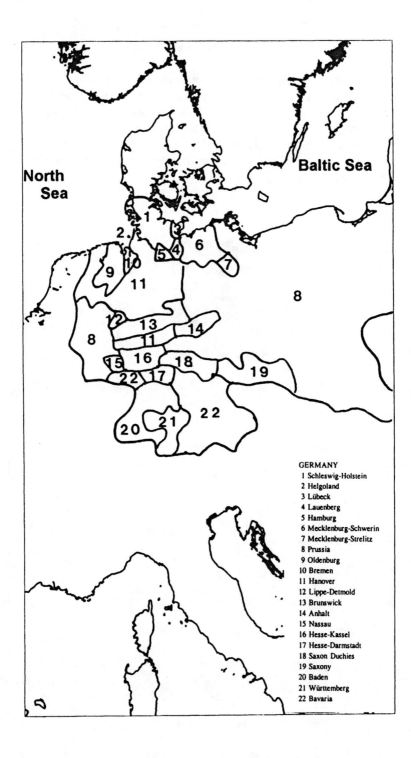

North
Sea

Baltic Sea

GERMANY
1 Schleswig-Holstein
2 Helgoland
3 Lübeck
4 Lauenberg
5 Hamburg
6 Mecklenburg-Schwerin
7 Mecklenburg-Strelitz
8 Prussia
9 Oldenburg
10 Bremen
11 Hanover
12 Lippe-Detmold
13 Brunswick
14 Anhalt
15 Nassau
16 Hesse-Kassel
17 Hesse-Darmstadt
18 Saxon Duchies
19 Saxony
20 Baden
21 Württemberg
22 Bavaria

CHAPTER 5

Germany

Members of the German race . . . look upon beer drinking as an essential element in man's social and moral nature, and think everybody a Puritan or fanatic who holds different views.
— J.E. Stebbins, 1874.

ANHALT (Freistaat Anhalt)

The Duke of Vanholt! an honourable gentleman to whom I must be no niggard of my cunning.
— Christopher Marlowe, 1588.

Area: 906 sq. miles (2,347 sq. km); Capital: Dessau
Population: 203,354 (est. 1871)

A principality, later a duchy, in eastern Germany founded by Frederick Barbarosa in 1180 and separated from the Duchy of Saxony in 1212. By 1603, due to inheritances and deaths in the ducal line, Anhalt was split into three smaller duchies; Anhalt-Dessau, Anhalt-Köthen and Anhalt-Bernberg. In 1847 the first two were merged and in 1863 the last. The reconstituted Duchy of Anhalt, which became a state in the German Reich in 1871, lasted from 1863 to 1918. Upon the abolition of the ducal regime in 1918 Anhalt became the Free State of Anhalt. This status continued until 1945 when Anhalt became part of the state of Anhalt-Saxony in the German Democratic Republic. In

1952 Anhalt ceased to exist when its territory was divided between Magdeburg and Halle. Catherine the Great, Empress of Russia, was of the Anhalt dynastic line.

Readings: *American Cyclopædia*, 1883; *Encyclopædia Britannica*, 1926.

ANHALT-BERNBERG

On each side of the river were beautiful rising grounds covered with vines. Pray may we not have the same in Scotland? Surely our climate differs little from that of Saxony. I saw too, here and there, old castles, Heerschaften's houses, seats of gentlemen. It pleased me. It was Scottish.
— James Boswell, 1764.

Area: 301 sq. miles (780 sq. km); Capital: Bernberg
Population: 15,716 (est. 1871)

In east-central Germany. Mentioned as early as 961 Bernberg was on an important trade route in the Middle Ages. Anhalt-Bernberg was a duchy in some form from 1251 to 1863 when, upon the extinction of its ruling family, it joined with Anhalt-Dessau to form the Duchy of Anhalt.

Readings: *Encyclopædia Britannica*, 1926; Pottle, 1953.

ANHALT-DESSAU

The forests of Dessau are magnificent, all of fine oaks, some of which are immensely large.
— James Boswell, 1764.

Area: 324 sq. miles (840 sq. km); Capital: Dessau
Population: 17,464 (est. 1871)

First mentioned as a German town in 1213, Anhalt-Dessau was a duchy north of Leipzig. Between 1603 and 1918 Dessau was the seat of the dukes, counts and princes of Anhalt. In 1847 Anhalt-Dessau merged with Anhalt-Bernberg to form the Duchy of Anhalt. The philosopher Moses Mendelssohn was born in Dessau in 1729 and the

Bauhaus school of architecture under Walter Gropius was located there from 1925 to 1933.

Readings: *Encyclopædia Britannica*, 1926; Pottle, 1953.

ANHALT-KÖTHEN (Anhalt-Cöthen)

The being served at every inn, since we came into Saxony, upon Dresden china, gives one an odd feel somehow.
— Hester Lynch Piozzi, 1789.

Area: 280 sq. miles (727 sq. km); Capital: Köthen
Population: 13,563 (est. 1871)

A principality, later duchy, in east-central Germany. Dating to 1115 Köthen had become an important market town by 1194. Anhalt-Köthen existed as a duchy from 1603 to 1847 when its royal line died out and it was added to the territory of the nearby duchy of Anhalt-Dessau. From 1717 to 1723 J.S. Bach was concertmaster in Köthen and wrote his Brandenburg Concertos there.

Readings: *American Cyclopædia*, 1883; *Encyclopædia Britannica*, 1926.

BADEN (Republik Baden; Freistaat Baden)

. . . I left my rheumatism in Baden-Baden. Baden-Baden is welcome to it. It was little, but it was all I had to give. I would have preferred to leave something that was catching, but it was not in my power.
— Mark Twain, 1880.

Area: 5,851 sq. miles (15,154 sq. km); Capital: Karlsruhe
Population: 1,461,428 (est. 1871)

In the extreme southwestern corner of Germany, dominated by the Rhine River and the Black Forest, Baden has been a recognizable entity since 1112. It was ruled by a margrave — a hereditary title from the Holy Roman Empire similar to a count. For about six hundred years Baden was divided into petty states. It was torn by bitter sectarian conflict during the Reformation, pillaged during the Thirty Years' War (1618-1648) and not reunited until 1771. During the French Revolution and the Napoleonic period Baden became a virtual French dependency and profited greatly by it. Margrave Charles Frederick married Napoleon's adopted daughter, quadrupled the size of his dominion, and made it a grand duchy in his father-in-law's Confederation of the Rhine. When Napoleon's power faded Charles Frederick changed sides at precisely the right moment. As a result Baden was able to join the German Confederation in 1815 as a sovereign state and keep most of its territorial acquisitions. The Grand Duchy of Baden became part of unified Germany in 1871. The last duke was deposed in 1918 and a provisional government proclaimed Baden a republic and a component free state of Germany. After World War II Baden was divided between American and French zones of occupation. It is now part of the German state of Baden-Württemberg.

The most fashionable health spa in Europe was located in the Black Forest town of Baden-Baden. Its warm mineral springs have been in use since Roman times.

Black Forest

Readings: *Encyclopædia Britannica*, 1926; Twain, 1880.

BAVARIA (Bayern; Freistaat Bayern)

[The Bavarian King] is fond of the opera, but not fond of sitting in the presence of an audience; therefore, it has sometimes occurred, in Munich, that when an opera has been concluded and the players were getting off their paint and finery, a command has come to them to get their paint and finery on again. Presently the king would arrive, solitary and alone, and the players would begin at the beginning and do the entire opera over again with only that one individual in the vast solemn theatre for an audience.
— Mark Twain, 1880.

Area: 30,562 sq. miles (79,155 sq. km); Capital: Munich
Population: 4,861,402 (est. 1871)

In southern Germany, bordered by Austria and Czechoslovakia (Czech Republic); divided by the Danube River. Originally inhabited by highly advanced Celtic peoples Bavaria was subdued by the Romans during the reign of Augustus (c. 15 B.C.). In 788, about the same time the country was christianized by Irish and Scottish monks, Bavaria was incorporated into Charlemagne's empire. Bavaria, which became a duchy and after 1806 a kingdom, was ruled by the Wittelsbach family from 1180 to 1918. Under Napoleon's tutelage Bavaria greatly expanded its territories at the expense of Austria. Bavaria joined the Allies for the final defeat of Napoleon (1814-1815). Linking itself with Prussia in the Franco-Prussian War Bavaria shared in the establishment of the German Empire in 1871. Until World War I Bavaria enjoyed a greater amount of independence than any other state in Germany. It retained separate military, postal, railway and telegraph systems and diplomatic service. The last king of Bavaria was deposed in 1918 and replaced by a short-lived soviet republic. The Nazi Party was established in Bavaria and in 1923 Adolf Hitler staged an unsuccessful coup in Munich. After World War II Bavaria was occupied by the Americans. Bavaria is now the largest land, or state, in Germany.

In the alpine village of Oberammergau a passion play has been enacted every ten years since 1633, in fulfillment of a vow.

Bavarian coat of arms

Readings: *Encyclopædia Britannica*, 1926; Twain, 1880.

BERG

> The Germans are exceedingly fond of Rhine wines; they are put up in tall slender bottles, and are considered a pleasant beverage. One tells them from vinegar by the label.
> — Mark Twain, 1880.

Area: 1,120 sq. miles (2,900 sq. km); Capital: Berg
Population: 878,000 (est. 1807)

A duchy of the Holy Roman Empire, on the Rhine between Cologne and Düsseldorf, Berg became a countship in 1108 and a duchy in 1380. A dispute over the succession to the throne of Berg was one of the causes of the Thirty Years' War in the 17th century. Napoleon made Berg a grand duchy in his Confederation of the Rhine in 1806. After Napoleon's defeat Berg became part of Prussia's Rhine province.

Readings: *Encyclopædia Britannica*, 1926; Twain, 1880.

BERGDORF

The surrounding district, exceptionally fertile marshland, is known as Die Vierlande, being divided into four parishes, whence the name is derived.
— *Encyclopædia Britannica*, 1926.

Area: 34 sq. miles (87 sq. km); Capital: Bergdorf
Population: 12,000 (est. 1861)

Bergdorf was a town in northern Germany that received civic rights in 1275. It was jointly owned by the free cities of Hamburg and Lübeck, an arrangement that lasted from 1420 to 1867 when Bergdorf was purchased outright by Hamburg.

Reading: *Encyclopædia Britannica*, 1926.

BREMEN / FREE HANSEATIC STATE OF BREMEN (Freie Hansestadt Bremen)

As one approaches the frontiers of a great country like Germany, a general interest in that country gives place to the particular interest in the first important town one proposes to visit. As we approached our port of debarkation, then, Bremen stood in the foreground and quite blocked our view of Germany.
— Henry Albert Phillips, 1929.

Area: 99 sq. miles (256 sq. km); Capital: Bremen
Population: 122,000 (est. 1871)

An important port in northwestern Germany on the Weser River about 43 miles (70 km) from the North Sea. Founded in 787 by

Charlemagne, Bremen became a prosperous trading center, joining the Hanseatic League in 1358. Occupying a fortified position, Bremen successfully asserted its independence for centuries. It accepted the Protestant Reformation in 1522 and became a free imperial city a century later. The conclusion of the Thirty Years' War saw Bremen placed under Swedish rule. The city, which was the oldest republic in Germany, did not regain its autonomy until 1741. Bremen was taken by France in 1806 and annexed. It joined the German Confederation in 1815 and merged with other states to form Imperial Germany in 1871.

At the Weser's estuary, separated from the rest of Bremen, was the port of Bremerhaven built on land purchased from Hanover. Bremerhaven was established to handle ships too large to sail up the river to Bremen.

Bremen became a state of the Federal Republic of Germany in 1947. Bremen today constitutes the smallest German state but is, economically, one of the most important.

Readings: *Encyclopædia Britannica*, 1926; Phillips, 1929.

BRUNSWICK (Braunschweig; Freistaat Braunschweig)

It is an old, silent, dull looking place, but has some good houses in it.
— Dorothy Wordsworth, 1798.

Area: 1,417 sq. miles (3,670 sq. km); Capital: Brunswick
Population: 311,715 (est. 1871)

A sovereign duchy in northwestern Germany now incorporated into the state of Lower Saxony. Brunswick became a duchy in 1235 but its power and influence did not match its ancient lineage. Its territory was repeatedly divided due to deaths and inheritances among its ruling family. The duchy was split into three main sections and six enclaves. Hanover was at times part of Brunswick. Brunswick was included in Napoleon's Kingdom of Westphalia (1806-1814) and in 1871 became part of the German Reich. In 1918 the dukes were overthrown and Brunswick became a state in the German Republic. The state of Brunswick ceased to exist in 1934. After World War II the territory that had been Brunswick was included in the British zone of occupation.

Brunswick coat of arms

Readings: De Selincourt, 1952; *Encyclopædia Britannica*, 1926.

CONFEDERATION OF THE RHINE (Rheinbund; Confédération du Rhin)

The lordly, lovely Rhine.
— Thomas Campbell, 1841.

Area: 125,000 sq. miles (324,000 sq. km); Capital: Frankfurt
Population: 15,000,000 (est. 1808)

The French, under Napoleon I, annexed all the German territories west of the Rhine and created a union, except for Austria and Prussia, of the German-speaking states that remained. Napoleon set up the Confederation of the Rhine in 1806 with himself as its protector. The union was created to control Germany and counterbalance Austria and Prussia. The principle member states were Bavaria, Württemburg, Baden, Hesse-Darmstadt, Berg and Westphalia. The member states retained their internal autonomy but were required to kowtow to Napoleon's foreign policy and supply troops and money for his armies. By enlarging the larger states at the expense of the smaller, Napoleon won the Confederation of the Rhine's support — until the French suffered a shattering defeat at the Battle of Leipzig in 1813. The Confederation of the Rhine lasted just six years but it paved the way for the eventual unification of Germany in 1871.

Readings: Connelly, 1985; *New Encyclopædia Britannica*, 1991.

EAST GERMANY / GERMAN DEMOCRATIC REPUBLIC
(Deutsche Demokratische Republik)

I love Germany so much I am glad there are two of them.
— François Mauriac, 1978.

Area: 41,824 sq. miles (108,333 sq. km); Capital: East Berlin
Population: 16,674,632 (est. 1988)

Bordered by West Germany, Czechoslovakia (Czech Republic), Poland and the Baltic Sea, East Germany grew out of the Soviet occupation zone after World War II. Non-Communist political parties were suppressed by the Soviets, and the German Democratic Republic was formally established in 1949. In its early years East Germany was burdened by harsh war reparations. Entire factories were dismantled and carted off to the Soviet Union. Even so, East Germany became the most prosperous and industrially developed of the Communist countries in Eastern Europe.

East Germany, from its founding, was a one-party totalitarian state. The regime was propped up by an all-pervasive secret police and internal security network. As a result of oppression and privation a major uprising occurred in 1953, which had to be put down by Soviet occupation troops. Between 1945 and 1961 about 3,000,000 people, many of them highly skilled, fled the country via West Berlin. The western half of Berlin existed as an island of the capitalist West in the middle of East Germany's territory. Beginning in 1961 the East Germans erected a barbed wire cordon, later a concrete wall with armed watchtowers and searchlights, around West Berlin to stem the flow. The size of East Germany's population in 1990 was roughly the same as it was in 1954. With the general collapse of Communism in Eastern Europe the German Democratic Republic was united with West Germany in 1990.

Lenin Square, East Berlin

Readings: *Collier's Encyclopedia*, 1994; *New Encyclopædia Britannica*, 1991.

FRANKFURT (Frankfurt am Main)

> It is rich and commercial — And in this character it holds a
> distinguished Rank in the Cities of the Empire.
> — Henry Crabb Robinson, 1800.

Area: 187 sq. miles (485 sq. km); Capital: Frankfurt
Population: 77,372 (est. 1864)

From a 1st-century A.D. Roman settlement on the river Main,
Frankfurt became one of Germany's oldest and most important cities.
From 1372 until 1806 Frankfurt was independent as a free city. During
those years the city developed into the most important financial and
commercial center in Germany. An international trade fair has been
held there since 1240 and a stock exchange was founded in 1585. It
was in Frankfurt that the Rothschild family's international banking
empire had its headquarters. The French suspended the city's
independence in 1806 when they made it the residence for the prince-
prime minister of their Confederation of the Rhine. In 1810 Napoleon
created the Grand Duchy of Frankfurt but that lasted barely five years.
Frankfurt resumed its status of a free city in 1815 and from 1816 to
1866 was the seat of the German Confederation's parliament. During
the Austro-Prussian War of 1866 Frankfurt had the misfortune to back
the losing side. Victorious Prussian troops marched into the city and
annexed it, thus ending Frankfurt's independence. Frankfurt was the
birthplace of Goethe and the home of the philosopher Arthur
Schopenhauer.

Frankfurt town hall

Readings: *Encyclopædia Britannica*, 1926; Sadler, 1869.

GERMAN CONFEDERATION (Deutscher Bund)

> Even in the narrowest and poorest and most ancient quarters of
> Frankfort neat and clean clothes were the rule.
> — Mark Twain, 1880

Area: 243,219 sq. miles (630,100 sq. km); Capital: Frankfurt
Population: 46,059,329 (est. 1864)

After the defeat of Napoleon I the Congress of Vienna (1815)
created the German Confederation to replace the Holy Roman Empire.
It consisted of thirty-four sovereign German states and four free cities.
The Emperor of Austria, and the Kings of Prussia, Denmark, the
Netherlands and England were also members by virtue of lands they
held in the former Holy Roman Empire. The Confederation was a
stillborn attempt at German unity due to rivalry between Prussia and
Austria. Prussia ended it after defeating Austria in the Seven Weeks'
War (1866).

Readings: *Collier's Encyclopedia*, 1994; *Encyclopædia Britannica*, 1926.

HAMBURG / FREE AND HANSEATIC CITY OF HAMBURG (Freie
und Hansestadt Hamburg)

> Hamburg is an ill, close-built town, swarming with inhabitants; and,
> from what I could learn, like all the other free towns, governed in a
> manner which bears hard on the poor, whilst narrowing the minds of
> the rich; the character of the man is lost in the Hamburger.
> — Mary Wollstonecraft, 1796.

Area: 148 sq. miles (385 sq. km); Capital: Hamburg
Population: 338,794 (est. 1871)

A large port in northwestern Germany, on the Elbe River. The city
was founded by Charlemagne as a missionary outpost around a moated
castle c. 811 and given a town charter in 1188. Hamburg, with its
access to the North Sea, negotiated an alliance with Lübeck on the
Baltic in 1241. From this arose the powerful Hanseatic League of
trading cities. By the 16th century the Hanseatic League had declined
but Hamburg continued its own economic ascendency. Merchant
convoys from Hamburg, sometimes escorted by men-of-war, traded

throughout Europe and with North and South America. The city was heavily fortified and maintained its independence throughout several turbulent centuries. Hamburg, although under nominal Danish suzerainty for 250 years, was a free imperial city from 1510. Apart from a brief occupation by Napoleon's army Hamburg remained independent until it joined the German Reich in 1871. It has the status of a land, or state, in Germany today and is the country's second-largest city.

Hamburg coat of arms

Readings: *American Cyclopædia*, 1883; *Encyclopædia Britannica*, 1926.

HANOVER (Hannover)

> To Hanover one should go, they say, to learn the best German. The disadvantage is that outside Hanover, which is only a small province, nobody understands this best German.
> — Jerome K. Jerome, 1900.

Area: 14,893 sq. miles (38,573 sq. km); Capital: Hanover
Population: 1,963,618 (est. 1871)

Hanover, in northwestern Germany, was a major city of the Hanseatic League. For many years it and its hinterland were part of the Duchy of Brunswick, becoming independent in 1636 as the Principality of Brunswick-Calenburg-Göttingen. By 1692 the principality had been raised to the status of an electorate in the Holy Roman Empire and was named after its principle city — Hanover. In common with many

German states Hanover lost its independence when it was forcibly included in Napoleon's Kingdom of Westphalia. The Congress of Vienna (1814-1815) restored Hanover's autonomy, enlarged Hanover's boundaries, and made it a kingdom.

In 1714 Elector George Louis of Hanover became King George I of England. For the next 123 years Hanover was in personal union with the British sovereign. The connection, which had some political and economic advantages for Hanover, came to an end when Queen Victoria was denied succession to the throne of Hanover in 1837. According to Hanoverian law a female could not be sovereign.

As a result of its active involvement on the Austrian side in a war with Prussia the Hanoverian kingdom was annexed by Prussia in 1866. Though it was a Prussian province for the next 80 years Hanover was never fully assimilated. Property of the Hanoverian king was used to finance the Prussian secret service, activities of which were partly devoted to countering the intrigues of the deposed royal family. After World War II Hanover was, for a short time, a separate German state. It is now part of the state of Lower Saxony.

Herrenhausen Castle, Hanover

Readings: *American Cyclopædia*, 1883; *Encyclopædia Britannica*, 1926.

HELGOLAND / HELIGOLAND

> The next thing will be to propose to give up Gibraltar: and soon nothing will be secure, and all our Colonies will wish to be free.
> — Queen Victoria, c. 1890, q. by James Morris.

Area: .25 sq. mile (.72 sq. km); Capital: Helgoland
Population: 2,307 (est. 1900)

Two rocky islets in the North Sea occupying a strategic position with respect to the mouth of the Elbe River, 40 miles (65 km) away, and the port of Hamburg. Helgoland, a name which was derived from "Holy Land," was often called the Gibraltar of the North Sea in the 19th century. The islands were the possession of Holland from 1402 to 1714 and of Denmark from 1714 to 1807. Helgoland was seized by the Royal Navy in 1807 and was officially ceded to Great Britain in 1814. Over Queen Victoria's objections Helgoland became part of Schleswig-Holstein in 1890 when Great Britain ceded it to Germany in exchange for concessions in Zanzibar and Uganda. Imperial Germany fortified the islands and established a naval base. The waters of Helgoland were the scene of important naval battles between Prussia and Denmark in 1864, and Great Britain and Germany in 1914, 1915 and 1917. After World War I the islands were demilitarized. When the Nazis came to power Helgoland was refortified. After World War II Helgoland again passed into British hands. In 1946 Helgolanders asked to be readmitted to the British realm. About 250 islanders claimed to have been born under the British flag but their petition was ignored. So determined were the British that Helgoland would never be used for war again that they actually changed the shape of the islands as a result of dynamiting its fortifications and submarine pens. The demolition was suspended during spring and autumn so as not to disturb migrating birds. Thereafter the Royal Air Force used Helgoland as a bombing range. Despite the devastation Helgoland's inhabitants wanted to come home. They did so in 1952 when the islands were returned to Germany. Helgoland is now a popular seaside resort.

The German anthem "Deutschland, Deutschland über Alles" was written on Helgoland in 1841 when the island was British territory. The island's stamps, which featured a portrait of Queen Victoria, were printed in Germany.

Readings: *American Cyclopædia*, 1883; *New Encyclopædia Britannica*, 1991.

HESSE-DARMSTADT (Hessen-Darmstadt) / Hesse (Volksstaat Hessen)

> Darmstadt is a sort of town perfectly new to us — all palaces, big houses, soldiers, and dullness — yet pretty — nay handsome.
> — Dorothy Wordsworth, 1820.

Area: 2,964 sq. miles (7,677 sq. km); Capital: Darmstadt
Population: 852,894 (est. 1871)

Originally a small and unimportant territory around the town of Darmstadt, Hesse-Darmstadt was created when the Landgraviate of Hesse was divided in 1567. Hesse-Darmstadt became more important as a result of enlargements after the Thirty Years' War and during the 18th and 19th centuries. It became a grand duchy and entered the German Confederation in 1815. Hesse-Darmstadt was allied with Prussia in the Franco-Prussian War and was one of the states that formed the German Empire in 1871. After the neighboring state of Hesse-Kassel was annexed by Prussia in 1866 Hesse-Darmstadt became known simply as Hesse. Upon the abolition of the grand duchy in 1918 Hesse-Darmstadt became a free state of the German Republic.

Readings: De Selincourt, 1952; *Encyclopædia Britannica*, 1926.

HESSE-HOMBURG (Hessen-Homburg)

> Do you know Homburg at all? It is very pretty — German pretty — and is cool and shady and comfortable generally, and still amusing enough, in spite of the death and burial of the gaming.
> — Henry James, 1873.

Area: 106 sq. miles (275 sq. km); Capital: Homburg-vor-der-Höhe
Population: 27,374 (est. 1864)

Founded in 1622 Hesse-Homburg became an independent langraviate when it was split from Hesse-Darmstadt in 1768. When the royal line became extinct in 1848 the state's territory was divided between Prussia and Hesse-Darmstadt. In the 19th century Homburg-vor-der-Höhe was famous for its gambling casino and its mineral springs.

Readings: *American Cyclopædia*, 1883; *Encyclopædia Britannica*, 1926.

HESSE-KASSEL (Hessen-Kassel; Hessen-Cassel)

> Cassell is to be seen rapidly only — there is a mixture of meanness & poverty with taste and splendour which is to me at least disgusting even to painfulness.
> — Henry Crabb Robinson, 1801.

Area: 3,699 sq. miles (9,581 sq. km); Capital: Kassel
Population: 745,063 (est. 1864)

In 1567 the historic Langraviate of Hesse was divided along dynastic lines and Hesse-Kassel was one of the new states created. Beginning in the Thirty Years' War (1618-1648), as a means of raising revenue, Hesse-Kassel hired out its soldiers as mercenaries. The British hired about 20,000 such soldiers to fight the rebels in the American Revolution. All German regiments fighting under British colors came to be called Hessians as a result.

Hesse-Kassel was the last electorate of the Holy Roman Empire. When the Holy Roman Empire was abolished (1806) the ruler of Hesse-Kassel, an archconservative, continued to call himself elector even though the title did not legally exist. He also dressed his army, to their embarrassment, in uniforms of an earlier day, complete with powdered pigtails. Hesse-Kassel attempted to remain neutral during the Napoleonic Wars but was occupied by the French anyway. Hesse-Kassel survived until 1866 when it was annexed by Prussia. In 1945 it became part of the German state of Hesse.

Readings: *Encyclopædia Britannica*, 1926; Sadler, 1869.

HOLY ROMAN EMPIRE (Sacrum Romanum Imperium; Heiliges Römisches Reich)

> The Empire was soon sinking into dotage among the cinders.
> — Patrick Leigh Fermor, 1977.

Area: 250,000 sq. miles (650,000 sq. km); Capital: Vienna
Population: 40,000,000 (est. 1800)

The name applied to a changing group of territories in Germany, Holland, Austria, Bohemia, Italy and parts of France—300 principalities and about 1,500 semi-independent states. The Holy Roman Empire grew out of a desire to unite Western Christendom under a single political ruler and revive the glories of the ancient Roman Empire. It was founded in 962 by Otto I of Germany who revived the earlier empire founded by Charlemagne in 800. The Holy Roman Empire was never a unified political entity although in its early centuries a feudal suzerainty was established over many of its constituent states. Inevitably, there were disputes between emperors and popes. By the 14th century the Empire had gone into steep decline and had become essentially a German institution; a loose federation of German princes under the House of Habsburg. But faced with the Protestant Reformation, nationalism and the notions of liberty and enlightenment unleashed by the French Revolution the Holy Roman Empire became an anachronistic shell. Nevertheless it survived until 1806. The last emperor, Francis II of Austria, realizing he could not defend the Holy Roman Empire against Napoleon's designs, resigned the crown and thus brought it to an end.

Readings: Fermor, 1977; *New Encyclopædia Britannica*, 1991.

LAUENBERG / SAXE-LAUENBERG

> It has very fertile soil, extensive forests, and a number of picturesque lakes.
> — *American Cyclopædia*, 1883.

Area: 453 sq. miles (1,173 sq. km); Capital: Ratzeburg
Population: 49,546 (est. 1871)

A duchy on the Elbe River in northern Germany founded in the 13th century. Lauenberg's independence came to an end in 1803 when it was occupied by the French. After the Battle of Leipzig in 1813 Lauenberg passed to Hanover and then to Prussia, which in turn gave most of it to Denmark, in exchange for territory in Pomerania. Lauenberg became Prussian again after the Danish-Prussian War of 1864. Prussian prime minister Otto Von Bismarck was created Duke of Lauenberg upon his retirement in 1890. Though united with the crown of Prussia, Lauenberg maintained a degree of autonomy until it was incorporated into the Kingdom of Prussia in 1876. The Duchy of Lauenberg was not formally abolished until 1918. Since 1946 Lauenberg has been part of the German state of Schleswig-Holstein.

Readings: *American Cyclopædia*, 1883; *Encyclopædia Britannica*, 1926.

LIPPE-DETMOLD / LIPPE (Freistaat Lippe)

It is traversed by chains of the Teutoburg Mountains, called here
Lippe'schen Wald, and drained by the Werre and other small
tributaries of the Weser.
— *American Cyclopædia*, 1883.

Area: 469 sq. miles (1,215 sq. km); Capital: Detmold
Population: 111,153 (est. 1871)

A small princely state in western Germany. The first count of
Lippe assumed his title in 1528 and soon after introduced the
Reformation into his domain. The territory became Lutheran in 1538
and Calvinist in 1605. Dynastic complications divided Lippe in the
early 17th century and it was not until 1720 that most of the Lippe
lands were reunited. The tiny state of Schaumburg-Lippe maintained a
separate independence until 1871. Lippe was included in Napoleon's
Confederation of the Rhine and joined the German Empire in 1871.
After 1918 a republican form of government was put in place until
abolished by the Nazis. Lippe has been included in the state of North-
Rhine Westphalia since 1946.

Readings: *American Cyclopædia*, 1883; *Encyclopædia Britannica*, 1926.

LÜBECK / FREE AND HANSEATIC CITY OF LÜBECK (Freie und Hansestadt Lübeck)

The building of this City is very beautifull, all of bricke, and
it hath most sweete walkes without the walles.
— Fynes Moryson, 1617.

Area: 115 sq. miles (298 sq. km); Capital: Lübeck
Population: 52,158 (est. 1871)

Founded in 1143, and created a free city in 1226, Lübeck grew to
become the most important German port on the Baltic Sea. An
agreement with the North Sea port of Hamburg in 1241 led to the
creation of the Hanseatic League of trading cities. Lübeck was the
League's unofficial headquarters. The city was occupied by Denmark
in 1801 and was integrated into the French Empire in 1810. Lübeck

regained its independence after Napoleon's defeat. As a free city it joined the German empire in 1871, and in 1918, the German Republic. It is now part of Schleswig-Holstein. The partition of Germany after World War II placed Lübeck almost directly on the East German border. German novelist Thomas Mann was born in Lübeck.

Holsten Gate, Lübeck

Readings: *American Cyclopædia*, 1883; *Encyclopædia Britannica*, 1926.

MECKLENBURG-SCHWERIN (Freistaat Mecklenburg-Schwerin)

> But the Duke of Mecklenburg-Schwerin was one of that class of petty sovereigns in Germany, who, if they conferred no honour on their rank and power, did not abuse them to the injury of their subjects.
> — Henry Crabb Robinson, 1807.

Area: 5,138 sq. miles (13,307 sq. km); Capital: Schwerin
Population: 557,897 (est. 1871)

Located in northeastern Germany on the Baltic Sea, Mecklenburg became a vassal of the Holy Roman Empire in 1170 and a duchy in 1348. As a result of complex dynastic disputes Mecklenburg was divided in 1701 and the duchy of Mecklenburg-Schwerin was created. Although compelled to join Napoleon's Confederation of the Rhine, Mecklenburg-Schwerin became the first duchy to leave it and fight against the French. Mecklenburg-Schwerin joined the German Empire in 1871 and became a free state in the Republic of Germany in 1918. Mecklenburg-Schwerin and Mecklenburg-Strelitz were united between 1934 and 1952. Mecklenburg-Schwerin became part of East Germany (German Democratic Republic) from 1946 to 1990. It is now included in the state of Mecklenburg-West Pomerania.

Readings: *Encyclopædia Britannica*, 1926; Sadler, 1869.

MECKLENBURG-STRELITZ (Freistaat Mecklenburg-Strelitz)

> The idea of a fashionable Bathing place in Mecklenberg! - How can
> people pretend to be fashionable or to bathe out of England.
> — Jane Austen, 1813.

Area: 1,053 sq. miles (2,727 sq. km); Capital: Neu-Strelitz
Population: 96,982 (est. 1871)

In northeastern Germany, divided in two by Mecklenburg-Schwerin. The historic duchy of Mecklenburg was split into Mecklenburg-Schwerin and Mecklenburg-Strelitz in 1701. Mecklenburg-Strelitz managed to preserve its independence through wars, invasions, revolutions and Napoleon Bonaparte until it joined the German Empire in 1871. The duchy was not abolished until 1918 after which time Mecklenburg-Strelitz became a free state within the Republic of Germany. Mecklenburg-Strelitz ceased to exist in 1934 when it was merged into the state of Mecklenburg. Its lands are now located in the state of Mecklenburg-West Pomerania.

Ploughman

Readings: *American Cyclopædia*, 1883; *Encyclopædia Britannica*, 1926.

NASSAU

> From its hills burst mineral streams of various descriptions, and
> besides the Selters or Seltzer water, which is drunk as a luxury in
> every quarter of the globe, there are bright sparkling remedies,
> prescribed for almost every disorder under the sun.
> — Sir F.B. Head, 1834.

Area: 1,830 sq. miles (4,790 sq. km); Capital: Wiesbaden
Population: 468,311 (est. 1864)

Founded in the 12th century Nassau was a duchy on the Rhine River in central Germany. During the 16th and 17th centuries it was partitioned and reformed along shifting dynastic lines a bewildering number of times. It was up to Napoleon I to unite the Duchy of Nassau in 1806. Despite Napoleon's eventual downfall Nassau maintained its independence until 1866 when, as a result of supporting Austria in a war with Prussia, it was annexed by the latter. After World War II most of what had been Nassau became part of the German state of Hesse.

One branch of the House of Nassau gave Great Britain William of Orange (King William III). Other branches of the family reign in the Netherlands and Luxembourg.

Readings: *American Cyclopædia*, 1883; *Encyclopædia Britannica*, 1926.

NORTH GERMAN CONFEDERATION (Norddeutscher Bund)

> The country round Berlin, the Mark of Brandenberg, is bitter, bad, deep sand almost a desert; I don't wonder the Great Frederick wanted something better.
> — Thomas Hood, 1836.

Area: 170,000 sq. miles (440,000 sq. km); Capital: Berlin
Population: 31,000,000 (est. 1871)

A union, under the hegemony of Prussia, of the German states north of the river Main. It was formed in 1867 after the Prussian victory over Austria the year before and the collapse of the German Confederation. The Prussian king and chancellor served as president and chancellor of the North German Confederation. The Confederation created economic unity and cleared the path for German unification in 1871. The North German Confederation comprised Prussia (80 percent of the total area and population) and twenty-one smaller states. Reluctant states were bullied into joining.

one-half Groschen stamp

Readings: *American Cyclopædia*, 1883; *New Encyclopædia Britannica*, 1991.

OLDENBURG (Freistaat Oldenburg)

> Oldenburg is a neat little town, with a good public walk, and a tolerable large palace, but it has no theatre, no university, no excellent situation, nothing to make it desirable as a residence.
> — Thomas Hodgskin, 1820.

Area: 2,480 sq. miles (6,423 sq. km); Capital: Oldenburg
Population: 314,778 (est. 1871)

Successively a countship, a duchy and a grand duchy in northwestern Germany, bordering the North Sea. Oldenburg also included enclaves in Schleswig and southwestern Germany. First mentioned in 1108 Oldenburg was a sovereign state until it became part of unified Germany in 1871. Oldenburg, a free state from 1918 to 1946, is now part of Lower Saxony.

Readings: *Encyclopædia Britannica*, 1926; Hodgskin, 1820.

PRUSSIA (Preussen; Freistaat Preussen)

> The only way to treat a Prussian is to step on his toes until *he* apologises.
> — Bavarian and Austrian proverb.

Area: 137,066 sq. miles (355,000 sq. km); Capital: Berlin
Population: 24,693,066 (est. 1871)

When Germans expanded east of the river Elbe in the 10th century, the Margravate (later Electorate) of Brandenburg was created to defend the northeastern border. The Hohenzollern dynasty took control of the area in the 15th century becoming the powerful Prince-Electors of Brandenburg. The Duchy of Prussia, a small Polish fief until 1660, was added to the domain of the Prince-Elector of Brandenburg in 1525. Gradually Prussia rose in prominence until its name came to be applied to all the lands of the Hohenzollerns. Due to skillful diplomacy, its efficient professional standing army (made up of mercenaries and conscripts), and its centralized bureaucracy Prussia was able to greatly expand its territory, becoming the most powerful Protestant state in Germany.

By 1701, with its militaristic and bureaucratic character firmly in place, the country became the Kingdom of Prussia and soon began to compete for leadership among the German-speaking states. Prussia went into temporary eclipse at the hands of Napoleon I, but after the defeat of the French, in which Prussia's army played a major role, lost territory was regained and new lands were added. Wars were fought and won against Denmark (1864), Austria (1866) and France (1871). Under Prussian hegemony Germany was unified in 1871 and Prussia's king became emperor. At its height Prussia comprised about two-thirds of Germany's area and population and completely dominated the country. When Germany became a republic in 1918 Prussia became the largest free state. After World War II the Allies, taking no chances of a Prussian resurgence, formally abolished the state in 1947. Its territory was divided between East and West Germany, Poland and the Soviet Union, and the name of Prussia vanished from the map of Europe.

Königsberg, Prussia

Readings: *American Cyclopædia*, 1883; *New Encyclopædia Britannica*, 1991.

REUSS-GREIZ

The present reigning princes (1875) are Henry XXII, of the elder line, son of Henry XX, and Henry XIV, of the younger line, son of Henry LXVII.
— *American Cyclopædia*, 1883.

Area: 148 sq. miles (383 sq. km); Capital: Greiz
Population: 45,094 (est. 1871)

A tiny principality in Saxony composed of three large parcels of land and several enclaves. The royal house of Reuss, so named because an early prince married a Russian princess, dates back to the 1100s. Reuss was divided in 1564 into Reuss-Greiz and Reuss-Schleiz. Reuss-Greiz maintained its independence until 1871. Reuss was reunited in 1919 before being incorporated into the state of Thuringia.

Every male born into the royal family of Reuss-Greiz, the elder line of the House of Reuss, from the 12th century to the abolition of the monarchy in 1918 was named Heinrich and designated by a number. In order to keep the numerical designators manageable the counting stopped after every 100th Heinrich was born. A new series of Heinrichs would then begin when the next boy was born.

Readings: *American Cyclopædia*, 1883; *Encyclopædia Britannica*, 1926.

REUSS-SCHLEIZ / REUSS-SCHLEIZ-GERA

Whenever the literary German dives into a sentence, that is the last you are going to see of him till he emerges on the other side of the Atlantic with his verb in his mouth.
— Mark Twain, 1889.

Area: 297 sq. miles (769 sq. km); Capital: Schleiz
Population: 89,032 (est. 1871)

A principality in the German region of Saxony that became a separate state when Reuss was divided in 1564. Every boy born in the royal family of Reuss-Schleiz was named Heinrich. In order to distinguish Reuss-Schleiz's Heinrichs from those of nearby Reuss-Greiz the first male born in a new century was designated Heinrich I, and the numbers continued to the end of the century. Thus the son of Heinrich LXVII (born in 1789), was Heinrich XIV (born in 1832). The former being the 67th Heinrich born in the 18th century and the latter the 14th Heinrich born in the 19th century.

Readings: *American Cyclopædia*, 1883; *Encyclopædia Britannica*, 1926.

SAAR TERRITORY (Sarre) / SAARLAND

Sit in any stuffy café at Saarbrücken, watch the guests eat red cabbage
and boiled pork, or sip fat steins of beer as the band plays heavy
Wagner music, and the place seems just another German industrial
center.
— Frederick Simpich, 1935.

Area: 991 sq. miles (2,567 sq. km); Capital: Saarbrücken
Population: 1,005,000 (est. 1957)

On the Franco-German border southeast of Luxembourg. After
World War I Saar, an important producer of coal, iron and steel, was
split from the defeated Germany. Its mines were ceded to France as
compensation for the destruction of coal mines in northern France
during the war. From 1920 to 1935 Saar was administered as a
territory by the League of Nations. The Saar Territory had no
sovereign rights and no permanent existence. As a result of a plebiscite
in 1935 Saar was returned to Germany and its important mines bought
back from France. After World War II the Saarland was again split
from Germany and occupied by the French. In 1947 Saar became a
French protectorate; a semi-independent state in a diplomatic, tariff and
economic union with France. After a 1955 referendum, whereby voters
overwhelmingly rejected a plan for Saar to be administered by the
Western European Union, France agreed in principle that the territory
should be returned to Germany. The transfer took place in 1957 and
since that time Saar has been a German state. Although France retained
certain economic privileges Saar's reintegration with Germany had been
completed by 1959.

Factory workers

Readings: *New Encyclopædia Britannica*, 1991; Simpich, 1935.

SAXE-ALTENBURG (Sachsen-Altenburg)

> It was a fine old castle. We had a very good dinner. The grand
> passage was lined with honest-looking guards . . . . I found the style
> of this court easy and cordial.
> — James Boswell, 1764.

Area: 509 sq. miles (1,318 sq. km); Capital: Altenburg
Population: 142,122 (est. 1871)

A sovereign Saxon duchy in the southern part of the former East
Germany. It was divided into two detached parts and twelve enclaves.
Altenburg was mentioned in 976 and became a trading center and royal
residence in the 12th century. After Saxony was divided Saxe-
Altenburg became a separate duchy between 1603 and 1672, and
between 1826 and 1918. The Duchy of Saxe-Altenburg was famous
among card players as the birthplace of the three-handed card game
skat.

Readings: *Encyclopædia Britannica*, 1926; Pottle, 1953.

SAXE-COBURG-GOTHA (Sachsen-Koburg-Gotha)

> They say this City was of old called Cotburg, that is, the City of dirt,
> and the dirty streets well deserve the name.
> — Fynes Moryson, 1617.

Area: 764 sq. miles (1,979 sq. km); Capital: Coburg
Population: 174,339 (est. 1871)

A sovereign duchy in Saxony which became a member of the
German Empire in 1871. It was made up of the two former duchies of
Coburg and Gotha, about 14 miles (22 km) apart, and eight enclaves.
After the ducal line of Gotha became extinct in 1825 it was merged
with Coburg. In the 19th and early 20th centuries the royal family of
Saxe-Coburg-Gotha was one of the best connected in Europe. Members
of the family were King Léopold I of Belgium, Albert the prince
consort of Queen Victoria, the prince consort of Portugal and the king
of Bulgaria.

Readings: *American Cyclopædia*, 1883; *Encyclopædia Britannica*, 1926.

SAXE-MEININGEN-HILDBURGHAUSEN (Sachsen-Meiningen-Hildburghausen)

At Meiningen, the Ducal House had created and supported a talented company of Players that had won renown for its extraordinary work throughout the whole of Germany. Since the War they have degenerated into a band of strolling mummers, without funds, wandering here and there to give a chance performance, complaining bitterly that they cannot hold together much longer.
— Henry Albert Phillips, 1929.

Area: 953 sq. miles (2,468 sq. km); Capital: Meiningen
Population: 187,884 (est. 1871)

An independent Saxon duchy founded in 1680 formed from the old duchy of Meiningen, the principality of Hildburghausen and a few small enclaves. Saxe-Meiningen-Hildburghausen sided with Austria during the Seven Weeks' War (1866) and was occupied by Prussia as a result. The last duke abdicated in 1918 and the duchy was incorporated into the state of Thuringia.

Readings: *Encyclopædia Britannica*, 1926; Phillips, 1929.

SAXE-WEIMAR-EISENACH

It is a very queer little place, although called the "Athens of Germany" on account of the great poets who have lived here . . .
— G. H. Lewes, 1854.

Area: 1,397 sq. miles (3,618 sq. km); Capital: Weimar
Population: 286,183 (est. 1871)

A Saxon duchy of three detached districts and twenty-four enclaves. Saxe-Weimar became independent in 1641 and absorbed the duchy of Saxe-Eisenach. The most notable ruler of Saxe-Weimar-Eisenach was Charles Augustus, a famous patron of the arts, who reigned from 1775 to 1828. Under his support Weimar became the home of the likes of Goethe, Herder, Schiller, Nietzsche and Franz Liszt. What was politically an unimportant duchy became the intellectual center of Germany. The last duke was deposed in 1918. In 1919 the German National Assembly convened in Weimar and adopted a constitution for a democratic republic, which came to be known as the Weimar Republic.

Readings: *American Cyclopædia*, 1883; *New Encyclopædia Britannica*, 1991.

SAXONY (Sachsen; Freistaat Sachsen)

> Saxony is a flat Country rich to the agricultural, poor to the picturesque Eye.
> — Henry Crabb Robinson, 1801.

Area: 5,778 sq. miles (14,965 sq. km); Capital: Dresden
Population: 2,556,244 (est. 1871)

A kingdom in the southeastern part of the former East Germany. Saxony, which became a duchy in 1485, was the cradle of the Protestant Reformation. After Napoleon I invaded Saxony he raised it to a kingdom. The kingdom became a loyal vassal of the French, and as a result its territory was reduced by half at the Congress of Vienna in 1815. Nevertheless Saxony survived as an independent kingdom until it joined the German Empire in 1871. The Saxon monarchy lasted until 1918. Becoming part of East Germany after World War II the state of Saxony was abolished in 1952. After German reunification in 1990 Saxony was reconstituted as a state.

Bridge construction

Readings: *Encyclopædia Britannica*, 1926; Sadler, 1869.

SCHAUMBURG-LIPPE (Schauenburg-Lippe; Freistaat Schaumburg-Lippe)

> Our chief passenger cargo consists of a picnic from the Schaumburg-Lippe country, all the women and girls being in the full peasant holiday costume of their little principality — red skirts with green embroidered hems, maroon or green close-fitting basque jackets with brass buttons. . . . Above all else the hair is braided, rolled in the shape of an old-fashioned cookie and then planted so as to half cover the forehead . . . it is too horrid!
> — Henry Albert Phillips, 1929.

Area: 131 sq. miles (339 sq. km); Capital: Bückeburg
Population: 32,059 (est. 1871)

One of the smallest princely states to join the German Empire and the least populous. Schaumburg-Lippe was founded in the 1640s as a branch of the House of Lippe. It joined the Confederation of the Rhine in 1807, the North German Confederation in 1866 and the German Reich in 1871. When the principality of Schaumburg-Lippe was abolished in 1918 a republican form of government was in place until suppressed by the Nazis. The lands that constituted Schaumburg-Lippe are now to be found in the German state of Lower Saxony.

Readings: *Encyclopædia Britannica*, 1926; Phillips, 1929.

SCHLESWIG-HOLSTEIN (Slesvig)

> That which offered the greatest novelty to our party, was the loud and incessant chorus of myriads of frogs. . . . To call it croaking, would convey a very erroneous idea of it, because it is really harmonious; and we gave to these reptiles the name of *Holstein nightingales*. . . .
> — E.D. Clarke, 1824.

Area: 7,338 sq. miles (19,005 sq. km); Capital: Schleswig
Population: 995,873 (est. 1871)

Two duchies straddling the border of Denmark and Germany, between the North and Baltic Seas. Schleswig, in the north, had a mixed German-Danish population while Holstein, to the south, was predominantly German. The two were linked together and ruled by the king of Denmark from 1460. Following a rebellion by the German population, who declared their independence, war broke out between Prussia and Denmark (1848-1850). After the Prussian-Austrian War with Denmark in 1864, and the Prussian War with Austria in 1866 the duchies of Holstein and Schleswig were annexed by Prussia. The northern portion of Schleswig, populated by Danes, was returned to Denmark in 1920 following a plebiscite.

Schleswig coat of arms

Readings: *American Cyclopædia*, 1883; *Encyclopædia Britannica*, 1926.

SCHWARZBURG-RUDOLSTADT

It is divided into the upper lordship of Rudolstadt, which is mountainous, and the lower of Frankhausen, which is less so.
— *American Cyclopædia*, 1883.

Area: 364 sq. miles (943 sq. km); Capital: Rudolstadt
Population: 75,523 (est. 1871)

A principality in Saxony which became a member state of the German Empire in 1871. Rudolstadt, recorded in 800, was ruled by the Schwarzburg family from 1335 to 1918.

Readings: *American Cyclopædia*, 1883; *Encyclopædia Britannica*, 1926.

SCHWARZBURG-SONDERHAUSEN

This is a fruitful fine country . . . but the people are probably as rude and as ignorant as in any part of Germany. The princes are said once to have been celebrated for learning. At present they are known only as good huntsmen.
— Thomas Hodgskin, 1820.

Area: 323 sq. miles (837 sq. km); Capital: Sonderhausen
Population: 67,191 (est. 1871)

A small Saxon principality, which joined the German Empire in 1871. Its princes were descended from one of the oldest royal houses in Germany. From the 13th century every male born in the ruling Schwarzburg family was named Günther. To keep all the Günthers distinguished they were given numbers and then prefixed names.

Readings: *Encyclopædia Britannica*, 1926; Hodgskin, 1820.

WALDECK / WALDECK-PYRMONT (Freistaat Waldeck)

Waldeck proper is mountainous and woody . . . possessing a poor and stony but carefully cultivated soil, and yields sufficient grain and potatoes for home consumption.
— *American Cyclopædia*, 1883.

Area: 466 sq. miles; Capital: Arolsen
Population: 56,218 (est. 1871)

Two parcels of land located between Westphalia and Hesse. Waldeck had been a principality for centuries when its monarchy was abolished in 1918. It was a free state from 1918 to 1919 at which time it was voluntarily absorbed by Prussia.

Readings: *Encyclopædia Britannica*, 1926; Hodgskin, 1820.

WEST BERLIN

He said that in Berlin, if you wanted to make a scandal in the theatre, you had to have a mother committing incest with *two* sons; one wasn't enough.
— Arnold Bennett, 1925.

Area: 185 sq. miles (480 sq. km); Capital: Berlin
Population: 2,068,313 (est. 1988)

Founded early in the 13th century Berlin became the capital of Prussia in 1701 and the capital of Germany between 1871 and 1945, and from 1990 to now. After the defeat of Germany in World War II Berlin was placed under a four-power (Great Britain, France, United

States, Soviet Union) military government, the Kommandatura, from 1945 to 1948. In 1948, when the other powers decided to unite their sectors, the Soviets withdrew, established a separate municipal government in their sector of the city, and blockaded West Berlin. The western allies launched an airlift and kept West Berlin alive. East Berlin became the capital of the German Democratic Republic (East Germany) in 1954. The British, French and American sectors became known as West Berlin. Although integrated culturally, politically and economically to the Federal Republic of Germany (West Germany) West Berlin, because it was physically surrounded by East German territory, had a precarious and ambiguous existence. Beginning in 1961 the East Germans constructed the infamous Berlin Wall to seal off this island of Western influence and stop a hemorrhage of emigration. Although West Berlin was officially under Allied military occupation and constitutionally not part of West Germany, in practice it was treated as if it were a German state. West Berlin sent representatives to the Bundestag (parliament) in Bonn but they could only debate, not vote. The West German military was not permitted in West Berlin. Upon the reunification of Germany in 1990 the Berlin Wall was torn down and East and West Berlin became one city again. The last foreign troops departed in 1994.

Halle Gate

Readings: Canby, 1984; *Collier's Encyclopedia*, 1994.

WESTPHALIA

Thy bread, Westphalia, thy brown bread I sing,
Bread which might make the dinner of a king . . .
— James Boswell, 1764.

Area: 14,627 sq. miles (37,884 sq. km); Capital: Kassel
Population: 2,000,000 (est. 1807)

The bread Boswell sang of was pumpernickel which originated in Westphalia. Westphalia, the western plain, was a historic region in northwestern Germany. The archbishop of Cologne was its nominal overlord from 1180 until 1803 when Westphalia was given to the Duchy of Hesse-Darmstadt. Napoleon I created the Kingdom of Westphalia, between the rivers Elbe and Rhine, for his brother Jerome in 1807. When King Jerome was expelled in 1813 his kingdom came to an end. Westphalia became a Prussian province in 1816.

Osthofen Gate,
Soest, Westphalia

Readings: *Encyclopædia Britannica*, 1926; Pottle, 1953.

WÜRTTEMBERG (Volkstaat Württemberg)

Stuttgart is a charming town, clean and bright, a smaller Dresden. It has the additional attraction of containing little that one need to go out of one's way to see: a medium-sized picture gallery, a small museum of antiquities, and half a palace, and you are through with the entire thing and can enjoy yourself.
— Jerome K. Jerome, 1900.

Area: 7,530 sq. miles (19,503 sq. km); Capital: Stuttgart
Population: 1,818,484 (est. 1871)

A compact state in what is now Baden-Württemberg. Württemberg, which goes back to the 11th century, was made a duchy of the Holy Roman Empire in 1495. Over the centuries that followed Württemberg was frequently devastated by warfare; including the French Revolutionary Wars. It was forced into an alliance with Napoleon I but as a reward for supplying troops for the French campaigns against Austria and Prussia Württemberg was more than doubled in size. Of

the 16,000 Württembergers who participated in the French invasion of
Russia only a few hundred survived. Upon receiving assurances that its
recent territorial acquisitions would be retained Württemberg changed
sides and joined the anti-Napoleonic coalition in 1813. After the defeat
of Napoleon Württemberg began to see Prussia as a threat. It resisted
Prussian hegemony until decisively defeated in the Seven Weeks' War
of 1866. Württemberg joined the German Empire in 1871 and was
given more autonomy than most German states.

Wangen town gate

Readings: *American Cyclopædia*, 1883; *Encyclopædia Britannica*, 1926.

WÜRZBURG

> In the course of the day I beheld a strange sight — a man beheaded
> for murder. . . . The executioner then stepped from behind, holding
> a broad sword under his cloak, and in an instant, with a back-handed
> blow, severed the head from the body. The headless trunk remained
> in the chair unmoved, as if nothing had happened.
> — Henry Crabb Robinson, 1804.

Area: 1,900 sq. miles (4,921 sq. km); Capital: Würzburg
Population: 250,000 (est. 1800)

Würzburg was a bishopric in Bavaria founded in 704. By the peace
of Lunéville (1801) the French secularized the bishopric and gave it to
Bavaria in 1803. In 1805 Napoleon I gave Würzburg to the former
grand-duke of Tuscany who needed some place to rule. The Grand
Duchy of Würzburg only lasted as long as Napoleon's forces were
there to support it. Würzburg was restored to Bavaria.

Readings: *Encyclopædia Britannica*, 1926; Sadler, 1869.

CHAPTER 6

Eastern Europe

> From Stettin, in the Baltic, to Trieste, in the Adriatic, an iron curtain
> has descended across the continent.
> - Winston Churchill, 1945.

ALLENSTEIN (Commission Interalliée Allenstein)

> I stumble upon a movie house of the nickelodeon days, a long dark illy
> ventilated hall. A rather awful pre-historic American comedy starring
> Hoot Gibson is being run and I find the audience fairly eating up this
> cowboy stuff away up here on the borders of Lithuania.
> - Henry Albert Phillips, 1929.

Area: 4,457 sq. miles (11,544 sq. km); Capital: Allenstein
Population: 540,000 (est. 1920)

After World War I the East Prussian districts of Allenstein,
Ortelesburg, Osterode, Sensburg, Johannisburg, Lotzen, Lyck and
Neidenburg were garrisoned by Allied troops under the terms of the
Versailles Treaty. An inter-Allied commission administered the districts
until a plebiscite could be held to determine their future. Preceded by
much lawlessness and turmoil the plebiscite was held on July 11, 1920.
98 percent of the electorate opted for Germany over Poland. Allied
troops withdrew on August 16, 1920, and the Allenstein districts were

returned to Germany. Since 1945 Allenstein has been part of the Polish province of Olsztyn.

German stamp overprinted for use in Allenstein

Readings: *Encyclopædia Britannica*, 1926; Phillips, 1929.

AUSTRO-HUNGARIAN EMPIRE (Österreichisch-Ungarisches Reich)

East of Vienna, the orient begins.
- Prince Metternich, attrib.

Area: 261,000 sq. miles (675,000 sq. km); Capitals: Vienna; Budapest
Population: 55,000,000 (est. 1914)

A multiethnic empire in central and eastern Europe which was under the Habsburg dynasty from 1867 to 1918. The Austrian Empire officially began in 1804 when Francis II, the last of the Holy Roman emperors, proclaimed himself emperor of Austria. Within the empire was Hungary whose population, the second largest ethnic group, grew increasingly rebellious and nationalistic. In order to keep the empire from breaking up, a historic constitutional compromise was reached with Hungary in 1867. Replacing the centralized Austrian Empire was a dual monarchy under which Hungary was recognized as a nation with separate citizenship, a parliament and complete internal autonomy. The empire was unified under a common monarch (emperor of Austria and apostolic king of Hungary) and joint ministries of foreign affairs, defence and finance. Customs and tariffs, currency and post office were also held in common (although separate stamps were issued). Quotas paid by each half of the empire to maintain these services were reconsidered every decade. The rest of the empire's districts had no part in this arrangement and were plagued by interethnic squabbles. Austria ruled Bohemia, Moravia, Galicia, Bukovinia, South Tirol and

Slovenia. Slovakia, Ruthenia, Transylvania and Croatia were subject to Hungary. Bosnia and Hercegovina, which were annexed in 1900, were ruled by the Finance Ministry because it could not be agreed whether the territories should be Austrian or Hungarian. The assassination of Archduke Franz Ferdinand, in Sarajevo, on 28 June, 1914, set off the chain of events that led to World War I and the downfall of the empire. After the war Austro-Hungary was split into Austria, Hungary, Czechoslovakia and parts of Romania, Yugoslavia, Poland, Italy and Russia.

Emperor Franz Josef

Readings: Canby, 1984; *Encyclopædia Britannica*, 1926.

PROTECTORATE OF BOHEMIA AND MORAVIA (Cechy a Morava; Böhmen und Mähren)

He who holds Bohemia holds mid-Europe.
— Bismarck, attrib.

Area: 27,500 sq. miles (71,225 sq. km); Capital: Prague
Population: 7,000,000 (est. 1930)

Bohemia was the western province of Czechoslovakia, and Moravia the central. Upon the German annexation of Czechoslovakia in 1939 a protectorate was established in Bohemia and Moravia. The government of the protectorate had some rights and powers but in practice was under the complete control of Nazi Germany. Bohemia and Moravia existed solely to serve the German war effort. The protectorate came to an end when Czechoslovakia was liberated from the Nazis in 1945. Bohemia and Moravia were restored to Czechoslovakia. In 1993, upon the dissolution of Czechoslovakia, Bohemia and Moravia were reconstituted as the Czech Republic.

Atlantic
Ocean

North
Sea

Baltic Sea

Mediterranean
Sea

20TH CENTURY EUROPE

1 Irish Free State
2 Saar
3 East Germany
4 West Berlin
5 Danzig
6 Marienwerder
7 Allenstein
8 Central Lithuania
9 Memel
10 North Ingermanland

11 Karelia
12 Bohemia and Moravia
13 Czechoslovakia
14 Upper Silesia
15 Western Ukraine
16 Carpatho-Ukraine
17 Union of Soviet Socialist
  Republics
18 Vichy France
19 Italian Social Republic

20 Trieste
21 Fiume
22 Kingdom of the Croats, Slovenes
  and Serbians
23 Serbia
24 Saseno
25 Crete
26 Dodecanese Islands
27 Castelrosso

Adolf Hitler

Readings: Canby, 1984; *New Encyclopædia Britannica*, 1991.

CARPATHO-UKRAINE (Karpats'ka Ukraïna) / SUBCARPATHIAN
RUTHENIA (Pidkarpatska Rus)

> Their language, which occupies a middle ground between Polish and
> Russian, is softer and more melodious than either.
> — *American Cyclopædia*, 1883.

Area: 4,901 sq. miles (12,694 sq. km); Capital: Uzhorod
Population: 604,670 (est. 1921)

Part of the Slavic Kievan state in the 10th century, Ruthenia came
under Hungarian rule. With the breakup of the Austro-Hungarian
Empire in 1918 the Ukrainian-populated district of Ruthenia, south of
the Carpathian mountains, was given to the new state of
Czechoslovakia, with guarantees given for its autonomy. As a result of
the infamous Munich Agreement of 1938, Czechoslovakia was
emasculated and Ruthenia forced to cede territory to Hungary. In 1939
Germany annexed what was left of Czechoslovakia, and the
independence of Ruthenia, as the Republic of Carpatho-Ukraine was
declared. The Republic was promptly invaded by Hungary and ruled by
that country until 1944. Carpatho-Ukraine then became part of the
Ukrainian Soviet Socialist Republic, the first time in centuries that the
population of Ruthenia had been united with other Ukrainians. It now
forms part of the Ukrainian Republic.

Readings: Kubijovyc, 1963; Struk, 1993.

CASTELROSSO (Castellorizo; Kastellórizon)

> An hour after sunup we were riding at anchor on what seemed the
> stage of a classic theatre. In a semicircle, tiers of white houses climbed
> against red-rocked hills.
> — Dorothy Hosmer, 1941.

Area: 3 sq. miles (8 sq. km); Capital: Castelrosso
Population: 2,238 (est. 1936)

The easternmost of the Dodecanese Islands in the Aegean Sea,
about 60 miles (100 km) east of Rhodes, within sight of the Turkish
coast. Populated entirely by Greeks Castelrosso was occupied, in turn,
by the Knights of St. John, the Sultan of Egypt, the King of Naples and
the Ottoman Turks. The latter held the island from 1512 until 1915
when, during World War I, it was captured by the French. The French
used the island as a refueling station. Castelrosso was not included in
the Italian colony of the Dodecanese Islands which was established in
1912 after the Italo-Turkish War. Italy, however, was eager to acquire
the island as a base for its penetration of Asia Minor. This was
achieved by a treaty with France and the island was ceded to Italy in
1923. Thereafter the chief Italian administrator in the Aegean referred
to himself as "Governor of Rhodes and Castelrosso" or "Governor-
General of the Dodecanese and Castelrosso." Following World War II
Castelrosso was given to Greece. The island's name was derived from
its red rocks and the Knights of St. John who called it Château-Roux
(Red Castle).

Castelrosso Castle

Readings: Hosmer, 1941; Shor, 1953.

CENTRAL LITHUANIA

So intense was the feeling during the 18 years of disagreement that all communication across the border was suspended, even postal service.
— Douglas Chandler, 1938.

Area: 16,176 sq. miles (41,957 sq. km); Capital: Vilnius
Population: 1,806,300 (est. 1904)

A disputed district between Poland and Lithuania. In 1919 the supreme council of the Allies fixed the border between Poland and Lithuania. The area around Vilnius, which had a mixed population, was assigned to Lithuania over Poland's protests. In 1920 a Polish freebooter seized Central Lithuania and the district had a semi-independent status until officially annexed by Poland in 1922. In 1939 the area was taken by the U.S.S.R. and added to the Lithuanian Soviet Socialist Republic.

Vilnius University

Readings: Chandler, 1938; *Encyclopædia Britannica*, 1926.

REPUBLIC OF CRACOW (Krakówska Rzeczpospolita) / FREE CITY OF CRACOW (Wolne Miasto Kraków)

The effects of cannon, grape, and musket-shot, are still discernible on the walls and houses. In a word, Cracow exhibits the remains of a magnificent capital in ruins: from the number of fallen and falling houses one would imagine it had lately been sacked and that the enemy had left it only yesterday.
— William Coxe, 1792.

Area: 500 sq. miles (1,300 sq. km); Capital: Cracow
Population: 95,000 (est. 1846)

Cracow is a city in southern Poland founded in the 9th century. It had a long and glorious past. Between 1320 and 1609 it was the capital of Poland and became one of Europe's greatest centers of culture and learning. However by the time Austria seized Cracow in 1795 it was in decline. Between 1809 and 1815 the city was included by Napoleon I in the Grand Duchy of Warsaw. At the conclusion of the Napoleonic Wars the Congress of Vienna made Cracow a free state under the protection of the three powers that had carved up the rest of Poland; Austria, Prussia and Russia. As the only part of Poland to be independent the ministate of Cracow, much to the annoyance of its powerful neighbors, became the center of Polish national aspirations. In 1846, when a rebellion broke out in Galicia, the Austrian-controlled part of Poland, Cracow was blamed for fomenting it. Austria, with the support of Prussia and Russia, suppressed the Republic of Cracow and annexed it. Since 1918 Cracow has been part of Poland.

View of Cracow

Readings: Canby, 1984; *Encyclopædia Britannica*, 1926.

CRETE (Candia; Kríti)

> The people of Crete unfortunately make more history than they can consume locally.
> — Saki, 1911.

Area: 3,190 sq. miles (8,262 sq. km); Capital: Canea
Population: 336,150 (est. 1913)

An island in the Aegean Sea south of the Greek mainland, the largest of the Greek islands. Crete was the center of the Minoan civilization, which reached its height about 1500 B.C. It then became the home of independent Greek city-states until conquered by the Romans in 67 B.C. Crete passed to Byzantium (A.D. 395), the Saracens (823), Venice (1204) and finally, after a twenty-two-year seige of the capital, to the Ottoman Turks (1669). The 19th and early 20th centuries in Crete were periods of nearly continuous revolt and agitation for union with Greece. In order to prevent the conflict between Greeks and Turks from spreading into the Balkans, Great Britain, France, Italy, Russia, Germany and Austro-Hungary intervened. Greek and Turkish troops were evacuated from the island and in 1898 Crete was converted into an international protectorate under Turkish suzerainty. Crete was given an autonomous government with a Greek prince as high commissioner. The Cretan assembly voted for union with Greece in 1908 but it was 1913 before this came about.

Hermes

Readings: Canby, 1984; *New Encyclopædia Britannica*, 1991.

KINGDOM OF THE CROATS, SLOVENES AND SERBIANS
(Kraljevina Srba, Hrvata, i Slovenaca)

> Belgrade reminded me at one time of Moscow, at another of some white Spanish city. The whole place is made by the crossing of straight lines: I never saw a curve.
> — Arthur Symons, 1903.

Area: 96,136 sq. miles (248,991 sq. km); Capital: Belgrade
Population: 13,930,918 (est. 1931)

A Balkan country on the eastern shore of the Adriatic Sea. In 1918, after a revolution in Austro-Hungary, the provinces of Bosnia, Dalmatia, Slovenia and Croatia joined Serbia, Montenegro and Macedonia to create the Kingdom of the Croats, Slovenes and Serbians, under the royal house of Serbia. This was the fulfilment of a movement begun in the 1840s to unite the South Slavs in a single independent state. In 1929 the name of the country was changed to the Kingdom of

Yugoslavia. A communist republic was established in 1945.
The country's always serious interethnic tensions boiled over
between 1991 and 1992 when Croatia, Slovenia, Bosnia-Hercegovina
and Macedonia seceded from Yugoslavia. Serbia and Montenegro
constitute a rump Yugoslav state calling itself the Federal Republic of
Yugoslavia.

King Alexander

Readings: Canby, 1984; *Collier's Encyclopedia*, 1994.

CZECHOSLOVAKIA / CZECHO-SLOVAK REPUBLIC
(Ceskoslovenská Republika) / CZECH AND SLOVAK FEDERATIVE
REPUBLIC (Ceská a Slovenská Federativni Republika)

"Where can I find the world's biggest cow?"
"In Czechoslovakia. Its head is in Prague but it gets milked in
Moscow."
— Czechoslovakian joke, q. by R.H. Bruce Lockhart.

Area: 49,382 sq. miles (127,899 sq. km); Capital: Prague
Population: 15,690,633 (est. 1990)

A landlocked nation bordered by Poland to the north, Ukraine to
the east, Hungary and Austria to the south and Germany to the West.
Czechoslovakia arose in 1918, out of the ashes of the Austro-Hungarian
Empire, as the homeland of the Czechs and Slovaks. There were also
significant minorities of Ukrainians and Germans. The latter, who had
begun to sympathize with the emerging Nazis, were the excuse for
German aggression. With the cowardly acquiesence of France and
Britain Germany annexed the German-speaking region of
Czechoslovakia, the Sudetenland, in 1938 while Hungary occupied the
Ukrainian region of Subcarpathian Ruthenia. The rest of

Czechoslovakia was taken over by Germany in 1939. The Czech lands, Bohemia and Moravia, became a German protectorate and Slovakia a puppet state. The Germans were driven out of Czechoslovakia by the Soviets in 1945. The country, minus Ruthenia, which was ceded to the U.S.S.R., was then reconstituted. By 1948 the Communists had gained the upper hand in Czechoslovakia and a people's republic was established. An attempt to create "socialism with a human face," the so-called Prague spring, was crushed by Soviet tanks in 1968. A declining economy and an unpopular government led to the fall of Communism in 1989. The end of Czechoslovakia came on January 1, 1993. On that day the country was peacefully split into the Czech Republic and the Republic of Slovakia.

Painting by Jan Zrzavy

Readings: Canby, 1984; *Collier's Encyclopedia*, 1994.

DANZIG (Freie Stadt Danzig)

The houses are in general lofty, and in antique taste. In most of the streets are planted trees, which at this season of the year afford an agreeable shade; but which in the winter must be very inconvenient, and ought to be removed.
— Sir. N.W. Wraxall, 1775.

Area: 754 sq. miles (1,953 sq. km); Capital: Danzig
Population: 407,000 (est. 1939)

A German port on the Baltic Sea. Following World War I the Treaty of Versailles called for the separation of Danzig from Germany. In 1919 Danzig was created a free state with its own legislature, flag, money and customs inspectors. It also had a League of Nations high commissioner. The city, which was 96 percent German, served as the principal port of Poland. Poland garrisoned the city and was awarded free transit rights and customs privileges. After 1924 Danzig was adversely affected when Poland opened the rival port of Gdynia, 10 miles (16 km) to the northwest. In 1938 Adolf Hitler demanded that Danzig be returned to Germany. Poland's refusal to allow this was used as an excuse for the German invasion of Poland on September 1, 1939, which started World War II. Since 1945 the city has been Polish and is now known as Gdansk.

Danzig coat of arms

Readings: Canby, 1984; Chandler, 1938.

DODECANESE ISLANDS (Dhodhekánisos) / ITALIAN ISLANDS OF THE AEGEAN (Isole Italiane dell' Egeo)

> From the number of the appellations which it bore at different periods, *Rhodes* might have at last received the name of the *poly-onomous* island.
> — E.D. Clarke, 1818.

Area: 1,031 sq. miles (2,670 sq. km); Capital: Rhodes
Population: 140,000 (est. 1941)

A group of islands off the coast of Turkey. Apart from small minorities of Muslims, Jews and a few imported Italian farmers the population was Greek. The name Dodecanese means "Twelve Islands" although there were in fact fourteen. The islands were occupied by the Turks in 1522. Twelve of the islands submitted peacefully to Turkish rule and, so long as they remitted an annual tax, were allowed to exercise local autonomy. The two largest islands, Rhodes and Cos, resisted the Turks and received no privileges as a result. The

Dodecanese Islands remained under Turkish rule until the Italo-Turkish War of 1912. After a single battle on Rhodes the archipelago was captured by Italy. At first the islanders supported the Italians believing their promises of autonomy and reunification with Greece. But Italy reneged on its promises and annexed the islands outright in 1923 changing the name to the Italian Islands of the Aegean. The major powers did not object. As a price for entering World War I Italy had secured Allied acceptance of its sovereignty over the islands. Italian rule, firm and efficient, was not overly popular. Italian became the official language and the islanders were forced to accept Italian nationality. As a result of this enforced Italianization there was large-scale out-migration. Upon Italy's surrender in World War II the Dodecanese Islands were occupied by the Germans (1943-1945) and then by the British. With the consent of their inhabitants the islands were given to Greece in 1947.

The islands, as the Italians called them, with their Greek names in parentheses, were: Scarpanto (Kárpathos), Patmo (Pátmos), Caso (Kásos), Stampalia (Astipálaia), Lisso (Lipsoí), Lero (Léros), Calino (Kálimnos), Nisiro (Nísiros), Piscopi (Tílos), Calchi (Khálki), Simi (Sími), Rodi (Rhodes), Coo (Cos) and Castelrosso (Kastellórizon).

Statue of Romulus and Remus and Roman wolf

Readings: Hosmer, 1941; Shor, 1953.

FIUME

The Italians of Fiume are more Italian than the Italians.
— Joseph Galtier, 1919.

Area: 271 sq. miles (702 sq. km); Capital: Fiume
Population: 106,532 (est. 1931)

A port and its hinterland at the northeastern end of the Adriatic Sea. Though long a Hungarian possession Fiume had a large Italian population was this which formed the basis for the Italian claim to the city after World War I. The newly formed Kingdom of the Croats, Slovenes and Serbians (Yugoslavia) claimed Fiume as well. A compromise was reached with the Treaty of Rapallo (1920) by which Fiume became a free state under Italian control, with Yugoslavia having transit rights. While negotiations were underway in 1919 Italian poet Gabriele D'Annunzio organized a thousand-member legion and "liberated" Fiume in the name of Italy. D'Annunzio ruled Fiume as a dictator until forcibly removed in 1921. When Mussolini's fascists came to power in 1924 Fiume was annexed by Italy. In 1912 the city was the tenth largest port in Europe, but under Italian management it went into serious decline. Occupied by German forces at the end of World War II Fiume was freed by Yugoslav partisans in 1945. The city, now known as Rijeka, is in Croatia.

Severing the Gordian Knot

Readings: *Encyclopædia Britannica*, 1926; Galtier, 1919.

KARELIA (Karjala)

The dark, slender, poetic, dreamy, singing Karelian . . .
— Henry Norman, 1914.

Area: 28,890 sq. miles (74,825 sq. km); Capital: Petrozavodsk
Population: 144,392 (est. 1920)

A Russian territory bordering Finland, inhabited by people closely related to the Finns. After the Russian Revolution an independent government was established in Karelia in 1919 and it was not until 1922 that the U.S.S.R. was fully in control. The territory became the Karelian Autonomous Soviet Republic in 1923 and the twelfth republic of the U.S.S.R. In 1940 it became the Karelo-Finnish Soviet Socialist Republic. Karelia's status was downgraded in 1956 when it again became an autonomous republic. With the breakup of the Soviet Union Karelia remains part of Russia. About 80 percent of Karelians now live in Finland.

Readings: *Encyclopædia Britannica*, 1926; *Great Soviet Encyclopedia*, 1975.

MARIENWERDER (Commission Interalliée Marienwerder)

It is one of the most beautiful towns in eastern Germany, has a large cathedral church, a gymnasium, a hospital for blind soldiers, and an ancient castle which is now used as a prison.
— *American Cyclopædia*, 1883.

Area: 11,450 sq. miles (29,655 sq. km); Capital: Marienwerder
Population: 138,000 (est. 1910)

Under the terms of the Versailles Treaty, after World War I, the West Prussian districts of Marienwerder, Stuhm, Rosenburg and Marienburg were allowed to hold a plebiscite to determine whether they would become German or Polish. Until the plebiscite was held on July 11, 1920, Marienwerder was administered by an Allied commission supported by troops. 92 percent of the voters chose in favor of Germany and the Allied forces withdrew a month later. Since 1945 Marienwerder has been part of the province of Gdansk in Poland.

Symbol of the Allied supervision
of the plebiscite

Readings: *American Cyclopædia*, 1883; *Encyclopædia Britannica*, 1926.

MEMEL TERRITORY (Memelland)

> I asked if there were any objects of curiosity at Memel. "There is not any thing that I know of," said the second brother, "except a pot-ash manufactory, and you may see a better one at Dantzic: the ships at the quay are our finest sight."
> — Sir N.W. Wraxall, 1775.

Area: 943 sq. miles (2,442 sq. km); Capital: Memel
Population: 151,960 (est. 1939)

An ice-free port on the eastern coast of the Baltic Sea. Memel, which in early times had belonged to Sweden and Russia, came under German control in 1763 and was included in East Prussia. The town of Memel had a German population from the 13th century but its hinterland was mostly Lithuanian. In 1919, following World War I, Memel was detached from Germany and administered by a commission of the Allied powers. Objecting to plans to turn Memel into a free state Lithuania seized it in 1923 and made it an autonomous region. The League of Nations sanctioned the annexation in 1924 but Germany never forgot the loss. When the Nazis came to power they threatened Lithuania and the territory was returned to Germany in 1939. Memelland was liberated by Soviet troops in 1944 and restored to the Lithuanian Soviet Socialist Republic. Renamed Klaipeda it now forms part of the Republic of Lithuania.

French stamp overprinted for use in Memel

Readings: Chandler, 1938; *Great Soviet Encyclopedia*, 1975.

MONTENEGRO

They rose to where their sovran eagle sails,
They kept their faith, their freedom on the height
Chaste, frugal, savage, arm'd by day and night
Against the Turk; whose inroad nowhere scales.
— Alfred Lord Tennyson, 1877.

Area: 5,333 sq. miles (13,812 sq. km); Capital: Podgorica
Population: 199,857 (est. 1920)

A rugged land in southern Yugoslavia bordering Serbia, Albania and the Adriatic Sea. Montenegro's history has been marked by guerrilla war, blood feud and vendetta. Its women served for the purpose of procreation and labor while its men attended to war, politics and poetry. The name Montenegro means "Black Mountains," a reference to Mt. Lovcén (5,738 ft.; 1,749 m), a redoubt in the wars against the Turks. Settled by Slavs in the 7th century Montenegro became part of Serbia in the 12th century. Although closely related to the Serbs the Montenegrans took advantage of Serbia's defeat by Turkey in 1389 to establish their own independence. Between the 16th and 19th centuries Montenegro was ruled by hereditary Orthodox Bishop-Princes who were able to keep their country relatively free of the Turks. Though at times forced to accept Turkish suzerainty Montenegro was the only country in the Balkans never completely subdued by Turkey. Montenegro became a secular principality in 1851 and a kingdom in 1910. Its independence was recognized, and its size doubled, by the Congress of Berlin in 1878. In 1912-1913 Montenegro joined Serbia, Bulgaria and Greece in a war against Turkey and again increased its territory. Montenegro supported Serbia in World War I and in 1918 became part of the Kingdom of the Croats, Slovenes and Serbians (Yugoslavia). Montenegro has remained part of Yugoslavia.

King Nicholas I

Readings: Canby, 1984; *Encyclopædia Britannica*, 1926.

NORTH INGERMANLAND (Pohjois Inkeri)

> . . . belonging to the Tchudic branch of the Finns, now reduced to
> about 18,000, in 200 small and wretched villages. The Ingrians are
> poor and ignorant, but begin to assimilate more with the Russians.
> — *American Cyclopædia*, 1883.

Capital: Kirjasalo

A Russian district north of St. Petersberg, between the Neva River
and Finland. It was inhabited by people closely related to the Finns. In
1920 North Ingermanland revolted against Soviet authority and set up
its own government. The new state, which sought union with Finland
had but a short life. It was invaded by Soviet troops and returned to
the U.S.S.R.

Readings: *American Cyclopædia*, 1883; *Encyclopædia Britannica*, 1926.

RAGUSA

> . . . a State which is little, but more ancient they say than Venice, and
> is called the mother of Venice . . .
> — Samuel Pepys, 1662.

Area: 530 sq. miles (1,372 sq. km); Capital: Ragusa
Population: 8,278 (est. 1870)

A port on the Adriatic coast of Croatia, now called Dubrovnik.
Considered to be the most picturesque city in the region Ragusa was
founded in the 7th century. From about the 9th century Ragusa was an
independent city-republic. Though it was at times a vassal of Venice,
Hungary and the Ottoman Empire it maintained its independence until
Napoleon I subjugated it in 1808 and gave it to Austria. In its heyday
Ragusa was a major center of Slavic culture and the home of a
merchant fleet of 300 vessels. Ragusan ships traded as far as North
America and India. The English word *argosy* is a reminder of the ships
of Ragusa. Ragusa had a population of 40,000 in the 15th century until
reduced by earthquake and plague.

View of Dubrovnik (Ragusa)

Readings: Canby, 1984; *Encyclopædia Britannica*, 1926.

SASENO (Sazan)

> Italy remains in possession of Saseno, her position there being very similar to that of Great Britain at Gibraltar. A submarine base has been established there, and heavy guns which in conjunction with others upon the Italian coast forty-seven miles distant, are capable of bringing effective fire to bear upon any vessel passing the Straits of Otranto.
> — J. Swire, 1929.

Area: 2 sq. miles (5 sq. km)

A treeless and waterless island on the coast of Albania occupying a strategic position on the narrow southern entrance of the Adriatic Sea. Italy occupied the island in 1914 and did not return it to Albania until 1947.

Readings: Canby, 1984; Swire, 1929.

SEPTINSULAR REPUBLIC / UNITED STATES OF THE IONIAN ISLANDS

> The constant use of garlic, and the rare use of soap, impress an Englishman very disagreeably.
> — British administrator, 19th c.

Area: 891 sq. miles (2,308 sq. km); Capital: Corfu
Population: 229,516 (est. 1870)

A group of six islands — Corfu (Kérkira), Cephalonia (Kefallinia), Zante (Zakynthos), Santa Maura (Lefkas), Ithica (Ithaki), Paxos (Pax) —in the Ionian Sea and a seventh, Cerigo (Kythera), in the Mediterranean Sea. Formerly part of the Venetian Republic the islands were transferred to France in 1797. A Russo-Turkish force (1798-1799) put an end to French rule and for the next few years the islands were independent as the Septinsular Republic. The French returned in 1807 and made the islands an integral part of the French Empire. The British captured Zante, Cephalonia and Cerigo in 1809, Santa Maura in 1810 and Paxos in 1814. In 1815, after the Napoleonic Wars were over, the rest of the islands surrendered and the archipelago was placed under British protection as the United States of the Ionian Islands. Although a senate and assembly were established the British high commissioner wielded the real power. The population came to resent Britain's despotic rule and after 1848 there were rebellions, especially on Cephalonia, which had to be put down with force. The assembly called for immediate union with Greece in 1850. The British ceded the Ionian islands to Greece in 1864 as a gesture of good will on the accession of a new Greek king.

View of Corfu

Readings: *Encyclopædia Britannica*, 1926; Morris, 1968.

SERBIA

> The sunset sky against which I first saw Belgrade, was like a crimson and orange and purple moth, barred with colours as hard and clear as enamel. Belgrade stood heaped white on its hill, all its windows on fire with light.
> — Arthur Symons, 1903.

Area: 18,050 sq. miles (48,303 sq. km); Capital: Belgrade
Population: 2,911,701 (est. 1910)

In eastern Yugoslavia bordering Hungary, Romania, Bulgaria, Macedonia, Albania, Montenegro, Bosnia and Croatia. The Serbians, a slavic people, settled in the region in the 7th century and accepted Orthodox Christianity between the 9th and 10th centuries. The Kingdom of Serbia was established in 1217 and lasted until it was crushed by the Turks at the Battle of Kosovo in 1389. Serbia revolted against its Turkish overlords (1804-1813, 1815-1817) and achieved increasing degrees of self-rule. Under Turkish suzerainty it became a principality in 1829. Following the Russo-Turkish War (1877-1878), in which Serbia was Russia's ally, Serbia was recognized as an independent principality. It became a kingdom in 1882. During the Balkan Wars (1912-1913) Serbia expanded its territory and became the leader of the movement to unite all the South Slav peoples. Tensions increased with Austro-Hungary, which had annexed nearby Bosnia-Hercegovina in 1908. In 1914, when a Serbian nationalist assassinated Austrian Archduke Franz Ferdinand in Bosnia, Austro-Hungary declared war on Serbia. Russia joined Serbia and within a few days the other European powers chose sides and World War I had begun. After the war, in which 23 percent of Serbia's population died, the Kingdom of the Croats, Slovenes and Serbians (Yugoslavia) was formed, with an expanded Serbia as the dominant partner. Between 1991 and 1992 Croatia, Slovenia, Bosnia and Macedonia seceded from Yugoslavia leaving Serbia, its autonomous provinces of Kosovo and Vojvodina, and Montenegro in a rump Yugoslavia.

King Peter and military aides

Readings: Canby, 1984; *New Encyclopædia Britannica*, 1991.

UNION OF SOVIET SOCIALIST REPUBLICS (Soyuz Sovetskikh
Sotsialisticheskikh Respublik) / SOVIET UNION

It is a riddle wrapped in a mystery inside an enigma.
— Sir Winston Churchill, 1939.

Area: 8,650,000 sq. miles (22,400,000 sq. km); Capital: Moscow
Population: 290,100,000 (est. 1991)

The biggest country in the world, covering a seventh of the planet's
land mass. The U.S.S.R. stretched from Poland to the Pacific Ocean,
from the Black Sea to the North Pole. Before 1917 most of what
became the U.S.S.R. had constituted the Russian Empire, an autocracy
ruled by the Tsar. Revolution broke out on March 8, 1917. A
provisional government was created and the Tsar forced to abdicate.
Factional disputes crippled the new government and the Bolsheviks
(Communists) led an insurrection in St. Petersberg in November. The
provisional government was arrested, the Tzar and his family executed,
and a Communist regime under V.I. Lenin took power. A bloody five-
year civil war left the Communists in complete control of the country.
The Union of Soviet Socialist Republics officially came into being in
1922. Under Lenin, and later Stalin, the U.S.S.R. became a totalitarian
dictatorship and began a ruthless march toward socialism and heavy
industry by means of forced collectivization and five-year plans. The
country did became a major economic and military power but at an
appalling cost in human lives and suffering.

Germany invaded the U.S.S.R. in 1941. By the time the Great
Patriotic War ended in 1945, with Germany's total defeat, as many as
27,000,000 Soviet citizens had perished. After the war the U.S.S.R.
devoted itself to reconstruction and the exportation of Communism
worldwide. Its increasingly confrontational stance with regard to the
Western countries led to a period of tension and suspicion known as the
Cold War.

The last Soviet leader, M. Gorbachev, who took office in 1985,
saw that his country could no longer compete with the West.
Gorbachev realized that economic and structural reforms (perestroika)
as well as openness and freedom (glasnost) were urgently needed.
Political reform lagged, however. As the grip of central authority
unraveled, many parts of the country were consumed by violent
nationalism. Russia declared itself a sovereign nation in 1990 and the

U.S.S.R. collapsed in 1991. It was replaced by Russia, Ukraine, Belarus (Belorussia), Armenia, Azerbaijan, Georgia, Moldova (Moldavia), Kazakhstan, Kirghizia, Tajikistan, Turkmenistan, Uzbekistan, Estonia, Latvia and Lithuania. Most of these have become loosely tied as the Commonwealth of Independent States.

Diamond brooch and amethyst

Readings: *Great Soviet Encyclopedia*, 1975; Jackson, 1989.

UPPER SILESIA (Ober Schlesien; Gorny Slask)

> Upper Silesia itself, where conditions exist which make those best acquainted with Central Europe keep a fearful finger on the pulse of events in those parts.
> — F.P. Cockerell, 1921.

Area: 1,628 sq. miles (4,217 sq. km); Capital: Katowice
Population: 2,280,902 (est. 1919)

Ruled by Prussia since 1742, and Austria before that, Upper Silesia was a mixed German-Polish area in eastern Germany on the Polish border. After World War I parts of Upper Silesia were claimed by Germany, Poland and Czechoslovakia. While its final status was being sorted out, from 1919 to 1922, Upper Silesia was governed by an inter-Allied commission of France, Great Britain and Italy. Allied troops occupied the territory, assisted by a special half-German half-Polish police force. Czech demands were settled in 1920 by the transfer of a small strip of territory. The more serious dispute between Germany and Poland, which resulted in three bloody Polish uprisings, remained to be dealt with. It was decided to hold a plebiscite in 1921 asking each commune in Upper Silesia whether it wanted to be German or Polish. Although a majority of the communes declared for Germany, Poland acquired the most economically important areas, including three-quarters of the coal mines and two-thirds of the iron and steel works. When Germany attacked Poland in 1939 Upper Silesia was annexed, its Polish inhabitants suppressed, and the territory subjected to forcible Germanization. In 1945 Poland retook Upper Silesia, and acquired Lower Silesia which had always been German. About 3,500,000 Germans fled Silesia which was then repopulated with Poles.

Dove of peace in the sky over Silesia

Readings: Cockerell, 1921; *Encyclopædia Britannica*, 1926.

GRAND DUCHY OF WARSAW (Grand-Duché de Varsovie; Wielkoksiestwo Warszawskie)

> This metropolis seems to me, like the Republic of which it is the nominal head, to unite the extremes of civilization and of barbarism, of magnificence and wretchedness, of splendour and misery.
> — Sir N. W. Wraxall, 1779.

Area: 58,300 sq. miles (151,000 sq. km); Capital: Warsaw
Population: 4,334,000 (est. 1810)

A restored Polish state created by Napoleon I (1807-1815). As Polish independence had been lost when its lands were partitioned by Russia, Prussia and Austria the Grand Duchy of Warsaw became the focal point of Polish nationalism. Under French influence serfdom was abolished, a constitution was written, and the Code Napoléon was introduced. Schools were established, the first Polish dictionary was published and the first census in Polish history was carried out. In response, the Poles proved to be Napoleon's most loyal allies. Polish soldiers fought in Spain, Italy and even served in Haiti and in the

Imperial Guard. Nearly 100,000 took part in the invasion of Russia. Though much was accomplished during its life the Grand Duchy of Warsaw perished with Napoleon. Poland again vanished from the map of Europe but the Grand Duchy's brief existence kept alive the dreams of Polish independence.

Copernicus statue, Warsaw

Readings: Canby, 1984; *New Encyclopædia Britannica*, 1991.

WESTERN UKRAINIAN NATIONAL REPUBLIC (Zakhidno-Ukrainska Narodnia Respublika)

. . . the estate parcelled out, cut in half by the new Polish frontier, the owner dead with his brains blown out, and his last penny gambled away in Paris.
— V. Sackville-West, 1926.

Area: 27,000 sq. miles (70,000 sq. km); Capital: Lvov
Population: 6,000 (est. 1918)

An independent republic created out of the former Austro-Hungarian provinces of Galicia and Bukovinia in 1918. Western Ukraine lasted less than a year before being forcibly divided and annexed by Romania and Poland. Both parts of Western Ukraine fell into Soviet hands after World War II and are now part of Ukraine.

Readings: Kubijovyc, 1963; Struk, 1993.

ZARA (Zadar)

Zara is noted all over the world for its maraschino.
— Kenneth McKenzie, 1912.

Area: 113 sq. miles (293 sq. km); Capital: Zara
Population: 20,314 (est. 1931)

Zara was a town at the end of a low-lying peninsula in Dalmatia, on the eastern coast of the Adriatic Sea. Founded in the 9th century B.C. Zara became the capital of Dalmatia. The town was made an Austrian possession in 1797 and, apart from a French interregnum during the Napoleonic Wars, remained Austrian until 1918. Briefly part of the Kingdom of the Croats, Slovenes and Serbians (Yugoslavia) Italy asserted that it had rights to the area because of a resident Italian minority. By an Italo-Yugoslav agreement in 1920 Italy received Zara and a few nearby islands in exchange for renouncing its claim to the rest of Dalmatia. Zara then became a free city under Italian sovereignty. The city, 75 percent destroyed in World War II, was liberated by partisans in 1944 and returned to Yugoslavia. It is now part of Croatia.

Zara was the home of maraschino, a sweet liqueur made from black cherries and honey.

Readings: McKenzie, 1912; *New Encyclopædia Britannica*, 1991.

CHAPTER 7

Middle East

To glance at the genuine son of the desert is to take the romance out of him for ever — to behold his steed is to long in charity to strip his harness off and let him fall to pieces.
— Mark Twain, 1869.

ABU DHABI (Abu Zaby)

Someone in Abu Dhabi must have bought the idea of New York on the strength of getting postcards of the place from a holidaying friend: the entire city had the appearance of something obtained ready made in bulk.
— Jonathan Raban, 1979.

Area: 26,000 sq. miles (67,340 sq. km); Capital: Abu Dhabi
Population: 32,000 (est. 1968)

Formerly an independent emirate on the Arabian shore of the Persian Gulf. Founded about 1795 Abu Dhabi was the youngest emirate in the region but became the most important. Traditionally it maintained a rivalry with the neighboring emirates of Ras al-Khaima and Sharjah. From 1820 Abu Dhabi came under increasing British influence. It was included in the British sponsored Trucial States Protectorate from 1892 to 1971 and is now part of the United Arab Emirates, encompassing about 70 percent of the total area. Abu Dhabi, which has about 10 percent of the world's petroleum reserves, has gone from extreme poverty to fabulous wealth in less than a single generation.

Readings: Osbourne, 1977; Raban, 1979.

ADEN COLONY / STATE OF ADEN

The Coal-hole of the East.
— Sir Richard Burton, 1860.

Area: 75 sq. miles (194 sq. km); Capital: Aden
Population: 138,441 (est. 1955)

Aden was an ancient port on a volcanic peninsula in southwest Arabia. Its strategic location, about 100 miles (260 km) east of the entrance to the Red Sea, attracted the British, who garrisoned it in 1800 and annexed it in 1839. Aden was seen as part of India's outer defenses and was a dependency of British India until it became a separate crown colony in 1937. The British fortified Aden and transformed it into an important coaling station.

The crown colony included the rocky volcanic island of Perim (5 sq. miles, 13 sq. km) in the strait of Bab el-Mandeb at the southern end of the Red Sea. The British took possession of Perim in 1857 using it as a coaling station and garrison.

The Kuria Muria Islands (28 sq. miles, 73 sq. km) on the coast of Muscat and Oman were also part of Aden Colony. The five islands in the archipelago were ceded by the Sultan of Muscat to Great Britain in 1854 for use as a cable station. The islands were retroceded to Muscat and Oman in 1967.

Aden Colony, renamed the State of Aden, joined the Federation of South Arabia in 1963 and subsequently became part of the People's Democratic Republic of Yemen.

King George VI and
Aidrus Mosque

Readings: Heravi, 1973; *Imperial Gazetteer of India*, 1908.

ADEN PROTECTORATE/ FEDERATION OF ARAB EMIRATES OF THE SOUTH / FEDERATION OF SOUTH ARABIA / PEOPLE'S REPUBLIC OF SOUTH YEMEN / PEOPLE'S DEMOCRATIC REPUBLIC OF YEMEN

Aden should mean oven. Only the camels seemed baked enough to suit it.
— Henry Adams, 1891.

Area: 112,000 sq. miles (290,000 sq. km); Capital: Aden
Population: 2,345,266 (est. 1988)

The remote desert hinterland of the port of Aden in southwestern Arabia. The area, divided into the Eastern and Western Aden Protectorates, came under British suzerainty between 1876 and 1914 and comprised sultanates, emirates and tribal confederations. Those in eastern Aden were the Kathiri State of Seiyun, the Qu'aiti State of Shir and Mukalla, and Mahra. The states of western Aden were Alawi, Aqrabi, Audhali, Beihan, Dathina, Dhala, Fadhli, Haushabi, Lahej, Lower Aulaqi, Lower Yafa, Maflahi, Shaib, Upper Aulaqi, Upper Yafa and Wahidi. The British aim was to forestall Yemeni annexation and protect their base in Aden.

The protectorate included the island of Kamaran (70 sq. miles, 181 sq. km) in the Red Sea. It was taken from the Turks by the British in 1915 and administered by the government of Aden through a civil administration. A quarantine station for Mecca pilgrims was maintained on the island until 1952. In 1967 Kamaran's inhabitants opted to join independent South Yemen. It was occupied by North Yemen in 1972.

In 1959 the states in about half of the Aden Protectorate formed the Federation of the Arab Emirates of the South, under British influence. Over the next six years Aden Colony and most of the remaining emirates joined. The grouping was renamed the Federation of South Arabia in 1963 and prepared for independence. Between August and October 1967 the states of the Federation were seized and abolished by the National Liberation Front (NLF). In Aden a rival organization, the Front for the Liberation of South Yemen (FLOSY) waged a civil war against the NLF and harassed the departing British. The last British forces had to shoot their way out of Aden on November 29, 1967. The

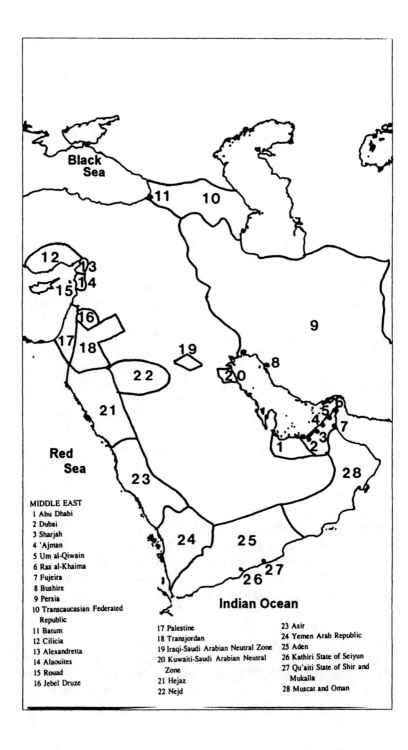

Black
Sea

11   10

12   13
15 14

16

17 18

19

22

9

8

20

6
5
4   7
3
2
1

21

Red
Sea

23

28

MIDDLE EAST
1 Abu Dhabi
2 Dubai
3 Sharjah
4 'Ajman
5 Um al-Qiwain
6 Ras al-Khaima
7 Fujeira
8 Bushire
9 Persia
10 Transcaucasian Federated
   Republic
11 Batum
12 Cilicia
13 Alexandretta
14 Alaouites
15 Rouad
16 Jebel Druze

24   25

26   27

Indian Ocean

17 Palestine
18 Transjordan
19 Iraqi-Saudi Arabian Neutral Zone
20 Kuwaiti-Saudi Arabian Neutral
   Zone
21 Hejaz
22 Nejd

23 Asir
24 Yemen Arab Republic
25 Aden
26 Kathiri State of Seiyun
27 Qu'aiti State of Shir and
   Mukalla
28 Muscat and Oman

next day the NLF-dominated People's Republic of South Yemen was proclaimed. It was renamed the People's Democratic Republic of Yemen in 1970. The Yemen Arab Republic (North Yemen) and the People's Democratic Republic of Yemen (South Yemen) were unified as the Yemen Arab Republic in 1990. The union has proven to be less than satisfactory. Both of the former Yemens kept their armed forces and there have been serious outbreaks of fighting.

People's Democratic Republic of Yemen coat of arms

Readings: Heravi, 1973; *Imperial Gazetteer of India*, 1908.

'AJMAN (Ujman)

> Ajman is tucked into Sharjah like a pocket-handkerchief.
> — Christine Osbourne, 1977.

Area: 100 sq. miles (260 sq. km); Capital: 'Ajman
Population: 4,200 (est. 1968)

The smallest emirate in the British protectorate of the Trucial States (1892-1971), comprising three noncontiguous enclaves. 'Ajman was first recognized as an autonomous state in 1820 when it signed a treaty with Great Britain. 'Ajman had no oil and was the poorest Trucial State. Prior to its joining the United Arab Emirates in 1971 'Ajman eked out a living from pearl diving and the sale of bogus postage stamps.

Sheik Rashid bin Humaid al Naimi and angelfish

Readings: Anthony, 1976; Osbourne, 1977.

ALAOUITES (Alawites) / LATAKIA (Lattaquié)

> What a country this is! I fear I shall spend the rest of my life travelling
> in it. Race after race, one on top of the other, the whole land strewn
> with the mighty relics of them.
> — Gertrude Bell, 1905.

Area: 2,500 sq. miles (6,475 sq. km); Capital: Latakia
Population: 278,000 (est. 1930)

On the Mediterranean coast of Syria inhabited mostly by members
of the 'Alawite sect of Shi'ite Islam. Alaouites, which had long been
under the rule of the Ottoman Turks, became part of the French
mandated territory of Syria after World War I. In 1924 Alaouites
became a separate unit in the French mandate. The name was changed
to Latakia in 1930 and it was under that name that the territory was
reincorporated into Syria in 1942. The region produces the famous
Latakia tobacco.

Syrian stamp overprinted
for use in Latakia

Readings: *Encyclopædia Britannica*, 1926; Heravi, 1973.

ALEXANDRETTA / HATAY

> Alexandretta . . . is very unwholesome by reason of the huge high hills hindringe the approach of the Sunne Beames, untill nine or ten a Clocke in the morning, lyeinge in a great Marsh full of boggs, foggs and Froggs.
> — Peter Mundy, c. 1620.

Area: 10,000 sq. miles (25,900 sq. km); Capital: Alexandretta
Population: 273,350 (est. 1939)

At the extreme northeast corner of the Mediterranean Sea. The town of Alexandretta was founded by Alexander the Great in 333 B.C. to celebrate a great victory over the Persians. Through the centuries that followed, the district around Alexandretta was ruled by Romans, Persians, Arabs, Byzantines and Ottoman Turks. Following Turkey's defeat in World War I Alexandretta became a League of Nations mandated territory awarded to France. It was attached to Syria (also a French mandated territory) by a special administrative regime. The inhabitants of Alexandretta were mostly Turkish and the territory was claimed by Turkey. The French mandate lasted from 1918 to 1937 when Alexandretta became the semi-independent territory of Hatay, a joint French-Turkish responsibility. Following a referendum, Hatay asked to be annexed by Turkey. This was done in 1939 over the protests of Syria.

Map of Hatay

Readings: Heravi, 1973; *New Encyclopædia Britannica*, 1991.

ASIR (Assir)

> Now, in the Assir, I was standing on a mountain-side forested with
> wild olives and junipers. A stream tumbled down the slope; its water,
> ice-cold at 9,000 feet, was in welcome contrast with the scanty, bitter
> water of the sands. There were wild flowers: jasmine and honeysuckle,
> wild roses, pinks and primulas. There were terraced fields of wheat
> and barley, vines and plots of vegetables. Far below me a yellow haze
> hid the desert to the east.
> — Wilfred Thesiger, 1959.

Area: 40,000 sq. miles (103,600 sq. km); Capital: Sabiyah
Population: 1,000,000 (est. 1923)

Asir, the "difficult country," was a mountainous land in
southwestern Arabia bordering the Red Sea. It broke away from Yemen
in the 19th century only to be occupied by the Ottoman Turks in 1872.
Asir took advantage of World War I to stage a revolt against the Turks
and re-establish its independence. To stave off Yemeni designs Asir
became a dependency of the Kingdom of Nejd in 1926. Subsequently
Asir became a province of the Kingdom of Saudi Arabia.

Readings: Thesiger, 1959; Wood, 1923.

BATUM (Batumi)

> Nobility is cheap in Georgia. There is only one rank, and that is
> prince.
> — John Foster Fraser, 1899.

Capital: Batum; Population: 45,000 (est. 1926)

A city and port on the Black Sea, in Georgia. Batum was
transferred to Russia from Turkey in 1878, fortified and turned into an
important naval base. At the end of World War I (1918) Batum was
captured by the Turks. They were replaced by the British who
administered Batum and its environs until 1920, under the terms of the
Treaty of Versailles. When the British withdrew, the Turks returned,
only to be driven out by the Red Army. Soviet power was established
in Batum in 1921. The city is now the capital of the Adjarian
Autonomous Republic, within the Republic of Georgia.

Stamp overprinted "British Occupation"

Readings: *Encyclopædia Britannica*, 1926; *Great Soviet Encyclopedia*, 1975..

BUSHIRE (Bushehr)

> At a distance, and seen from the harbour, Bushire is not unlike Cadiz. Its Moorish buildings, the whiteness of its houses and blueness of the sea, give it, on a fine day, a picturesque and taking appearance, speedily dissipated, however, on closer acquaintance; for Bushire is incredibly filthy.
> — Harry de Windt, 1891.

Area: 40 sq. miles (104 sq. km); Capital: Bushire
Population: 25,000 (est. 1910)

Bushire was an important port in Persia (Iran); the terminus of trade routes to Russia, India and Turkey. The town was on a peninsula separated from the mainland by a marsh. From 1763 the British East India Company made Bushire the base of their operations in the Persian Gulf and in the 19th century the city became a virtual British colony. The British based a fleet of gunboats in the port for the suppression of piracy and the British agent in Bushire, the Political Resident in the Persian Gulf (PRPG), became the most powerful official in the region. Persian objections caused the Resident to be transferred to Bahrain in the late 1940s although the office of PRPG was not abolished until 1971. Bushire was occupied by British troops during the Anglo-Persian War (1856-1857) and during World War I (1915).

Readings: Heravi, 1973; *Imperial Gazetteer of India*, 1908.

CILICIA (Cilicie)

Saffron, sought for in Cilicia's soil.
— Edmund Spenser, 1596.

Area: 6,238 sq. miles (16,156 sq. km); Capital: Seyhan
Population: 383,645 (est. 1920)

On the Mediterranean coast of Turkey, an ancient country valued for its strategic passes linking Syria with Asia Minor. Cilicia was dominated by Hittites, Assyrians, Persians, Macedonians, Selucids, Romans, Arabs, Byzantines and Ottoman Turks. Between 1918 and 1923 Cilicia was governed by France as a League of Nations mandated territory. It was then returned to Turkey.

French stamp overprinted O.M.F. (Occupation Militaire Française)

Readings: Canby, 1984; *Encyclopædia Britannica*, 1926.

DUBAI (Dubayy)

It is a fantastic dream city in which the warm evening haze mingles with the pink hues of twilight to create an impression of unreality and hallucination.
— M. Philippe Lannois, 1976.

Area: 1,510 sq. miles (3,911 sq. km); Capital: Dubai
Population: 70,000 (est. 1968)

Dubai was founded as an emirate in the 18th century but remained a dependency of Abu Dhabi until 1833. In that year dissident pearl divers from Abu Dhabi migrated to Dubai and established Dubai's independence. Dubai was the second largest of the Trucial States, a protectorate established by the British in 1892. Since 1971 it has been part of the United Arab Emirates. Many observers have thought Dubai to be the most beautiful city on the Persian Gulf.

Moonfish

Readings: Anthony, 1976; Osbourne, 1977.

FUJEIRA (Fujairah; al-Fujayrah)

> Until the road between Sharjah and Khor Fakkan was opened in 1975, one almost needed a magic carpet to reach Fujairah, the alternative being an 8-hour back-trip through the *wadis*.
> — Christine Osbourne, 1977.

Area: 440 sq. miles (1,140 sq. miles); Capital: Fujeira
Population: 10,000 (est. 1968)

The only emirate in the British-dominated Trucial States Protectorate (1892-1971) with no territory on the Persian Gulf. Fujeira bordered the Gulf of Oman. Sharjah annexed Fujeira about 1850 and thereafter had to contend with numerous rebellions. Fujeira did succeed in establishing a degree of autonomy by the end of the 19th century but was not recognized by the British as an autonomous state until 1952. Since 1971 it has been part of the United Arab Emirates.

Butterflies

Readings: Anthony, 1976; Osbourne, 1977.

HEJAZ (Hedjaz)

> The inhabitants here are few; so are their cities; their dwellings being
> in sequestrate dens, and hair-cloth tents: the most of their wealth
> consisteth in camels, dromedaries, and goats.
> — William Lithgow, 1614.

Area: 150,000 sq. miles (388,500 sq. km); Capital: Mecca
Population: 1,000,000 (est. 1932)

In western Arabia, on the Red Sea. Because it was the birthplace
of the prophet Mohammed and contained the holy cities of Mecca and
Medina, Hejaz was an important country for Muslims. It was overrun
by the Ottoman Turks in 1517 and remained under their rule until
1916. In that year Husein, Sherif of Mecca, joined the Allies in World
War I and, under the influence of T.E. Lawrence (Lawrence of
Arabia), rebelled against Turkey. Husein declared himself King of
Hejaz and his country's independence was recognized internationally.
But due to the complexities of Arabian politics Husein's reign was a
short one. In 1924 Hejaz was conquered by the forces of Ibn Saud,
Sultan of Nejd. Ibn Saud became King of Hejaz in 1926 and for a few
years Hejaz and Nejd were united through the person of their common

monarch. In 1932 the Kingdom of Saudi Arabia was created in which Hejaz became a province.

Hejaz coat of arms

Readings: Heravi, 1973; Wood, 1923.

KINGDOMS OF HEJAZ, NEJD AND DEPENDENCIES

The most striking feature of Es-Saud's plain palace is a white-tiled reception hall, where he sits under a kerosene lamp of great size blinding the eyes of all who face him.
— Junius B. Wood, 1923.

Area: 170,000 sq. miles (440,000 sq. km); Capitals: Mecca, Riyadh
Population: 4,000,000 (est. 1932)

Kingdoms in Arabia united under the personal union of Abdul Aziz ibn Abdur Rahman al-Faisal al Saud. Ibn Saud proclaimed himself Sultan of Nejd and its dependencies in 1921 and King of Hejaz in 1926. The union that resulted was reorganized in 1932 as the Kingdom of Saudi Arabia.

Readings: Heravi, 1973; Wood, 1923.

IRAQI-SAUDI ARABIAN NEUTRAL ZONE

Area: 1,717 sq. miles (4,446 sq. km)

A remote diamond-shaped desert region on the border of Iraq and Saudi Arabia. The Zone, demarcated in 1922 and administered jointly by the two countries, was divided according to a 1975 agreement. The Neutral Zone had no permanent population although nomads from both countries had rights for grazing and access to wells.

Readings: *New Encyclopædia Britannica*, 1991; *Statesman's Yearbook*, 1975-1976.

JEBEL DRUZE (Jabal ad-Druze)

Imagine a very huge giant emptying out giant-size sackfuls of big basalt boulders, as a child might empty out paper-bagfuls of monkey nuts. Make the top of the heap rise five or six thousand feet above sea level, and sprinkle the higher altitudes of the boulder dump with dwarf oaks. That is the best notion that I can give you of the Jabal Druz.
— Arnold Toynbee, 1958.

Area: 2,124 sq. miles (5,500 sq. km); Capital: El Suweideh
Population: 51,780 (est. 1929)

The Druze are a close-knit Islamic sect in Lebanon, Syria and Israel who have maintained their distinctiveness, often in the face of persecution, for more than a thousand years. Jebel Druze was a Druze dominated region in southeastern Syria. After the defeat of Turkey in World War I it became a French administered League of Nations mandated territory. The Druze were a difficult people to govern. In 1925 the Druze tribes throughout Syria and Lebanon revolted against the French who had unwisely attempted to supersede Druze tribal hierarchy and traditions. It took two years of fighting to pacify the region. Thereafter Jebel Druze was kept under tight control and the population's inclination toward xenophobia and isolation encouraged them to remain untouched by Arab nationalism. Jebel Druze was incorporated into Syria in 1942 where it now forms an administrative district.

Readings: *Collier's Encyclopedia*, 1994; *Encyclopædia Britannica*, 1926.

KATHIRI STATE OF SEIYUN

There is a feeling of gigantic and naked force about it all, and one thinks what it was when these hills were boiling out their stream of fire, hissing them into the sea, and wonders at anything so fragile as man living on these ancient desolations.
— Freya Stark, 1953.

Capital: Seiyun

A semi-independent emirate in the arid interior of Hadhramaut, southern Arabia. Seiyun was a powerful local state from 1500 until the early 19th century when it was challenged by the rising Qu'aiti State of Shir and Mukalla. The British supported the Qu'aitis and the Kathiri state was reduced. Under a treaty imposed in 1918 Seiyun was cut off from its access to the sea and its territory completely surrounded by that of Shir and Mukalla. The state maintained its autonomy, resisting British pressure to join the Federation of South Arabia, until 1967 when it was overrun by the National Liberation Front and incorporated into the People's Republic of South Yemen.

Sultan Ja'far bin Mansur al Kathiri and view of Seiyun

Readings: *New Encyclopædia Britannica*, 1991; *Statesman's Yearbook*, 1967-1968.

KUWAITI-SAUDI ARABIAN NEUTRAL ZONE

Area: 3,560 sq. miles (9,220 sq. km)

An arid district on the Persian Gulf claimed by Kuwait and Saudi Arabia. The Neutral Zone was jointly administered by Kuwait and Saudi Arabia from 1922 until 1966. The Zone had no permanent population and was of interest only to small groups of nomadic herders until were discovered there huge petroleum resources. Kuwait and Saudi Arabia partitioned the Zone in 1969 and agreed to share the oil revenue equally.

Readings: *New Encyclopædia Britannica*, 1991; *Statesman's Yearbook*, 1969-1970.

MUSCAT AND OMAN

> It was of the people of Muscat that the English ship's captain being instructed, on visiting strange places, to make a report of the manners and customs of the inhabitants, penned the famous saying: "As to manners they have none; and their customs are beastly."
> — George Curzon, 1892.

Area: 105,000 sq. miles (272,000 sq. km); Capital: Muscat
Population: 750,000 (est. 1964)

A sultanate in southeastern Arabia. Muscat and Oman was under Portuguese influence for about 150 years until they were driven out in 1650. The country then established its own power in the Persian Gulf and as far as Persia (Iran) and Zanzibar. Though it remained independent Muscat and Oman signed a treaty of friendship with Great Britain and, during the course of the 19th and early 20th centuries, came under the British sphere of influence. The country, which had remained in the Middle Ages, was ruled with absolute power by Sultan Said bin Taimur from 1932 to 1970. His repressive policies — there were only 6 miles of paved roads in the country, bicycles and sunglasses were banned — led to a revolt in the southern province of Dhofar which was put down with British assistance in 1965. The Sultan was overthrown, with British help, by his son Qaboos in 1970 who began to modernize the country with the aid of newfound oil wealth. He started by renaming it the Sultanate of Oman in 1970. Oman province, in the interior, was semi-independent from 1913 to 1955.

British stamp overprinted for use in Muscat and Oman

Readings: Anthony, 1976; Range, 1995.

NEJD (Najd)

> . . . the lofty table-lands and the broad pastures of Nijd, combined
> with the attention paid by the people to purity of blood, have rendered
> it the greatest breeding country in Arabia.
> — Sir Richard Burton, 1855.

Area: 500,000 sq. miles (1,395,000 sq. km); Capital: Riyadh
Population: 3,000,000 (est. 1932)

A kingdom in central Arabia associated with Wahhabism, a
conservative Muslim reform movement that arose in the 15th century.
The Saud family unified the tribes of Nejd in a religio-political
confederation dedicated to defeating the Turks and to spreading
Wahhabism and Saudi political authority throughout Arabia. After a
long period of turmoil with the Ottoman Turks and local princes the
Saudis achieved their goals. In World War I and the years following,
Abdul Aziz ibn Saud confirmed Nejd's independence and conquered
Hejaz, Asir and the other districts of Arabia. In 1921 ibn Saud became
sultan of Nejd and its dependencies and in 1926, king of Hejaz. The
country was reorganized as the Kingdom of Saudi Arabia in 1932. Nejd
was famous for its fine breeds of horses and camels.

Readings: Heravi, 1973; Wood, 1923.

OTTOMAN EMPIRE

> What energy can be expected of a people with no heels to their shoes?
> — Lord Palmerston, c. 1865.

Area: 1,450,000 sq. miles (3,750,000 sq. km); Capital: Constantinople
Population: 36,323,539 (est. 1910)

The Ottoman Turks were descendants of Turkomen mercenaries who appeared in Anatolia (Asia Minor) in the 11th century. By the end of the 13th century Osman I, after whom the empire derived its name, had established a powerful new state. The Ottoman Empire was an expansionist Islamic state that, at its peak in the 16th century under Sultan Suleiman the Magnificent, controlled Anatolia, the Middle East, the Arabian peninsula, Persia (Iran), Crimea, North Africa and southeastern Europe. The Empire, which went into decline after Suleiman, survived for another three centuries. By the late 19th and early 20th centuries the Ottoman Empire had become increasingly decadent and had suffered defeats at the hands of Russia, Austria and the nationalist forces in Greece and Serbia. France took Algeria and Tunisia, Italy seized Libya, and Great Britain acquired Cyprus and Egypt. The Sultanate had earned itself the unenviable nickname of "the Sick Man of Europe." In 1908 a revolution by the so-called Young Turks movement ended the autocratic power of the Sultan and brought forth long overdue political, financial and administrative reforms. Unwisely the Young Turks brought their country into World War I on the side of Germany and Austro-Hungary. The defeat of the Central Powers in 1918 resulted in the breakup of the Ottoman Empire. The Turks came to accept the loss of their Balkan and Arab territories but resisted foreign control and dismemberment of Anatolia. After the Turkish War of Independence (1918-1923) the secular Republic of Turkey was established under the dynamic leadership of Kemal Ataturk.

Sultan Mohammed V and map of the Dardanelles

Readings: Canby, 1984; *New Encyclopædia Britannica*, 1991.

PALESTINE

This is the land that flowed with milk and honey. As a matter of fact
it flows now chiefly with stones.
— Lilian Leland, 1890.

Area: 10,429 sq. miles (27,011 sq. km); Capital: Jerusalem
Population: 1,933,673 (est. 1947)

At the eastern end of the Mediterranean Sea, an ancient land bridge
between Asia and Africa. Palestine had been an obscure Turkish
province for 400 years when British troops occupied it in 1917. The
British established a civil administration in 1920 and the League of
Nations gave them a mandate over Palestine in 1923. At that time the
population was overwhelmingly Arab with a Jewish minority. Over the
course of the mandate there was heavy Jewish immigration, often
illegal, and the demographic balance began to shift in their favor.
Meanwhile the British had a confused and contradictory policy. They
issued the Balfour Declaration in 1917, which supported the
establishment of a Jewish homeland in Palestine. Yet in other political
accords they supported the creation of an independent Arab state or
international status. Palestine was subjected to recurring violence
between Arabs and Jews as well as Jewish terrorism against the British
and an Arab rebellion. The British withdrew from Palestine in 1948 but
the United Nations plan for partitioning Palestine into separate Jewish
and Arab states satisfied no one. The independent Jewish state of Israel
was proclaimed on May 14, 1948, and within hours war broke out with
the adjacent Arab states. When the fighting ended early in 1949 Israel
had survived and expanded its borders by a third. The part of Palestine
that came to be known as the West Bank was in Transjordanian hands
and was formally annexed by Jordan in 1950.

Citadel at Jerusalem

Readings: *Encyclopædia Britannica*, 1926; Heravi, 1973.

PERSIA

> Well in this country the men wear flowing robes of green and white
> and brown, the women lift the veil of a Raphael Madonna to look at
> you as you pass.
> — Gertrude Bell, 1892.

Area: 634,724 sq. miles (1,644,000 sq. km); Capital: Tehran
Population: 10,000,000 (est. 1932)

Bordered by British India (Pakistan) and Afghanistan in the east,
Turkey and Iraq in the west, the Soviet Union in the north and the
Persian Gulf to the south. The origin of Persia can be traced to Cyrus
the Great who created a monarchy that would last from 549 B.C. until
the last Shah, Muhammad Reza Pahlavi, was deposed in 1979. By the
19th century Persia's great days of empire and wealth were long gone.
The ruling house had grown decadent and the country was in turmoil.
Persia was under pressure from the Russians thrusting south and the
British moving west from India and north from the Persian Gulf. The
Anglo-Russian Entente of 1907 preserved Persia's independence but at
the cost of dividing the country into Russian and British zones of
influence. The next year Persia's vast petroleum deposits were
discovered. This led to an increased Russian-British rivalry that lasted
until after World War II. The country was known abroad as Persia,
from the ancient Greek name Persis. Since 1935 the older and more
correct name, Iran, "Land of the Aryans," has been used exclusively.
During its last years as Persia, the country attempted to free itself from
foreign domination and lay the basis for a modern state. Reforms
reduced the power of conservative Shi'ite Muslim clergy and freed
women from the veil.

Shah Ahmed

Readings: Canby, 1984; *New Encyclopædia Britannica*, 1991.

QU'AITI STATE OF SHIR AND MUKALLA

This is a charming little town to look at, rather like a picture by
Carpaccio, only white.
— Freya Stark, 1953.

Area: 58,000 sq. miles (150,000 sq. km); Capital: al-Mukalla

An emirate that covered most of Hadhramaut in southwestern
Arabia inland to the Rub 'al-Khali, the Arabian desert. The Qu'aiti
tribe rose to prominence in the 19th century. They fought for local
supremacy against the Kathiri sultanate until the British compelled the
two states to sign a peace treaty in 1918. Shir and Mukalla did not join
the Federation of South Arabia, retaining its autonomy until absorbed
by the People's Republic of South Yemen in 1967. Men from the state
traditionally migrated to India where they served as mercenaries in
Hyderabad.

Sultan Sir Saleh bin Ghalib al Qu'aiti and Mukalla Harbor

Readings: *New Encyclopædia Britannica*, 1991; *Statesman's Yearbook*, 1967-
1968.

RAS AL-KHAIMA (Ra's al-Khaymah)

Any remark by a local pertaining to development in Ras al-Khaimah
terminates with a confident "When we have our oil." Not "if we
discover oil" or "should we discover oil," but a very positive "when."
— Christine Osbourne, 1977.

Area: 660 sq. miles (1,709 sq. km); Capital: Ras al-Khaima
Population: 25,000 (est. 1968)

A small emirate, made up of two tracts of land, in the northern part of the Omani Promontory near the Strait of Hormuz. The Portuguese built a fort in Ras al-Khaima in 1622 but were supplanted by the Persians (Iranians) and then the Dutch. By the 19th century Ras al-Khaima was a dependent emirate of Sharjah and a major pirate base. The British attacked the pirates of Ras al-Khaima in 1809. Attacking again they destroyed the pirates and the town in 1819. Although part of the Trucial States Protectorate (1892-1971) Ras al-Khaima was not recognized by the British as a separate emirate until 1952. It is now one of the United Arab Emirates, having joined the federation in 1972 a year after the other emirates. The name Ras al-Khaima means "the tent point" and was derived from a navigational aid once located there.

Readings: Anthony, 1976; Osbourne, 1977.

ROUAD (Ile Rouad; Arwad; Aradus)

> Aradus is the only island on the Syrian coast mentioned by the historians of the Crusades.
> — *American Cyclopædia*, 1883.

Area: 1 sq. mile (3 sq. km); Capital: Rouad
Population: 2,500 (est. 1916)

A low, flat, rocky island in the eastern Mediterranean Sea off the Syrian coast. Settled since the second millennium B.C., Rouad was mentioned in the Bible and at various times has been controlled by Phoenicians, Assyrians, Babylonians, Persians, Romans, Crusaders, Arabs and Turks. The Turks used the island as a detention center for political prisoners. In ancient times Rouad was heavily fortified, had dependencies on the mainland, and maintained a powerful fleet, even though it had no natural soil, no harbor and no freshwater. There was said to be a freshwater spring on the ocean floor midway between Rouad and the mainland. In a crisis water was cleverly piped up to boats on the surface. In 1916 the French drove out the Ottoman Turks and occupied the island, the first part of the Syrian coast captured during World War I. The French administered Rouad from 1916 to 1920 when it was added to their mandated territories in Syria.

French stamp overprinted
for use in Rouad

Readings: *American Cyclopædia*, 1883; *Encyclopædia Britannica*, 1926.

SHARJAH AND DEPENDENCIES

Smile, you're in Sharjah.
— Signpost, q. by Christine Osborne, 1977.

Area: 1,000 sq. miles (2,600 sq. km); Capital: Sharjah
Population: 35,000 (est. 1968)

In the early 19th century Sharjah was a notorious pirate base on the Persian Gulf. The British attacked Sharjah in 1819 and forced it and the other emirates in the region to sign a peace treaty. Sharjah was grouped with six other emirates in 1892 to form the Trucial States Protectorate. That arrangement lasted until 1971 when the British withdrew and the United Arab Emirates was formed. At various times Abu Dhabi and Umm al-Qiwain were dependencies of Sharjah, as were the towns of Khor Fakkan, Dhiba and Kalba on the Gulf of Oman. Dhiba was shared with Fujeira and Oman while Kalba existed as a semi-independent emirate from 1939 until 1952.

Red Crescent and Sheik Saqr ibn Sultan al Qasimi

Readings: Anthony, 1976; Osbourne, 1977.

TRANSCAUCASIAN FEDERATED REPUBLIC / TRANSCAUCASIAN SOVIET FEDERATED REPUBLIC (Zakavkazye)

> The Alps incline you to altruism. . . . The Caucasus don't do that.
> They frighten you; their scowl makes you shiver.
> — John Foster Fraser, 1899.

Area: 74,970 sq. miles (194,171 sq. km); Capital: Tiflis
Population: 5,683,767 (est. 1920)

A federal republic south of the Caucasus Mountains and east of the Black Sea. Made up of Armenia, Azerbaijan and Georgia the Transcaucasian Federated Republic was proclaimed in 1917 during the Russian Revolution. It was invaded almost immediately by Turkish forces and broken into its constituent parts, each of which declared independence. However, civil war erupted and by 1921 the Bolsheviks were in control. The republic was reconstituted as the Transcaucasian Soviet Federated Republic and within a year was absorbed into the U.S.S.R. In 1936 the Transcaucasian Republic became the soviet republics of Armenia, Azerbaijan and Georgia. All of these re-established their independence upon the breakup of the U.S.S.R.

Coat of arms of the republic

Readings: *Great Soviet Encyclopedia*, 1975; Shukman, 1988.

TRANSJORDAN / KERAK

> [The Dead Sea] was spread out before me, motionless as a lake of molten lead. . . . The water is exceedingly clear and transparent but its taste and smell are a compound of all that is bad.
> — John Lloyd Stephens, 1837.

Area: 34,443 sq. miles (89,207 sq. km); Capital: Amman
Population: 1,500,000 (est. 1950)

A state occupying the east bank of the Jordan River and the Dead Sea. Although one of the oldest continuously inhabited places in the world Transjordan, as a political entity, was a creation of the 20th century. The Ottoman Turks had ruled Transjordan since 1517. When they were defeated in World War I Transjordan was included in the League of Nations mandated territory of Palestine awarded to the British. In practice Transjordan was treated as a separate entity and its population assured that they would not be included in any Jewish homeland to be established. By a treaty with Great Britain in 1928 Transjordan became a constitutional monarchy under British protection. In 1948 it was recognized as the independent Hashemite Kingdom of Transjordan, *hashemite* signifying a descendent of the prophet Mohammed. In common with other Arab states Transjordan opposed the partition of Palestine into separate Jewish and Arab areas and fought in the first Arab-Israeli war. At war's end Transjordan occupied the West Bank of the Jordan River, an area that had been awarded to the Arabs under the United Nations partition plan for Palestine. Transjordan was renamed the Hashemite Kingdom of Jordan in 1949 and formally annexed the West Bank in 1950.

Parliament building in Amman

Readings: Heravi, 1973; Wood, 1923.

TRUCIAL STATES / TRUCIAL OMAN / TRUCIAL COAST

No arm of the sea has been, or is of greater interest alike to the geologist and archaeologist, the historian and geographer, the merchant and the student of strategy, than the inland water known as the Persian Gulf.
— Sir Arnold Wilson, 1928.

Area: 32,300 sq. miles (83,657 sq. km); Capital: Dubai
Population: 180,200 (est. 1968)

On the southern shore of the Persian Gulf in an area once known as the Pirate Coast; for the most part a monotonous desert plain. The Trucial States was made up of seven Omani emirates — Abu Dhabi, 'Ajman, Dubai, Fujeira, Ras al-Khaima, Sharjah and Umm al-Qiwain. In the early 19th century pirates from Ras al-Khaima and Sharjah brazenly attacked British shipping in the Persian Gulf and the Gulf of Oman, often killing or ransoming the crews. In response the British dispatched a punitive expedition from Bombay in 1809 and a stronger one in 1819, which razed Ras al-Khaima. All the emirates in the region, whether involved in piracy or not, were forced to sign a treaty and accept British supremacy. Additional agreements brought the emirates more and more into the British orbit. The emirates were considered poor and benighted places and the British did not much care what they did on land as long as there was peace at sea. With the signing of the Treaty of Maritime Peace in Perpetuity in 1853 the area became known as the Trucial Coast. Beginning in 1892 the emirates were combined into the protectorate of the Trucial States, or Trucial Oman. The British were interested in keeping the French and Turks out of the area. The protectorate was supervised by the Government of British India until 1947 and thereafter by the British Foreign Office. When the British withdrew from the Persian Gulf in 1971 six of the emirates federated to form the United Arab Emirates (U.A.E.). Ras al-Khaima joined the federation in 1972. The original plan called for Qatar and Bahrain to join the federation but they opted for separate independence. Each of the emirates makes a contribution to the budget of the U.A.E. but retains a measure of autonomy and separate hereditary rulers. Decisions must have the approval of at least five of the emirs including those of Dubai and Abu Dhabi, the most important states. The former Trucial States possess enormous petroleum reserves. In less than a generation the emirates have gone from being one of the poorest spots on the globe to one of the richest.

Readings: Anthony, 1976; Osbourne, 1977.

UMM AL-QIWAIN (Umm al-Qaiwain; Umm al-Qaywayn)

> The drive into Umm al Qaiwain affords a charming view of this somnolent little town of coconut-ice-coloured houses stacked around the bay.
> — Christine Osbourne, 1977.

Area: 290 sq. miles (750 sq. km); Capital: Umm al-Qiwain
Population: 4,000 (est. 1968)

The second smallest and least populous of the Trucial States. Umm al-Qiwain was a vassal of Sharjah from the early 19th century and a pirate port. The first recognition of its autonomy came in 1820 when it signed a treaty with Great Britain. Umm al-Qiwain was part of the British protectorate of the Trucial States from 1892 to 1971 and is now one of the United Arab Emirates.

Sheik Ahmed bin Rashid al Mulla and ruins

Readings: Anthony, 1976; Osbourne, 1977.

YEMEN ARAB REPUBLIC (North Yemen)

> Smaller, darker and much scruffier than the Gulf Arabs, the Yemenis had bird's-egg skulls and curiously knotty faces. They wore plastic sandals, midi-length skirts and jackets which appeared to have once been the top halves of the cheapest and shiniest Hong Kong suits. What, I wondered, had happened to the trousers?
> — Jonathan Raban, 1979.

Area: 73,300 sq. miles (189,069 sq. km); Capital: San'a
Population: 8,595,000 (est. 1988)

A mountainous country in the southwest corner of the Arabian Peninsula, bordered by the Red Sea. Inhabited since at least 2,000 B.C. and known to the Romans as Arabia Felix (Happy Arabia), Yemen (which means "the right side," from its position when one gazes east from Mecca) was long one of the world's most isolated lands. Although the Ottoman Turks exercised a degree of control over the Red

Sea coast Yemen was ruled by a dynasty of kings and imams founded in the 11th century. The Turks were expelled as a result of World War I but otherwise things remained as they were until 1962 when a group of army officers overthrew the monarchy and declared Yemen a republic. The republican forces were supported by Egypt and the royalists by Saudi Arabia in a civil war that raged until 1967. Between 1958 and 1961 Yemen was loosely united with the United Arab Republic (Syria and Egypt) in a federation known as the United Arab States. In 1990 the Yemen Arab Republic (North Yemen) united with the People's Democratic Republic of Yemen (South Yemen) to form the Republic of Yemen. The new state has been afflicted by periods of turmoil and civil war. The famous mocha coffee originated in Yemen.

Arabian red legged partridge

Readings: Heravi, 1973; *New Encyclopædia Britannica*, 1991.

CHAPTER 8

India and Central Asia

The territories of the native princes are for the most part not the most fertile tracts of India; and one cannot avoid a suspicion that their comparative poverty has been the cause of their continued immunity from annexation.
— Wilfred Scawen Blunt, 1885.

ALWAR (Alwur; Ulwar)

Besides antelope, "ravine deer," and the usual small game in the plains, tigers, hyenas, and sambar in the hilly country and leopards almost everywhere, wild hog are fairly numerous in parts, and wolves are occasionally met with.
— Imperial Gazetteer of India, 1908.

Area: 3,158 sq. miles (8,179 sq. km); Capital: Alwar
Population: 823,055 (est. 1941)

In north-central India, south of Delhi. Alwar was founded in the middle of the 18th century by Rajput warriors. The state was created from petty chieftainships that had owed their allegiance to Jaipur and Bharatpur. Thereafter, Alwar's relationship with those states was not always cordial. In 1803 Alwar signed a treaty of alliance and defence with Great Britain. Due to an armed intervention in Jaipur Alwar was prohibited from political contact with other states without British consent.

Readings: *Encyclopædia Britannica*, 1926; *Imperial Gazetteer of India*, 1908.

BAHAWALPUR (Bhawalpur)

"In Bahawalpur," says a local proverb, "rain changes into storms of wind."
— Imperial Gazetteer of India, 1908.

Area: 15,918 sq. miles (41,227 sq. km); Capital: Bahawalpur
Population: 1,822,000 (est. 1951)

A Muslim state between Punjab and Sind, along the Sutlej River. The nawabs of Bahawalpur, who claimed to be descended from the uncle of the Prophet, established a state in 1748 that became independent in 1802. In order to stave off conquest by Sikh armies Bahawalpur asked for, and received, British protection in 1833. This arrangement lasted until 1947 when the ruler of Bahawalpur decided to join Pakistan.

Amir Khan V and sahiwal bull

Readings: *Imperial Gazetteer of India*, 1908; Burki, 1991.

BANGANAPALLE

No opium is grown, and the Nawab gets his supply from Madras on licences countersigned by the Political Agent.
— Imperial Gazetteer of India, 1908.

Area: 255 sq. miles (660 sq. km); Capital: Banganapalle
Population: 32,264 (est. 1901)

In southern India surrounded by Madras. From 1923 until Indian independence Banganapalle was supervised by the British as part of the Madras States Agency. In 1953 it was merged with Madras state.

Readings: *Encyclopædia Britannica*, 1926; *Imperial Gazetteer of India*, 1908.

BANSWARA

> The climate is relaxing and generally unpleasant.
> — *Imperial Gazetteer of India*, 1908.

Area: 1,946 sq. miles (5,040 sq. km); Capital: Banswara
Population: 165,350 (est. 1901)

In the southern district of Rajputana. Banswara "the forest country" was founded c. 1530. Ruled by a Rajput dynasty it became a tributary of the Maratha Empire. Banswara's rajah petitioned the British to become a tributary in 1812, on condition the Marathas were driven out. A treaty in 1818 brought this into effect. The British protected Banswara against external threats and rebellious chieftains in return for the right to oversee the state's administration. Banswara merged with the Union of Rajasthan in 1948. The petty state of Kushalgarh was in a feudatory relationship with Banswara.

Readings: *Encyclopædia Britannica*, 1926; *Imperial Gazetteer of India*, 1908.

BARODA

> I wonder how old the town is. There are patches of building — massive structures, monuments, apparently — that are so battered and worn, and seemingly so tired and so burdened with the weight of age, and so dulled and stupefied with trying to remember things they forgot before history began, that they give one the feeling that they must have been a part of original Creation.
> — Mark Twain, 1897.

Area: 8,236 sq. miles (21,331 sq. km); Capital Baroda City
Population: 2,855,010 (est. 1941)

A state in west-central India consisting of four noncontiguous

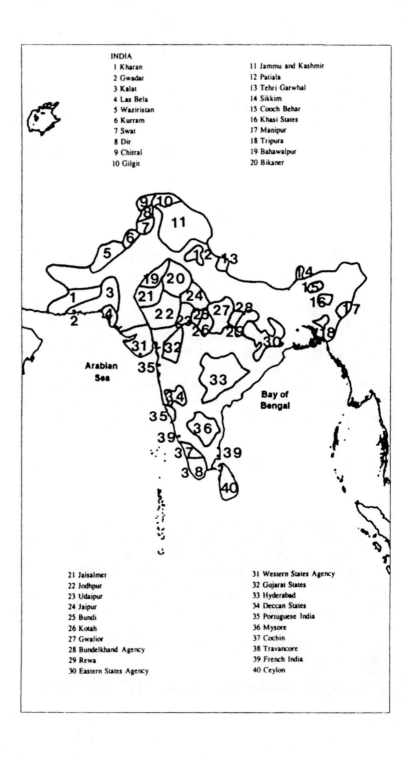

INDIA

1 Kharan
2 Gwadar
3 Kalat
4 Las Bela
5 Waziristan
6 Kurram
7 Swat
8 Dir
9 Chitral
10 Gilgit

11 Jammu and Kashmir
12 Patiala
13 Tehri Garwhal
14 Sikkim
15 Cooch Behar
16 Khasi States
17 Manipur
18 Tripura
19 Bahawalpur
20 Bikaner

Arabian
Sea

Bay of
Bengal

21 Jaisalmer
22 Jodhpur
23 Udaipur
24 Jaipur
25 Bundi
26 Kotah
27 Gwalior
28 Bundelkhand Agency
29 Rewa
30 Eastern States Agency

31 Western States Agency
32 Gujarat States
33 Hyderabad
34 Deccan States
35 Portuguese India
36 Mysore
37 Cochin
38 Travancore
39 French India
40 Ceylon

territories. The Baroda princes were part of the powerful Maratha Confederacy in the 18th century and by 1734 they had carved out their own state. The British established a residency in Baroda in 1802 and assumed the role of suzerain. In 1875, to settle a dynastic feud and end gross misgovernment, the British deposed the reigning prince and installed a 13-year-old boy, from a distant branch of the royal family, on the throne. The boy became Sayaji Rao III and ruled for 63 years. During his enlightened rule Baroda became the most progressive princely state in India. Compulsory education was introduced and important social and political reforms were carried out. Baroda now forms part of Gujarat State.

Readings: *Encyclopædia Britannica*, 1926; *Imperial Gazetteer of India*, 1908.

BENARES (Banaras)

The city fascinated me and repelled me, like Yoga, like India.
— F. Yeats-Brown, 1930.

Area: 875 sq. miles (2,266 sq. km); Capital: Ramnagar
Population: 362,735 (est. 1921)

Benares (Varanasi), on the Ganges river, was reputed to be the oldest city in India although the state of Benares was the youngest princely state. In 1911 the British government took the unusual step of elevating the family domains of the maharajah of Benares to that of a princely state. Although the maharajahs had been granted special privileges in 1738, and their lands a special administrative status in 1794, they had never enjoyed the autonomy of other Indian princes. Benares became part of Uttar Pradesh in 1950. The city of Benares was never part of Benares state and was located across the Ganges river from the state's capital.

Readings: *Encyclopædia Britannica*, 1926; *Imperial Gazetteer of India*, 1908.

BHARATPUR (Bhurtpore)

The only important manufactures are the *chauris* or fly-whisks made of ivory or sandal-wood.
— *Imperial Gazetteer of India*, 1908.

Area: 1,982 sq. miles (5,133 sq. km); Capital: Bharatpur
Population: 626,665 (est. 1901)

Bharatpur, a powerful state in eastern Rajputana, was founded in the 18th century. The East India Company concluded a treaty with Bharatpur in 1803, but the next year the state's rajah turned against the British. After a British army besieged Bharatpur a new treaty was negotiated in 1805 and a large indemnity was levied. A dispute over the succession to the throne led to a second British invasion of the state in 1826. After 1853 Bharatpur came under British management.

Readings: *Encyclopædia Britannica*, 1926; *Imperial Gazetteer of India*, 1908.

BHOPAL

Bhopal is the only principality in India whose evolution and development has been due to a succession of women Rulers.
— Rosita Forbes, 1939.

Area: 6,878 sq. miles (17,814 sq. km); Capital: Bhopal
Population: 836,474 (est. 1951)

The largest Muslim state in central India. An Afghan adventurer drove out the Moghuls and established the princely state of Bhopal in 1723. His dynasty ruled, with British support, until 1947. Bhopal, feeling threatened by the Marathas, concluded a treaty of protection with the British at the outbreak of the Pindari War in 1817. The state became known for its progress in social policy, public health and education. These reforms were instituted by Sultan Jahan Begum, India's only female ruler. Beginning her reign in 1901 she was the third woman in a row to rule Bhopal. For a few years after India's independence Bhopal remained a separate state, until it was merged with Madhya Pradesh in 1956. In 1984 Bhopal witnessed the worst industrial accident in history. Poisonous gas escaping from a pesticide factory killed as many as 3,500 people and disabled 200,000.

From Bhopal the British exercised control over the nearby petty states of Rajgarh, Narsinghgarh, Kilchipur, Kurwai, Muksudingurh, Mahomedgurh, Basoda, Pathari, Larawut and Seronje.

Bhopal coat of arms

Readings: *Imperial Gazetteer of India*, 1908; *New Encyclopædia Britannica*, 1991.

BIKANER (Bikanir)

In Bikanir city the camel comes into his own and proves that he is not only civilized, but sophisticated.
— Rosita Forbes, 1939.

Area: 23,315 sq. miles (60,386 sq. km); Capital: Bikaner
Population: 659,386 (est. 1921)

A state in the Rajputana Agency, in the Thar or Great Indian Desert. There were no rivers in Bikaner and the state was entirely dependent on water from irrigation and wells. Bikaner was founded c. 1488 by a Rajput chieftain. Its history in the 18th and early 19th century was one of intermittent war with the neighboring state of Jodhpur. Order was restored by the British in 1818 when Bikaner became a protected state. It is now in Rajasthan.

Readings: Forbes, 1939; *Imperial Gazetteer of India*, 1908.

BILASPUR / KAHLUR

There I left the king or rajah of your favourite village of Bilaspur, a most promising young rogue who amused himself last year by making one of his elephants crush to death anyone in his wretched little empire he chose and, having tired of his prime minister, hanged him just for a change.
— Victor Jacquemont, 1831.

Area: 448 sq. miles (1,160 sq. km); Capital: Bilaspur
Population: 98,000 (est. 1921)

A small Punjab hill state northwest of Simla. The British became involved in Bilaspur in 1815 when they drove out Gurkha invaders and restored the state's rajah. After the First Sikh War in 1846 Bilaspur came under British protection. It became part of India in 1948 and is now in the state of Himachal Pradesh.

Readings: *Encyclopædia Britannica*, 1926; *Imperial Gazetteer of India*, 1908.

BUKHARA (Bokhara; Buchara) / BUKHARA PEOPLE'S SOVIET REPUBLIC

The nineteenth century can scarcely be considered as yet to have got a firm hold upon Bokhara.
— G.N. Curzon, 1889.

Area: 70,345 sq. miles (182,193 sq. km); Bukhara
Population: 2,200,000 (est. 1920)

Founded in the 16th century Bukhara was a feudal Uzbeki-dominated khanate in central Asia. At its greatest extent Bukhara ruled most of what became Soviet central Asia, Afghanistan and northern Persia (Iran). Bukhara fell victim to Russian expansionism when it was invaded in 1868 and turned into a protectorate. The Khanate, although greatly reduced in power, existed until overthrown by Bolshevik troops in 1920. An Islamic counterrevolutionary movement launched a major rebellion that was not quelled until 1923. The nominally independent Bukhara People's Soviet Republic was established in 1920 and existed until the country was absorbed by the U.S.S.R. in 1924. The lands of the former Bukhara Khanate are now included in the Uzbekistan Republic and the Republic of Tajikistan.

50th anniversary,
Uzbek Soviet Republic

Readings: *Encyclopædia Britannica*, 1926; *Great Soviet Encyclopedia*, 1975.

BUNDELKHAND AGENCY

Bundelcund, a province cut up and subdivided into numerous petty principalities or baronies, the greater proportion of which are not more productive in revenue than the unpretending estates of some of the richer commoners of England.
— Captain Mundy, 1833.

Area: 9,851 sq. miles (25,514 sq. km); Capital: Nowgong
Population: 1,308,326 (est. 1941)

A historic region in central India comprising a number of small hill states. The Rajputs, who settled Bundelkhand in the 14th century, waged a guerrilla war against the Muslims of Delhi for centuries. The Marathas took control of the area in 1792. By the Treaty of Poona (1817) the British replaced the Marathas. The Bundelkhand Agency was created by the British to supervise the native states of Orchha, Panna, Samthar, Charkhari, Chhatarpur, Datia, Bijawar, Ajaigarh and fifteen others, the smallest being only four square miles (10 sq. km).

Charkhari State in Budelkhand Agency

Readings: *Imperial Gazetteer of India*, 1908; Mundy, 1833.

BUNDI (Boondee)

. . . but the Palace of Boondi, even in broad daylight, is such a Palace as men build for themselves in uneasy dreams — the work of goblins more than men.
— Rudyard Kipling, 1899.

Area: 2,220 sq. miles (5,750 sq. km); Capital: Bundi
Population: 250,000 (est. 1941)

A native feudatory state in the Rajputana Agency. Bundi was created in the 17th century when an older state, Haraoti, was divided. By a treaty with the British in 1818 Bundi became a protected tributary. Between the 17th and 19th centuries a distinctive school of Indian miniature painting arose in Bundi.

Bundi coat of arms

Readings: *Imperial Gazetteer of India*, 1908; Kipling, 1899.

CEYLON

> There is so much vegetable luxuriance in Ceylon, that even the marrow in people's bones is vegetable marrow. My!
> — Edward Lear, 1875.

Area: 25,332 sq. miles (65,610 sq. km); Capital: Colombo
Population: 12,747,755 (est. 1971)

Shaped like a teardrop, Ceylon was an island country separated from the southern tip of India by a narrow channel. The country gained its independence from Great Britain in 1948 and was renamed Sri Lanka, "beautiful island," in 1972. Ceylon's recorded history goes back to the 5th century B.C. The Portuguese, who arrived in 1505, finding Ceylon divided into a number of petty kingdoms, were able to control most of the island until driven out by the Dutch 150 years later. The Dutch made themselves masters of Ceylon until they were replaced by the British East India Company in 1796. Following charges of mismanagement Ceylon became a crown colony in 1802 and retained that status for 146 years. The British conquered the last independent Ceylonese kingdom in 1818. Because of its colonial past many residents of Sri Lanka today have Portuguese or Dutch surnames.

Buddhist Sinhalese were the dominant ethnic group in Ceylon. A source of conflict emerged when the British imported large numbers of Hindu Tamils from south India for use as laborers in the island's tea plantations. In recent years Sri Lanka has been convulsed by a bloody rebellion carried out by the minority Tamils.

King George V and rubber tapper

Readings: *Encyclopædia Britannica*, 1926; *Imperial Gazetteer of India*, 1908.

CHAMBA

Chamba is too hot to be pleasant . . . it is as well to hurry on to a better climate.
— General A.A.A. Kinloch, 1904.

Area: 3,127 sq. miles (8,099 sq. km); Capital: Chamba
Population: 168,908 (est. 1941)

A mountainous state in northern Punjab bordering Kashmir. Founded in the 6th century Chamba managed to preserve its independence for centuries, although at times it was subject to powerful neighbors such as Kashmir, the Moghul Empire and the Sikhs. Chamba came under the influence of Great Britain in 1846 when it was declared to be independent of Kashmir and a protected state.

King George VI

Readings: *Encyclopædia Britannica*, 1926; *Imperial Gazetteer of India*, 1908.

CHITRAL (Chitar) / QASHQAR

The name sounds like a shot from a rifle echoing down the craggy slopes of a frontier gorge.
— John Harris, 1975.

Area: 4,500 sq. miles (11,655 sq. km); Capital: Chitral
Population: 105,724 (est. 1951)

In the Hindu Kush Mountains. Chitral was a tribal area in the extreme northwest of British India, bordering Afghanistan and Chinese Turkestan. Recognizing the strategic importance of Chitral's mountain passes the British established a suzerainty over the country in 1889. The British controlled Chitral's foreign affairs and maintained a garrison there until Pakistan's independence in 1947.

Readings: Harris, 1975; *Imperial Gazetteer of India*, 1908.

COCHIN

In olden days elephants were generally caught in pits, and even now, in Cochin, the villagers sometimes resort to this method when a rogue is uprooting their crops or pulling down the small bridges because he happens to like the taste of home-made mortar.
— Rosita Forbes, 1939.

Area: 1,480 sq. miles (3,833 sq. km); Capital: Ernakulam
Population: 1,422,875 (est. 1941)

A feudatory state in the Madras States Agency in southwestern India. Cochin was occupied by the Portuguese in 1503 and from 1663 to 1796 was in Dutch hands. From then until 1947 the state was a British vassal. A Jewish community lived in Cochin from the first century and the Apostle Thomas is said to have come ashore there, bringing Christianity to India. In 1949 Cochin joined its southern neighbor to form the state of Travancore-Cochin, renamed Kerala in 1956. The port of Cochin, the most important harbor in south India, was a British enclave and not part of Cochin state.

Maharaja Sri Kerala Varma

Readings: Forbes, 1939; *Imperial Gazetteer of India*, 1908.

COOCH BEHAR (Kuch Behar)

> Insanity is more common than elsewhere in Bengal, and deaf-mutism
> and leprosy are also prevalent.
> — *Imperial Gazetteer of India*, 1908.

Area: 1,318 sq. miles (3,414 sq. km); Capital: Cooch Behar
Population: 592,489 (est. 1921)

A semi-independent state in northern Bengal, entirely surrounded
by British territory. Independent from about 1550 Cooch Behar became
a vassal of the Moghul Empire. After British troops intervened in a
dynastic dispute in 1772 the British East India Company replaced the
Moghuls. In 1950 Cooch Behar became part of the state of West
Bengal.

Readings: *Encyclopædia Britannica*, 1926; *Imperial Gazetteer of India*, 1908.

COORG (Kodagu)

> To a considerable number of Coorgs the cultivation of cardomoms was
> formerly second in importance only to that of rice, and the possession
> of a fine cardamom jungle was regarded as a mine of wealth.
> — *Imperial Gazetteer of India*, 1908.

Area: 1,582 sq. miles (4,097 sq. km); Capital: Mercara
Population: 111,830 (est. 1871)

A landlocked state in southwest India. Independent from the 9th century Coorg became a British province in 1834 when its last rajah, described as "a monster of sensuality and cruelty," was deposed. Because of its isolation Coorg was constituted as a separate province of British India. Rugged and hilly, Coorg was sometimes called the "Wales of India."

Readings: *Encyclopædia Britannica*, 1926; *Imperial Gazetteer of India*, 1908.

DECCAN STATES / KHOLPUR AND DECCAN STATES AGENCY

... the danger one runs there is that of dying of starvation, thirst and ataxic fevers, rather than of being attacked by marauding bands.
— Victor Jacquemont, 1830.

Area: 10,870 sq. miles (28,153 sq. km); Capital: Kholhapur
Population: 2,600,000 (est. 1901)

A group of small feudatory states in the hill country south of Bombay. The states included were: Akalkot, Aundh, Bhor, Jamkhandi, Janjira, Jath, Kolhapur, Kurundwadh, Miraj, Mudhol, Phaltan, Ramdurg, Sangli, Sawantwadi, Savanur and Wadi. At one time part of the powerful Maratha Confederacy the Deccan States entered into various political arrangements with the British during the 19th century. In 1933 they were grouped as the Kholpur and Deccan States Agency and were integrated with India in 1947.

Readings: *Encyclopædia Britannica*, 1926; *Imperial Gazetteer of India*, 1908.

DEWAS SENIOR and DEWAS JUNIOR

Water is supplied from a double system of water-works, one belonging to each branch, and is distributed through the town by stand-pipes.
— *Imperial Gazetteer of India*, 1908.

Senior — Area: 446 sq. miles (1,155 sq. km); Capital: Dewas
Population: 62,312 (est. 1901)
Junior — Area: 440 sq. miles (1,140 sq. km); Capital: Dewas
Population: 54,904 (est. 1901)

Dewas was a native state in central India founded by two brothers in 1728. From 1841, when the Dewas was divided in two, descendants of the brothers ruled each part of Dewas as a separate ministate — Dewas Senior and Dewas Junior. The town of Dewas served as joint capital. Although geographically intertwined the two divisions of Dewas maintained distinct administrations. The two sides of the capital's main street were ruled by different princes with separate arrangements for things like electrical power and water supply. Since 1956 both divisions of Dewas have been part of Madhya Pradesh.

Readings: *Encyclopædia Britannica*, 1926; *Imperial Gazetteer of India*, 1908.

DHAR

The site is picturesque, the town lying somewhat lower than the surrounding country; its numerous lakes and many shady trees forming a striking contrast to the barren yellow downs which enfold it on all sides.
— *Imperial Gazetteer of India*, 1908.

Area: 1,800 sq. miles (4,662 sq. km); Capital: Dhar
Population: 243,521 (est. 1941)

A feudatory state in central India. Founded by the Rajputs in the 9th century Dhar was captured by the Muslims in the 14th century. It was a Maratha vassal from 1742 until it entered into a political arrangement with Great Britain in 1819. The former state of Dhar is now in western Madhya Pradesh.

Readings: *Encyclopædia Britannica*, 1926; *Imperial Gazetteer of India*, 1908.

DHOLPUR (Dhawalpur)

The plain of Dholpur, north of the Chambal River, has been the battleground of innumerable armies. Invader after invader followed this age-old road from Delhi to the Deccan.
— Rosita Forbes, 1939.

Area: 1,155 sq. miles (2,991 sq. km); Capital: Dholpur
Population: 270,973 (est. 1901)

The town of Dholpur, in east-central Rajputana, was founded in the

11th century and the state had its own rajah by 1450. The British concluded their first treaty with the ruler of Dholpur in 1799. Eventually Dholpur became a protected native state.

Readings: Forbes, 1939; *Imperial Gazetteer of India*, 1908.

DIR

Dir, a tumbledown fort surrounded by a dirty straggling village.
— John Harris, 1975.

Area: 3,000 sq. miles (7,770 sq. km); Capital: Dir
Population: 148,648 (est. 1951)

A semi-independent tribal area in a remote corner of the North-West Frontier Province. The British established a protectorate over Dir in 1896 to guard the state's strategic passes. The town of Dir is reputed to have been founded by a 17th-century holy man.

Readings: Harris, 1975; *Imperial Gazetteer of India*, 1908.

EASTERN STATES AGENCY

. . . tigers are almost as careless as the forest dwellers who are always getting eaten when their minds are on other matters.
— Rosita Forbes, 1939.

Area: 55,235 sq. miles (143,000 sq. km); Population: 6,800,000 (est. 1941)

An amalgamation of autonomous princely states in east central India. Between 1948 and 1949 the Agency merged with Orissa and Madhya Pradesh. The most important states were: Atgarh, Athmalik, Bamra, Baramba, Bastar, Baudh, Bonal, Changbhakar, Chhulkhadan, Daspalla, Dhenkanal, Gangpur, Hindol, Jashpur, Kalahandi, Kanker, Kawardha, Keonjhar, Khairagarh, Khandpara, Korea, Nandgaon, Narsingpur, Nayagarh, Nilgiri, Pal Lahara, Patna, Rairakhol, Ralgarh, Ranpur, Sakit, Sarangarh, Sonepur, Surguja, Talchar, Tigiria, Udaipur.

Readings: Forbes, 1939; *Imperial Gazetteer of India*, 1908.

FARIDKOT

The country is a dead level, sandy in the west, but more fertile to the east, where the Sirhind Canal irrigates a large area.
— *Imperial Gazetteer of India*, 1908.

Area: 638 sq. miles (1,652 sq. km); Capital: Faridkot
Population: 164,364 (est. 1941)

In southwestern Punjab. Faridkot, founded in the reign of the Mughal emperor Akbar, was seized by the Sikhs in 1803. By treaty the British established a protectorate in 1809. Because of its loyalty to the British during the Sikh Wars and the 1857 Sepoy Mutiny, Faridkot was enlarged.

Readings: *Encyclopædia Britannica*, 1926; *Imperial Gazetteer of India*, 1908.

FRENCH INDIA (Établissements Français de l'Inde)

"From India!" said he, as he took it up, "Pondicherry postmark! What can this be?" Opening it hurriedly, out there jumped five little dried orange pips, which pattered down upon his plate.
— Sir Arthur Conan Doyle, 1891.

Area: 196 sq. miles (508 sq. km); Capital: Pondichéry
Population: 323,295 (est. 1941)

The French established themselves in India in 1668. After repeated conflicts with the British the French were permitted, in 1814, to retain five enclaves — Pondichéry, Karikal and Yanaon on the southeast coast; Mahé on the southwest coast; and Chandernagor, on the River Hooghly, north of Calcutta. After a referendum, Chandernagor was annexed by India in 1952. The remaining enclaves were peacefully merged with India in 1954. Pondichéry, Karikal, Yanaon and Malé were created a union territory in 1962.

Apsara carving

Readings: *Encyclopædia Britannica*, 1926; *Imperial Gazetteer of India*, 1908.

GILGIT AGENCY

Gilgit had a strange and enduring charm. . . . Eternal snows reflected the sunlight and every season had its own peculiar beauty while, despite its height of 5,000 feet above sea level, the temperature was mild and severe cold was practically unknown.
— John Harris, 1975.

Capital: Gilgit

A remote mountainous region of glaciers and ice-fields near the borders of Afghanistan, Russia and China. A region of mixed races speaking many languages, Gilgit was composed of a number of petty states — Hunza, Nagar, Ashkuman, Yasir, Ghizar, Chilas and others. These states sent tribute in grain or gold to Kashmir but were otherwise independent. Hunza also sent tribute to China. The British, who were the suzerain power of Kashmir, established the Gilgit Agency in 1889 to keep a watch over this turbulent and strategic area. They also wanted to monitor the Russians who were constantly probing the region. Although claimed by India, Gilgit today is part of Pakistani administered Kashmir.

Gilgit mountains

Readings: Harris, 1975; *Imperial Gazetteer of India*, 1908.

GUJARAT STATES

> . . . we marched nearly without intermission, day and night; and so insupportable was the heat, and so suffocating the dust, that of the three large oxen of *Guzarate* which drew my carriage, one had died, another was in a dying state, and the third was unable to proceed from fatigue.
> — Francois Bernier, 1656-1658.

Area: 5,350 sq. miles (13,850 sq. km); Population: 510,000 (est. 1901)

A region in west-central India bordering the Arabian Sea. Between 1401 and 1572 Gujarat was independent. It passed to the Mughal Empire and then to the Marathas. The British East India Company took control of Gujarat after the Third Maratha War (1817-1819) and the region was divided into British territory and a host of petty princely states. The principle states were: Balasinor, Bansada, Baria, Cambay (Khambat), Chota Udepur (Chota Udaipur), Dangs, Dharampur, Jawhar, Rajpeepla (Rajpipla), Sachin, Sant, Surgana, Uinawada. The Gujarat States are now in the state of Gujarat.

Readings: *Encyclopædia Britannica*, 1926; *Imperial Gazetteer of India*, 1908.

GWADAR (Gwadur)

> On the hill overlooking the town is a stone dam of fine workmanship.
> — *Imperial Gazetteer of India*, 1908.

Area: 300 sq. miles (777 sq. km); Capital: Gwadar
Population: 17,000 (est. 1981)

A town and peninsula in Baluchistan, on the Arabian Sea. The Khan of Kalat permitted an exiled Omani sultan to settle in Gwadar in 1784. From then until 1958, when it was sold to Pakistan for £3,000,000, Gwadar was ruled by Oman. The town, which had long supplied Baluchi mercenaries for the Omani army, became a major smuggling port in the 20th century.

Readings: Anthony, 1976; *Imperial Gazetteer of India*, 1908.

GWALIOR

We went this evening to see the Fort and Palace, and very beautiful it was, so like Bluebeard's abode.
— Emily Eden, 1840.

Area: 26,382 sq. miles (68,329 sq. km); Capital: Lashkar
Population: 4,006,159 (est. 1941)

Gwalior was the foremost Maratha state in central India. The state was established in 1751 and lasted until 1947, when it merged with Madhya Pradesh. Gwalior was invaded by British troops after the First Maratha War of 1780 and after the Sepoy Mutiny in 1858. From their residency at Gwalior the British exerted a supervisory control over the state as well as the petty states of Raghugarh, Khaniadhana, Paron, Garha, Umri and Bhadaura. Gwalior was known for its colossal Jain rock sculptures.

Queen Victoria

Readings: *Encyclopædia Britannica*, 1926; *Imperial Gazetteer of India*, 1908.

HYDERABAD

Hyderabad is like a great flower bed.
— Wilfred Scawen Blunt, 1909.

Area: 82,313 sq. miles (213,000 sq. km); Capital: Hyderabad
Population: 10,338,534 (est. 1941)

The largest and most populous of the Indian princely states. Though Hindus were in the majority Hyderabad was ruled by Muslim nizams from the 14th century. In 1724 one of Hyderabad's rulers defeated the Moghuls and declared independence. The state then became caught up in the British-French struggle for dominance in south India. Hyderabad cast its lot for the British and the nizam took to styling himself "Faithful Ally of the British Government." Hyderabad and Great Britain formed an alliance in 1766 and the state became a protectorate in 1798, the first in India. When India and Pakistan became independent in 1947 the Nizam of Hyderabad was not inclined to join either country. Indian troops occupied the state and Hyderabad was forcibly merged with India in 1948. The last Nizam of Hyderabad was reputedly one of the wealthiest men in the world and had 250 women in his harem.

Hyderabad soldier returning from World War II

Readings: *Encyclopædia Britannica*, 1926; *Imperial Gazetteer of India*, 1908.

INDORE (Indur) / HOLKAR

> The Canadian Presbyterian Mission have their head-quarters in the Residency, and also carry on work in Indore city. In 1901 native Christians numbered 91.
> — *Imperial Gazetteer of India*, 1908.

Area: 9,934 sq. miles (25,729 sq. km); Capital: Indore
Population: 1,514,000 (est. 1941)

An important state in central India, founded in the 18th century. Defeated by the British, Indore entered into a treaty relationship with them in 1818. Even so, Indore was often racked by turmoil and revolt that required British intervention and pacification.

Maharaja Tukoji Rao III

Readings: *Encylopædia Britannica*, 1926; *Imperial Gazetteer of India*, 1908.

JAIPUR (Jeypore)

> Jeypore is sometimes extolled as the finest specimen of a native city, European in design, but Oriental in structure and form, that is to be seen in the East. The "rose-red city" . . . struck me, when I was in India, as a pretentious plaster fraud.
> — George Curzon, 1892.

Area: 15,610 sq. miles (40,430 sq. km); Capital: Jaipur
Population: 3,040,876 (est. 1941)

The most important native state in the Rajputana Agency. Ruled by Rajputs the state of Jaipur was founded in 1128. It rose to great power under the Moghuls but by 1800 was in disarray. By treaty Jaipur was placed under British protection in 1818.

Lord Curzon notwithstanding, Jaipur town is famous as one of the most beautiful cities in India. It was unique in India for having a regular gridiron plan comprising nine rectangular blocks. Jaipur was called the pink city because most of its buildings were constructed of rosecoloured sandstone.

Chariot of Surya

Readings: *Encyclopædia Britannica*, 1926; *Imperial Gazetteer of India*, 1908.

JAISALMER (Jeysulmere)

The State is visited by constant scarcities, caused by short rainfall or damage done by locusts; indeed hardly a year passes in which a failure of crops does not occur in some part of Jaisalmer.
— *Imperial Gazetteer of India*, 1908.

Area: 16,062 sq. miles (41,600 sq. km); Capital: Jaisalmer
Population: 73,370 (est. 1901)

On a major caravan route Jaisalmer was located almost completely in the sandy wastes of the Great Indian Desert and its population were mostly wandering herders. Jaisalmer reached its greatest power in the 12th century but declined after being sacked by the Muslims in the 14th century. The state was a vassal of the Mughal Empire before transferring its allegiance to the British in 1818. Jaisalmer became part of the Indian state of Rajasthan in 1949.

Readings: *Encyclopædia Britannica*, 1926; *Imperial Gazetteer of India*, 1908.

JAMMU AND KASHMIR (Jumoo and Cashmere)

Who has not heard of the Vale of CASHMERE
With its roses the brightest that earth ever gave,
Its temples and grottos, and fountains as clear
As the love-lighted eyes that hang over their wave?
— Thomas Moore, 1817.

Area: 86,100 sq. miles (223,000 sq. km); Capital: Srinigar
Population: 4,021,616 (est. 1941)

A Himalayan state in the north of the Indian subcontinent, famed for its beauty and its healthful climate. The state was formed in 1846 when the British installed the Rajah of Jammu as Maharajah of Jammu and Kashmir. By establishing a protected state in Kashmir the British were able to guard the northern flank of their Indian empire from Russian and Chinese encroachments. Although the maharajahs were Hindus about two-thirds of their subjects were Muslims. When India and Pakistan became independent in 1947 both countries claimed Jammu and Kashmir, India, on the basis of a decision by the maharajah to join the state to India and Pakistan on religious, cultural and ethnic grounds. India and Pakistan have fought three wars over Kashmir. A cease-fire line was drawn in 1972 with Pakistan acquiring about 40 percent of the territory, in the north and west, and India the rest. The Pakistani area of Jammu and Kashmir has been organized as the state of Azad "free" Kashmir. The dispute over Kashmir remains unresolved and has been further complicated by Chinese incursions and a Kashmiri independence movement.

Kashmir stag

Readings: *Encyclopædia Britannica*, 1926; *Imperial Gazetteer of India*, 1908.

JHALAWAR

> Owing to its geographical position, the State has generally a very good rainfall, and scarcities and famines are uncommon.
> — *Imperial Gazetteer of India*, 1908.

Area: 813 sq. miles (2,106 sq. km); Capital: Jhairrapatan
Population: 123,000 (est. 1941)

Jhalawar was created a separate British dependency in 1838 when, because of dynastic squabbles, the state of Kotah was divided. In 1897 most of its territory was returned to Kotah. The remainder formed the boundaries of Jhalawar until the state was incorporated into the Indian state of Rajasthan.

Readings: *Encyclopædia Britannica*, 1926; *Imperial Gazetteer of India*, 1908.

JIND (Jhind, Jeend)

[The Rajah] is a handsome, wild-looking young man of twenty-two, and is said to divide his inclinations and his time pretty equally between his zenana and his stable. Of the former addiction we have, of course, no means of judging.
— Captain Mundy, 1833.

Area: 1,299 sq. miles (3,364 sq. km); Capital: Sangur
Population: 361,812 (est. 1941)

A Sikh state near Delhi which came under British suzerainty in 1809. Jind, made up of three separate tracts of land, was founded in 1763 by Sikh chieftains and recognized by the Mughal emperors. Jind was always a loyal ally of the British in India and was rewarded by having its territory enlarged. It is now in Haryana state.

Readings: *Imperial Gazetteer of India*, 1908; Mundy, 1833.

JODHPUR / MARWAR

The *anars* [pomegranates] of the *Kagli-ca-bagh*, or "Ravens' Garden," are sent to the most remote parts as presents. Their beautiful ruby tint affords an abundant resource to the Rajpoot bard, who describes it as "sparkling in the ambrosial cup."
— James Tod, 1829.

Area: 35,066 sq. miles (90,821 sq. km); Capital: Jodhpur
Population: 1,848,825 (est. 1921)

The largest state in the Rajputana Agency Jodhpur was founded c. 1212 and reached its greatest power about three hundred years later. Invaded by the Mughal emperor, Akbar, Jodhpur became a vassal. In

1679 the emperor Aurangzeb invaded and plundered the state and ordered a mass conversion to Islam. In response, Jodhpur, Jaipur and Udaipur created a Hindu alliance against the Muslims. Dynastic quarrels eventually weakened the alliance and it came under the control of the Marathas, a Hindu warrior caste. Jodhpur was a British dependency from 1818 to 1947.

Readings: *Encyclopædia Britannica*, 1926; *Imperial Gazetteer of India*, 1908.

KALAT

> [Mirage]: In Kalat . . . the Balooch calls it *Lum pari ab*, the "Minstrel's white lake," from an old legend that a *Lum* or travelling minstrel, crossing the desert, saw the bright fresh water, as he thought, sparkling in the sun, with green trees and cool banks, and emptied out the muddy liquid from his leathern bottle that he might more quickly speed to the pool; the end being that he perished of thirst.
> — Edwin Arnold, 1886.

Area: 30,799 sq. miles (79,769 sq. km); Capital: Kalat
Population: 282,546 (est. 1951)

The Khan of Kalat headed a confederacy of chiefs on the Persian (Iranian) frontier. Kalat, which became part of the Moghul Empire in the 16th century, reached the height of its size and importance in the 18th century. Over the next two hundred years Kalat's power was steadily diminished. The British occupied Kalat during the First Afghan War (1839-1841) to protect their line of communication and made it a protected state in 1876. Kalat joined Pakistan in 1948. Ten years later the Khan led a revolt and declared his state independent. Pakistan quickly snuffed out the secession.

Readings: Arnold, 1886; *Imperial Gazetteer of India*, 1908.

KAPURTHALA

The city of Kapurthala is an anomaly. It has the tinsel fragility of an exhibition. A scrap of Paris laid at the foot of the Himalayas, it has the temporary quality of exile, but the effect is enchanting.
— Rosita Forbes, 1939.

Area: 630 sq. miles (1,632 sq. km); Capital: Kapurthala
Population: 284,275 (est. 1921)

A Sikh state in Punjab surrounded by British territory. Founded in the 11th century Kapurthala became a princely state in 1780 and lasted until 1948, when it was absorbed by India. Kapurthala was hostile to the British during the Sikh wars but by the Sepoy Mutiny of 1857 had become an ally.

Readings: Forbes, 1939; *Imperial Gazetteer of India*, 1908.

KHAIRPUR (Khyrpoor)

The town, which is irregularly built, consists of a collection of mud hovels, intermingled with a few houses of a better class.
— *Imperial Gazetteer of India*, 1908.

Area: 6,050 sq. miles (15,670 sq. km); Capital: Khairpur
Population: 319,408 (est. 1951)

The princely state of Khairpur was founded in the Sind region of south-central Pakistan in 1783. An arid country, it was irrigated by five canals from the Indus River. In return for allowing them free passage on the Indus the British recognized the state of Khairpur in 1832. It was the only state in Sind that did not resist the British annexation in 1843. As a result Khairpur retained its autonomy until it became part of Pakistan in 1947. Khairpur was a Pakistani state until 1955.

Readings: *Encyclopædia Britannica*, 1926; *Imperial Gazetteer of India*, 1908.

KHARAN / KHARAN KALAT

> Order is maintained by a force of about 450 men, armed with swords,
> matchlocks, and breechloaders. . . . The chief possesses three muzzle-
> loading cannon and a mortar.
> — *Imperial Gazetteer of India*, 1908.

Area: 18,508 sq. miles (47,935 sq. km); Capital: Kharan
Population: 54,000 (est. 1951)

A remote princely state, mostly desert, on the border with Persia
(Iran). The region, known for its turbulent tribes, came under British
protection in 1884 and joined Pakistan in 1948.

Readings: *Encyclopædia Britannica*, 1926; *Imperial Gazetteer of India*, 1908.

KHASI STATES

> Malaria lurks in the low ranges of hills on the north, but the
> climate of the high plateau is extremely healthy, and is admirably
> adapted to European constitutions.
> — *Imperial Gazetteer of India*, 1908.

Area: 3,600 sq. miles (9,324 sq. km); Capital: Shillong
Population: 180,000 (est. 1932)

A collection of twenty-five semi-independent chieftainships in
Assam. As long as they acknowledged British supremacy the Khasi
States were left alone. The territory had the second-highest average
rainfall in the world — 450 inches (11,430 millimeters). Because of its
highlands Khasi was sometimes called the "Scotland of the East."

Readings: *Encyclopædia Britannica*, 1926; *Imperial Gazetteer of India*, 1908.

KHIVA (Chiva) / KHOREZM PEOPLE'S SOVIET REPUBLIC

If the mountains on the south supply a perpetual variety of shape and summit, there is a more than equivalent monotony in the spectacle that extends as far as the eye can reach to the north. Here nothing is visible but a wide and doleful plain, wholly destitute, or all but destitute, of vegetation, and sweeping with unbroken uniformity to a blurred horizon.
— G.N. Curzon, 1889.

Area: 24,015 sq. miles (62,200 sq. km); Capital: Khiva
Population: 600,000 (est. 1920)

A khanate in central Asia that was independent from the 16th to the 19th century. The Russians launched military campaigns against Khiva in 1717 and 1839 but the country's geographical isolation and great desert wastes protected it until 1873 when it finally became a Russian protectorate. The Khan remained on his throne but as a mere figurehead. In the aftermath of the Russian Revolution (1917) the khanate was abolished, and the Khorezm People's Soviet Republic was set up in its place. Despite a determined anti-Bolshevik rebellion the Communists were victorious and the Republic was absorbed by the U.S.S.R. in 1924. It now forms part of the Republic of Uzbekistan.

40th anniversary of Uzbek Soviet Republic

Readings: Curzon, 1889; Skrine and Ross, 1899.

KISHANGARH (Kishengarh)

> The town and fort occupy a unique position on the banks of an old lake, over a square mile in extent . . . in the centre of which is a small garden.
> — *Imperial Gazetteer of India*, 1908.

Area: 858 sq. miles (1,222 sq. km); Capital: Kishangarh
Population: 105,000 (est. 1941)

A feudatory state in Rajputana, northwest India, founded by the younger son of the Rajah of Jaipur during the reign of the emperor Akbar. Kishangarh was in a treaty relationship with Great Britain from 1818 to 1947. A style of painting characterized by its religious feeling and portraiture arose in Kishangarh during the 18th century.

Kishangarh
painting

Readings: *Encyclopædia Britannica*, 1926; *Imperial Gazetteer of India*, 1908.

KOKAND / FERGHANA

> Had Kokand possessed a firm and politic ruler, its absorption might have been indefinitely postponed. The reverse was the case; for the Khan . . . was detested by his subjects, and rebellions frequently recurred which kept the whole of Central Asia in a ferment.
> — Francis Skrine and Edward Ross, 1899.

Area: 53,000 sq. miles (137,000 sq. km); Capital: Kokand
Population: 1,571,243 (est. 1897)

A khanate of central Asia that became a major center of trade and Islamic culture. Kokand lasted as an independent state from the early 18th century until it was created a province of Russian Turkistan in 1876. Successful Russian incursions on Kokand had begun in 1855 with the acquisition of a border fort. The country was completely conquered (1864-1865) but remained nominally independent. An 1875 uprising against Russian rule changed that. The rebellion was put down and Kokand was annexed by Russia in 1876. During the Russian Revolution (1918) an Islamic government arose in Kokand but was toppled with great brutality by the Bolsheviks. The city of Kokand was burned and 60 percent of its inhabitants massacred. The former Kokand is now part of the Republic of Uzbekistan.

Readings: *Great Soviet Encyclopedia*, 1975; Skrine and Ross, 1899

KOTAH (Kota)

> The solitary bridge at Kotah gave passage to the Moghul hordes and the Chambal, so insignificant a river compared to the Indus or the Ganges, was on more than one historic occasion the Rubicon which changed the fate of nations.
> — Rosita Forbes, 1939.

Area: 5,684 sq. miles (14,721 sq. km); Capital: Kotah
Population: 544,879 (est. 1901)

A state in the eastern part of the Rajputana Agency created in the 17th century when an older state, Haraoti, was subdivided. Kotah became a British protectorate in 1818 and part of India in 1947. As a result of dynastic complications Kotah was itself divided in 1838 and the state of Jhalawar came into being.

Readings: *Encyclopædia Britannica*, 1926; *Imperial Gazetteer of India*, 1908.

KURRAM

> I knew the Kurram to be a delightful fishing stream in 1879. . . . The
> chronic state of unrest of this region no doubt prevented exploitation,
> and probably more will be heard of the fishing as time goes by.
> — Lieut.-Col. P.R. Bairnsfather, 1904.

Area: 1,278 sq. miles (3,310 sq. km); Capital: Kurram
Population: 54,257 (est. 1901)

A tribal district on the Afghan border in the North-West Frontier
Province. Though it had long sent tribute to Afghanistan Kurram was
not brought under direct Afghan control until 1848 when a governor
was appointed. During the Second Afghan War Kurram assisted the
British advance and, as a result, had its independence recognized in
1880. By 1890, however, a British protectorate had been established.

Readings: *Encyclopædia Britannica*, 1926; *Imperial Gazetteer of India*, 1908.

LAS BELA (Lasbela; Lus Beyla; Bela)

> From November to February the air is crisp and cool causing
> pneumonia among the ill-clad inhabitants.
> — *Imperial Gazetteer of India*, 1908.

Area: 7,043 sq. miles (18,241 sq. km); Capital: Bela
Population: 76,000 (est. 1951)

Occupying a stretch of coast on the Arabian Sea and an inland
alluvial valley, Las Bela was on the centuries-old trade route from India
to Persia (Iran). The state, which became part of Pakistan in 1948, had
been ruled by a Jam (or Cham) under the British Raj.

Readings: *Encyclopædia Britannica*, 1926; *Imperial Gazetteer of India*, 1908.

MAKRAN (Mekran)

> To guard against the damp and the mosquitoes, every native of Makran possesses a mosquito-curtain.
> — *Imperial Gazetteer of India*, 1908.

Area: 23,197 sq. miles (60,000 sq. km); Capital: Makran
Population: 143,000 (est. 1951)

A state on the Arabian Sea bordering Persia (Iran) Makran was subject to the Khan of Kelat, who in turn was subject to British political supervision. As part of their treaty obligations to Kalat columns of British troops were sent to Makran in 1898 and 1901 to put down rebellions. Alexander the Great's retreat from India in 325 B.C. took him through Makran. It is now Pakistani territory.

Readings: *Encyclopædia Britannica*, 1926; *Imperial Gazetteer of India*, 1908.

MALER KOTLA (Malerkotla)

> The country is a level plain, unbroken by a single hill or stream, and varied only by sand-drifts which occur in all directions and in some parts assume the shape of regular ridges.
> — *Imperial Gazetteer of India*, 1908.

Area: 168 sq. miles (435 sq. km); Capital: Maler Kotla
Population: 80,322 (est. 1921)

A state in Punjab ruled by Muslim nawabs of Afghan descent. The state became independent of the Moghul Empire in the 18th century. In the face of Sikh aggression Maler Kotla came under British protection in 1809.

Readings: *Encyclopædia Britannica*, 1926; *Imperial Gazetteer of India*, 1908.

MANDI

> Wildflowers — such as anemone, dog violet, and pimpernel — grow abundantly in the hills in March and April.
> — *Imperial Gazetteer of India*, 1908.

Area: 1,200 sq. miles (3,108 sq. km); Capital: Mandi

Population: 185,048 (est. 1921)

A hill state in northern Punjab. Mandi, which means marketplace, was founded in 1527. Because of its location on a large river and at the junction of two roads Mandi became an important trading center, especially with Tibet. The state came within the British sphere of influence in 1846 after the First Sikh War. It is now in Himachal Pradesh.

Readings: *Encyclopædia Britannica*, 1926; *Imperial Gazetteer of India*, 1908.

MANIPUR

They wore very few clothes, and their necks were adorned with many necklaces made of gaudily-coloured glass beads. Their ears were split to a hideous extent, and in the loops thus formed they stuffed all kinds of things — rolls of paper (of which they are particularly fond), and rings of bamboo, which stretched them out and made them look enormous.
— Ethel St. Clair Grimwood, 1891.

Area: 8,456 sq. miles (21,901 sq. km); Capital: Imphal
Population: 577,635 (est. 1951)

On the border with Burma (Myanmar). The British became involved in Manipur when its rajah requested assistance to repel Burmese invaders in 1762 and 1824. The British exercised suzerainty from 1891 to 1947. Manipur was then ruled as an Indian union territory until it became a state in 1972.

Readings: *Encyclopædia Britannica*, 1926; *Imperial Gazetteer of India*, 1908.

MYSORE

In Mysore it is easy to become enthusiastic, for there is none of that stagnatory feeling induced by too many unproductive points of view.
— Rosita Forbes, 1939.

Area: 29,475 sq. miles (76,340 sq. km); Capital: Bangalore
Population: 7,000,000 (est. 1941)

An important landlocked princely state in southwestern India. In the mid-18th century Hyder Ali, a Muslim peasant adventurer, seized power in mostly Hindu Mysore. He and his son, Tippu Sultan, extended the state's boundaries by virtue of their military skill and made themselves powerful princes. Beginning in 1767 they fought four wars with the British. At the conclusion of the last war in 1799 Tippu Sultan was killed. The British conquered Mysore and restored the state's ancient Hindu dynasty. Because of gross maladministration British commissioners governed Mysore between 1831 and 1881, after which time a maharajah was returned to the throne. In 1947 Mysore became a state within the Indian union, with its last maharajah becoming governor. Mysore has since been expanded and renamed Karnataka.

Readings: Forbes, 1939; *Imperial Gazetteer of India*, 1908.

NABHA

It is surrounded by a mud wall containing six gates. In the heart of the town is a fort, with a masonry rampart and four towers.
— *Imperial Gazetteer of India*, 1908.

Area: 966 sq. miles (2,502 sq. km); Capital: Nabha
Population: 340,000 (est. 1941)

A Sikh state in Punjab, comprising thirteen separate pieces of land, founded in 1763. As a defense against aggressive neighbors Nabha received British protection in 1809. Its loyalty to the British during the Sepoy Mutiny of 1857 resulted in Nabha's expansion.

King Edward VII

Readings: *Encyclopædia Britannica*, 1926; *Imperial Gazetter of India*, 1908.

PATIALA (Puttiala)

> Nobody knows the size of the late Maharajah's family, but he was credited with at least eighty-seven sons and daughters, just as he was credited with the largest diamond in India, and an overdraft even bigger than his treasure of jewels and gold.
> — Rosita Forbes, 1939.

Area: 5,942 sq. miles (15,390 sq. km); Capital: Patiala
Population: 1,936,259 (est. 1941)

Founded by Sikhs in 1763 Patiala became the most important princely state in Punjab. By 1809, however, it had to turn to the British to maintain its independence. This was the beginning of a close relationship with the British that lasted until Indian independence in 1947. Sikh troops from Patiala fought alongside the British during the Sepoy Mutiny, in the North-West Frontier, China, Egypt, South Africa, and the two world wars. In 1948 Patiala and eight smaller Sikh states were merged into the Patiala and East Punjab States Union, referred to by its initials PEPSU. PEPSU was incorporated into Punjab State in 1956.

King George VI

Readings: Forbes, 1939; *Imperial Gazetteer of India*, 1908.

PORTUGUESE INDIA (India Portugesa)

> The Towne hath in it all sorts of Cloysters and Churches as Lisbon hath, onely it wanteth Nunnes, for the men cannot get the women to travell so farre, where they should be shut up, and forsake Venus.
> — John Huighen van Linschoten, 1583.

Area: 1,538 sq. miles (3,983 sq. km); Capital: Nova Goa
Population: 650,000 (est. 1960)

The major part of Portuguese India was Goa, a territory on the Arabian Sea, south of Bombay. The Portuguese also controlled the town of Damao (Daman) on the coast north of Bombay, the nearby landlocked enclaves of Dadra and Nagar Haveli, and the small island of Diu on the coast of Gujarat. The Portuguese established themselves in Goa in 1510, and it became important as a place of trade and missionary work. Nearly 40 percent of the population were Roman Catholics.

Indian nationalists occupied Dadra and Nagar Haveli in 1954. The districts were formally annexed by India in 1961 and created a union territory, which remains. The rest of Portuguese India was seized by Indian troops in 1961 and was also made a union territory. Goa was separated in 1987 and raised to the status of a state. Daman and Diu were united as a union territory in the same year.

Coins from the reign of King Manuel I of Portugal

Readings: *Encyclopædia Britannica*, 1926; *Imperial Gazetteer of India*, 1908.

PUDUKKOTTAI (Pudukottah)

> There are 108 arrack (spirit) and 233 toddy (fermented palm-juice) shops, one foreign liquor shop, and also one shop in the chief town for the sale of opium and *ganja*.
> — *Imperial Gazetteer of India*, 1908.

Area: 1,179 sq. miles (3,054 sq. km); Capital: Pudukkottai
Population: 400,594 (est. 1931)

A feudatory state in the Madras States Agency. Pudukkottai was created in 1753 by the British as a reward for the local chieftain who had assisted them during the Second Carnatic War. The state became part of Madras in 1953.

Readings: *Encyclopædia Britannica*, 1926; *Imperial Gazetteer of India*, 1908.

RAMPUR

> Rampore jungle . . . has generally a herd of bison in its neighbourhood. The remains of an old fort form a most picturesque and comfortable dwelling there.
> — Capt. A.G. Arbuthnot, 1904.

Area: 892 sq. miles (2,310 sq. km); Capital: Rampur
Population: 453,607 (est. 1921)

Situated near the Ganges River, Rampur was a Muslim-ruled state founded in the 18th century. Since 1949 it has been part of Uttar Pradesh.

Readings: *Encyclopædia Britannica*, 1926; *Imperial Gazetteer of India*, 1908.

REWA (Rewah; Riwa)

> The Rewah jungles are well-known for their tigers.
> — *Imperial Gazetteer of India*, 1908.

Area: 13,000 sq. Miles (33,670 sq. km); Capital Rewa
Population: 1,587,445 (est. 1921)

A princely state in the Central India Agency now in northeastern Madhya Pradesh. The state, founded by Rajputs c. 1400, was under British protection from 1812 to 1947.

Readings: *Encyclopædia Britannica*, 1926; *Imperial Gazetteer of India*, 1908.

SANDUR (Sundoor; Sundur)

> In 1728 it was seized by an ancestor of the present Raja. . . . He belonged to a family called Ghorpades, which name was earned, according to tradition, by one of them who scaled a precipitous fort by clinging to an iguana (ghorpad) which was crawling up it.
> — *Imperial Gazetteer of India*, 1908.

Area: 161 sq. miles (417 sq. km); Capital: Sandur
Population: 11,200 (est. 1901)

A petty state in the Madras States Agency ruled by a rajah. The state was merged with Madras in 1953.

Readings: *Encyclopædia Britannica*, 1926; *Imperial Gazetteer of India*, 1908.

SIKKIM (Denjong)

In front of me was Sikkim, which is dominated by the enormous mass of Kinchinjunga (Five Treasures of the Great Snows), the last of the Himalayan giants for me to see. I took my horse's reins in my hand and walked slowly down towards the Indian plain.
— Heinrich Harrer, 1953.

Area: 2,740 sq. miles (7,096 sq. km); Capital: Gangtok
Population: 208,609 (est. 1971)

A remote and rugged country in the Himalayas bordered by Nepal, Tibet and Bhutan. Sikkim, which had long been a sovereign state, was a dependency of Tibet until the British took their place in 1890. After India's independence in 1947 Sikkim entered into a dependent relationship with that country. India did not approve of Sikkim's attempts to exercise independence. The king, or Chogyal, was deposed and the country was annexed by India in 1975, becoming the twenty-second state. The abominable snowman or yeti, called in Sikkim, Nee-gued, is thought by many to roam the country's desolate mountain slopes and glaciers. It can be recognized by its high-pitched whistling shriek and unpleasant odor.

Readings: *Encyclopædia Britannica*, 1926; *Imperial Gazetteer of India*, 1908.

SIRMOOR (Sirmur; Sirmaur) / NAHAN

The climate of Nahan is very healthy, but at certain times of the year it is impossible to travel through the forests in the surrounding vallies without exposing oneself to almost certain death.
— Victor Jacquemont, 1831.

Area: 1,046 sq. miles (2,709 sq. km); Capital: Nahan
Population: 148,568 (est. 1941)

A princely state in the Himalayan foothills. Sirmoor was conquered by the Gurkhas in 1803. When the British expelled them in 1815 they established a protectorate.

Readings: *Encyclopædia Britannica*, 1926; *Imperial Gazetteer of India*, 1908.

SIROHI

The place is famous for its sword-blades, daggers and knives.
— *Imperial Gazetteer of India*, 1908.

Area: 1,964 sq. miles (5,087 sq. km); Capital: Sirohi
Population: 154,544 (est. 1901)

A princely state in Rajputana founded in the 15th century. During the 19th century Sirohi was involved in wars with Jodhpur which claimed suzerainty over it. The protection of Great Britain was sought and granted in 1823. Sirohi merged with Bombay state in 1949 and became part of Rajasthan in 1950.

Readings: *Encyclopædia Britannica*, 1926; *Imperial Gazetteer of India*, 1908.

SWAT

. . . a hot fertile place, well watered and green with corn, interspersed with fruit trees and wild flowers, and overlooked by the snowcapped mountains beyond. . . .
— John Harris, 1975.

Area: 4,000 sq. miles (10,360 sq. km); Capital: Swat
Population: 518,596 (est. 1951)

Swat was a semi-independent tribal area in a nearly inaccessible part of the North-West Frontier Province. Entry to the territory was through the Malakand Pass, scene of a fierce battle between British and Pathans in 1895. Further uprisings occurred in 1897. The British set up a political agency in 1896 to keep watch over Swat's strategic mountain passes. Since 1947 Swat has been part of Pakistan.

Readings: Harris, 1975; *Imperial Gazetteer of India*, 1908.

TEHRI GARHWAL

The State lies entirely in the Himalayas, and contains a tangled series
of ridges with innumerable spurs separated by narrow valleys.
— *Imperial Gazetteer of India*, 1908.

Area: 4,502 sq. miles (11,660 sq. km); Capital: Tehri
Population: 318,482 (est. 1941)

A state in the Himalayas, on the Tibetan border. Tehri Garhwal
was created by the British after a war with Nepal in 1815.

Readings: *Encyclopædia Britannica*, 1926; *Imperial Gazetteer of India*, 1908.

TONK

The old town, picturesquely situated on the slopes of a small range of
hills, is surrounded by a wall and is somewhat closely packed.
— *Imperial Gazetteer of India*, 1908.

Area: 2,553 sq. miles (6,612 sq. km); Capital: Tonk
Population: 273,201 (est. 1901)

The state of Tonk comprised six separate pieces of land in
Rajputana. Its founder was a predatory Pathan chieftain who seized the
lands between 1798 and 1817. Tonk submitted to British overlordship
in 1818 and is now part of Rajasthan.

Readings: *Encyclopædia Britannica*, 1926; *Imperial Gazetteer of India*, 1908.

TRAVANCORE

For here, whether it be among the Nayer landowners in mid-jungle or
in the admirably modern capital of Trivandrum, women rule. They
rule, not by the generosity of men, but by traditional right. For
Travancore is a matriarchate. . . . In effect, every male of the royal
house has the right to reign, but none can transmit that right.
— Rosita Forbes, 1939.

Area: 7,662 sq. miles (17,844 sq. km); Capital: Trivandrum
Population: 6,070,018 (est. 1041)

In the extreme southwest of the country, Travancore was India's third most populous native state. It was known for having a high level of literacy, good administration and prosperity. About 25 percent of the population were Christians. Formerly composed of many petty states Travancore was unified and became independent, under a Hindu dynasty, in the mid-18th century. Travancore allied itself with the British during the latter's wars with the French and during the Sepoy Mutiny. The state was placed under British protection in 1795. In 1949 Travancore united with the adjacent state of Cochin to form Travancore-Cochin, renamed Kerala in 1956.

Sir Bala
Rama Varma

Readings: Forbes, 1939; *Imperial Gazetteer of India*, 1908.

TRIPURA / HILL TIPPERA

The hills are clothed for the most part with bamboo jungle, while the low ground is well timbered and covered with cane-breaks and thatching grass.
— *Imperial Gazetteer of India*, 1908.

Area: 4,051 sq. miles (10,492 sq. km); Capital: Agartala
Population: 645,707 (est. 1951)

A semi-independent hill state in Assam, which came under the British East India Company in 1765. From 1808 Tripura's rajahs had to receive British approval before they could assume the throne. Maharajahs ruled Tripura for 1,300 years. The last died in 1947. In the early part of the 20th century the state was renamed Hill Tippera and attached to the province of Eastern Bengal and Assam. Tripura has been an Indian state since 1972.

Readings: *Encyclopædia Britannica*, 1926; *Imperial Gazetteer of India*, 1908.

UDAIPUR (Udaypur; Oodeypore) / MEWAR

Drab and burned in the dry months, in August with the surrounding
hills clothed in fresh verdure, the trees refoliaged in feathery green
gossamer, and the blue lakes filled to the brim by the rains and bound
by ornate marble dams reflecting the multicolored palaces on the
shore, Udaipur was to me an enchanted spot.
— Richard Haliburton, 1925.

Area: 12,915 sq. miles (33,450 sq. km); Capital: Udaipur
Population: 1,406,990 (est. 1921)

A very old princely state in the Rajputana Agency. Its rulers, who
settled the area in the 8th century, were recognized as the highest
ranking Rajput princes in India. Udaipur fiercely defended its
independence against invading Muslims. When its capital was captured
by Akbar in 1568 a new capital was created in the town of Udaipur.
The state suffered at the hands of the Marathas and as a result formed
an alliance with Great Britain in 1817. The coinage of Udaipur bore the
inscription "Friend of London" on the reverse.

Readings: Haliburton, 1925; *Imperial Gazetteer of India*, 1908.

WAZIRISTAN

. . . the country within a day's ride of [the] most important garrison
is an absolute *terra incognita*, and that there is absolutely no security
for British life a mile or two beyond our border.
— Lord Lytton, 1877.

Area: 4,373 sq. miles (11,326 sq. km); Capital: Kaniguram
Population: 395,000 (est. 1961)

A barren and mountainous region of the North-West Frontier
Province. The Waziris were a very warlike people given to blood
feuds, raiding and brigandage. Unfortunately their country sat astride
strategic passes to India that the British could not ignore. From 1852,
until the British established a political administration at the turn of the
century, Waziristan was the scene of seven large-scale military

operations. The unrest continued into the 20th century with the last important military campaign occurring in 1937. The territory was administered, as much as it ever was, through the Agencies of North and South Waziristan. In order to keep the peace the British and the Pakistanis after them gave subsidies to the tribal chiefs.

It was in North Waziristan that Aircraftsman Shaw (better known as T.E. Lawrence — Lawrence of Arabia) fled, for a time, from unwanted fame.

Readings: *Encyclopædia Britannica*, 1926; *Imperial Gazetteer of India*, 1908.

WESTERN INDIAN STATES AGENCY

> Idar is surrounded by a brick wall in fair preservation, through which a road passes by a stone gateway, marked with many red hands each recording a victim to the rite of *sati*.
> — *Imperial Gazetteer of India*, 1908.

Area: 20,882 sq. miles (54,000 sq. km); Capital: Rajkot
Population: 4,000,000 (est. 1941)

A complicated grouping of princely states in western India, north of Bombay. From 1924 until 1947 they were under the supervision of an agent to the governor-general of British India. The major states were: Bhavnagar, Cutch, Darangadhra, Dhrol, Gondal, Idar, Jasdan, Junagadh, Kathiawar, Limbdi, Morvi, Nowanuggur, Palkana, Porbandar, Radhanpur, Sabar Kantha, Soruth, Vijayanagar, Wadhwan, Wankaner. The Western States Agency is now included in Gujarat.

Sir Lakhdhirji Waghji the Thakur Sahib of Morvi

Readings: *Encyclopædia Britannica*, 1926; *Imperial Gazetteer of India*, 1908.

CHAPTER 9

East Asia

The East looks to itself; it knows nothing of the greater world of
which you are a citizen, asks nothing of you and of your civilization.
— Gertrude Bell, 1894.

ANNAM

All Annamites talk as though they had cleft palates.
— Crosbie Garstin, 1928.

Area: 39,758 sq. miles (102,973 sq. km); Capital: Hué
Population: 4,820,000 (est. 1930)

A kingdom under French protection in central Vietnam. The
French, who had intervened in the affairs of Annam as early as 1787,
helped the Emperor of Annam unify Vietnam in 1802. The French
continued to intervene for commercial reasons and to protect
missionaries and Vietnamese Christians. Annam became a French
protectorate in 1883 and its emperor a mere figurehead. It was grouped
with Cochin China, Tonkin and Cambodia to form French Indochina
in 1887. Annam was occupied by the Japanese during World War II.
After the war it witnessed fierce fighting between French and Vietminh
(communist) forces. When peace was made in 1954 Annam was
partitioned between the Democratic Republic of Vietnam (North

Vietnam) and the Republic of Vietnam (South Vietnam). The last
emperor of Annam was deposed in 1955.

Readings: *Encyclopædia Britannica*, 1926; Olson, 1988.

BURMA (Union of Burma; Socialist Republic of the Union of Burma)

> On the road to Mandalay
> Where the flying fishes play,
> an' the dawn comes up like thunder outer China 'crost the Bay.
> — Rudyard Kipling, 1890.

Area: 261,228 sq. miles (676,577 sq. km); Capital: Rangoon
Population: 39,297,000 (est. 1990)

Bordering China, Laos, Siam (Thailand), East Pakistan
(Bangladesh) and India. The British East India Company had
representatives in Burma from 1612. In order to protect their Indian
domains, and to keep the French out of the country, the British fought
three wars with Burma between 1825 and 1885. The result was that
Burma was completely conquered and became a province of British
India. Burma, still under British control, was separated from India in
1937. Between 1942 and 1945 Burma was overrun by the Japanese and
saw many battles on its territory. The British returned after the war and
granted Burma its independence in 1948. The country was known as
the Union of Burma until 1974 when it changed its name to the
Socialist Republic of the Union of Burma. Since 1962 the army has
ruled Burma and the country has isolated itself from the outside world.
Government corruption and mismanagement have turned resource-rich
Burma into one of the world's poorest countries. In 1989 the name of
the country was changed to the Union of Myanmar. The earlier name
remains in common use however.

King George VI

Readings: Imperial Gazetteer of India, 1908; New Encyclopedia Britannica,
1991.

COCHIN CHINA (Cochinchine)

> As we drove into the town, it became plain that Saigon was, in fact,
> an achievement, unique, a French city flowering alone out of a tropical
> swamp in the farthest corner of Asia.
> — Osbert Sitwell, 1939.

Area: 26,476 sq. miles (68,573 sq. km); Capital: Saigon
Population: 4,392,886 (est. 1929)

The southernmost part of Vietnam, in French Indochina, largely composed of the flood plain of the Mekong River Delta. Prior to the 18th century Cochin China was the name used by Europeans for all of Vietnam. To avenge the murder of some French missionaries Napoleon III sent a punitive expedition to Cochin China in 1859 and seized Saigon. Three years later the Emperor of Annam was forced to cede three eastern districts of Cochin China to France and a colony was created. France annexed the remainder of Cochin China in 1867 and the colony was incorporated into French Indochina in 1887. Cochin China was reborn between 1946 and 1949 when it became an autonomous republic within Indochina. It subsequently became part of South Vietnam.

Readings: *Encyclopædia Britannica*, 1926; Olson, 1988.

DUTCH EAST INDIES (Nederlands Oost-Indië; Nederlandsch-Indië)

> Java is the most beautiful dumb-bell in the world. Her conventional
> Dutch overlords have put their own dull and ugly stamp upon a tame
> and passive race, and the result is painful. There is an atrocious
> harmlessness about the people, an utter negativity, that makes one
> want to stick pins into them or start a revolution.
> — Richard Haliburton, 1925.

Area: 733,296 sq. miles (1,899,228 sq. km); Capital: Batavia
Population: 60,731,025 (est. 1930)

A huge archipelago consisting of Sumatra, Java, Bali, Celebes, Timor, Borneo, New Guinea and thousands of other islands. Europeans arrived in the East Indies in the 16th century in search of spices, especially cloves and nutmeg. Spices, which came from only a few

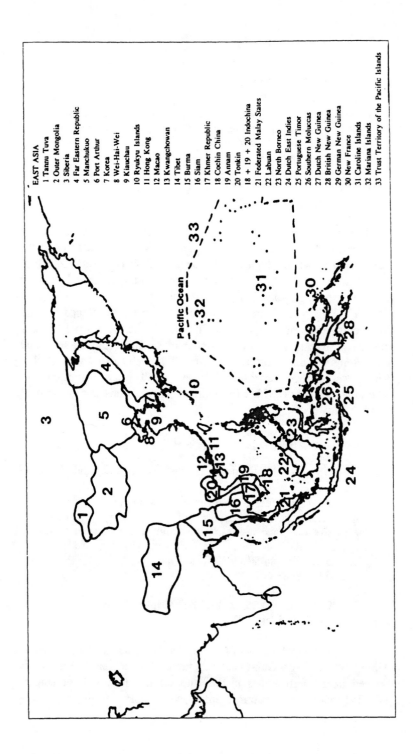

EAST ASIA

1 Tannu Tuva
2 Outer Mongolia
3 Siberia
4 Far Eastern Republic
5 Manchukuo
6 Port Arthur
7 Korea
8 Wei-Hai-Wei
9 Kiauchau
10 Ryukyu Islands
11 Hong Kong
12 Macao
13 Kwangchowan
14 Tibet
15 Burma
16 Siam
17 Khmer Republic
18 Cochin China
19 Annam
20 Tonkin
18 + 19 + 20 Indochina
21 Federated Malay States
22 Labuan
23 North Borneo
24 Dutch East Indies
25 Portuguese Timor
26 Southern Moluccas
27 Dutch New Guinea
28 British New Guinea
29 German New Guinea
30 New France
31 Caroline Islands
32 Mariana Islands
33 Trust Territory of the Pacific Islands

Pacific Ocean

small islands, were enormously expensive as they were Europe's only known means of preserving food. The Portuguese, English and Spanish all competed for control of the spice trade but it was the Dutch who became supreme. The Dutch East India Company, founded in 1602, drove out the competition and conquered and ruled most of the islands until it was dissolved in 1798. After an interregnum of British rule the Dutch regained the Indies in 1816 and ruled them as a colony until World War II. During the colonial period the Dutch fought major wars in Java and Sumatra and expanded their authority throughout the archipelago. Between 1942 and 1945 Japanese troops occupied almost all of the Dutch East Indies. At war's end the Dutch attempted to re-establish their rule ignoring the proclamation of an independent Indonesia by nationalists. Despite major "police actions" in Sumatra and Java in 1947 and 1948 the Dutch were compelled to transfer sovereignty in 1949 to the United States of Indonesia. The Dutch retained the western portion of New Guinea until 1962.

Dancer from Celebes

Readings: *Collier's Encyclopedia*, 1994; Haliburton, 1925.

DUTCH NEW GUINEA (Nederlands Nieuw-Guinea) / WEST IRIAN

Besides leeches there was not much to distract or to amuse us.
— A.F.R. Wollaston, 1912.

Area: 162,928 sq. miles (421,982 sq. km); Capital: Hollandia
Population: 730,000 (est. 1959)

The western half of the island of New Guinea and adjacent smaller islands. The Dutch claimed western New Guinea in 1828 but did not establish permanent outposts until 1898. The territory, remote, neglected and inhospitable to Europeans, was used as a place of exile for communists and other undesirables. Most of Dutch New Guinea was unexplored even in the 20th century and Dutch administration seldom extended beyond the coastal fringe. The territory was part of the Dutch East Indies until the latter achieved independence as Indonesia in 1949. Dutch New Guinea was renamed West Irian and placed under U.N. administration in 1962. It was transferred to Indonesia in 1963 with the stipulation that a plebiscite be held in 1969 to determine the territory's future. The plebiscite was held with the result that the former Dutch New Guinea became the Indonesian province of Irian Jaya.

Bird of paradise

Readings: *Encyclopedia of Papua and New Guinea*, 1972; Wollaston, 1912.

EAST INDONESIA (Negara Indonesia Timur)

> The distractions of Macassar at any time, and particularly during the rainy season, are hardly such as to earn it the reputation of a spa.
> — S.J. Perelman, 1948.

Area: 60,729 sq. miles (157,287 sq. km); Capital: Makassar
Population: 6,348,000 (est. 1961)

A short-lived state centered around the Molucca Islands and Celebes, Bali and Timor. East Indonesia was part of a Dutch attempt to re-establish themselves in the East Indies after World War II. The so-called state of East Indonesia was set up in 1946 but was incorporated into Indonesia when Dutch forces were defeated in 1950.

Readings: Canby, 1984; *New Encyclopædia Britannica*, 1991.

FAR EASTERN REPUBLIC (Dalnevostochnaya Respublika) / CHITA REPUBLIC (Chitinskaya Respublika)

Lake Baikal derives its name of Holy Sea from the fact that Our Saviour, when visiting this part of Asia, is supposed to have mounted to the summit of Oikon, an island about sixty miles long by fifteen broad, in the middle of the lake and surveyed the surrounding countries. Having blessed the land on the north and west, He turned to the south-west, and, stretching out His hands, cried, *"Beyond this shall be desolation."*
— Harry de Windt, 1889.

Area: 1,200,000 sq. miles (3,100,000 sq. km); Capital: Chita
Population: 1,500,000 (est. 1920)

In Siberia, southwest and east of Lake Baikal, bordering Outer Mongolia and Manchuria. In the upheaval brought about by the Russian Revolution and Civil War the important Pacific port of Vladivostock fell into the hands of counterrevolutionary forces supported by the Japanese army. Lenin, who felt that the newly created U.S.S.R. was not yet ready to confront the Japanese, created the Far Eastern or Chita Republic as a buffer in 1920. The Far Eastern Republic was never intended to be a permanent feature and its independence was never more than nominal. Once the Soviets had entrenched their power in Siberia the Japanese withdrew from Vladivostock. The Far Eastern Republic was absorbed by the U.S.S.R. in 1922.

Lake Baikal, at a maximum depth of 6,365 feet (1,939 m), is the deepest lake in the world and has the greatest volume of fresh water.

Readings: *Great Soviet Encyclopedia*, 1975; Jackson, 1989.

HONG KONG

A barren Island with hardly a House upon it.
— Lord Palmerston, 1841.

Area: 415 sq. miles (1,075 sq. km); Capital: Victoria; Population: 5,810,000 (est. 1992)

A British crown colony on the coast of southern China. The island of Hong Kong was ceded in perpetuity to the British after the First

Opium War (1842) and the mainland territory of Kowloon after the Second Opium War (1860). In 1898 the New Territories, land beyond Kowloon and a few islands, were added to the colony under a ninety-nine-year lease. When the British first occupied Hong Kong it was a barren rock inhabited by a few fishermen and frequented only by pirates and opium smugglers. It has since been transformed into a commercial dynamo attracting thousands of immigrants from all over China. When the Communists took control of Mainland China in 1949 they left Hong Kong untouched as 40 percent of China's foreign exchange was earned via the colony. Under an agreement with China all of Hong Kong was returned to China when the New Territories lease expired in 1997. Hong Kong then become a special administrative region with autonomy and the right to enjoy its capitalist lifestyle for fifty years. Hong Kong means "fragrant harbor."

Symbolic flower, Festival of Hong Kong

Readings: Canby, 1984; Dillon, 1979.

INDOCHINA (Indochine) / FRENCH INDOCHINA (Indochine Française) / INDOCHINESE UNION (L'Union Indochinoise)

Indo-China was French too, but there were mosquito nets, punkahs, brain-fever birds, and creepy crawlies.
— Viscount Northcliffe, 1923.

Area: 280,849 sq. miles (727,396 sq. km); Capital: Hanoi
Population: 27,030,000 (est. 1949)

A grouping of territories in southeast Asia — the colony of Cochin China and the protected monarchies of Annam, Tonkin, Cambodia and Laos — under French domination. Between 1900 and 1946 the leased territory of Kwangchowan, in southern China, was also attached to Indochina. The name *Indochina* reflects the supposed union of Indian and Chinese influences in the region.

Following in the wake of mercenaries, missionaries and traders France seized Saigon in 1859. By treaty and force of arms France took control of the entire region establishing Indochina in 1887. The capital moved from Saigon to Hanoi in 1902. Afterward the governor-general of French Indochina spent six months of the year in each city. The French did much to develop Indochina materially but there was always resistance to their rule. During World War II, although nominally under Vichy rule, Indochina was occupied by the Japanese. Following the war northern Indochina was occupied by the Chinese and southern Indochina by the British for the purpose of disarming the Japanese. The French then moved to reassert their control as the nationalist forces, especially the communist-led Vietminh in the north (assisted by the Chinese), moved to stop them. War broke out in 1946 and continued until the French defeat at Dien Bien Phu in 1954. In that year Laos and Cambodia became independent and Vietnam was partitioned. Tonkin and northern Assam became the Democratic Republic of Vietnam (North Vietnam) while Cochin China and southern Annam became the Republic of Vietnam (South Vietnam).

Airplane

Readings: Northcliffe, 1923; Olson, 1988.

KAREN STATES (Karen-Ni)

In their spontaneous readiness to accept Christianity they are probably unique among the more backward races of Asia.
— *Imperial Gazetteer of India*, 1908.

Area: 4,280 sq. miles (11,085 sq. km); Capital: Loikaw
Population: 300,000 (est. 1960)

Five small hill states inhabited by Karen tribes in southeastern Burma (Myanmar), on the border with Siam (Thailand). The Karen states existed in a feudatory arrangement with the British from 1892 until the independence of Burma in 1948. As the Karen States had never been integrated into preindependence Burma the Burmese/Myanmar government has had difficulty bringing this about. A sporadic civil war has been waged for more than forty years between the government and Karen insurgents.

Readings: *Imperial Gazetteer of India*, 1908; *New Encyclopædia Britannica*, 1991.

KHMER REPUBLIC / KAMPUCHEA

[Angkor Wat]: It calls you silently, irresistibly, day and night. People go out there alone, at all hours, and when met with are not communicative. Unable to sleep in the stifling small hours, I have wandered out along the causeway and up into the vast still temple and met with other pajamaed figures smoking their pipes apart in silence on the moon-bathed heights of the sanctuary.
— Crosbie Garstin, 1928.

Area: 69,898 sq. miles (181,035 sq. km); Capital: Phnom Penh
Population: 8,300,000 (est. 1990)

Until 1954 a protectorate in French Indochina, bordered by Vietnam, Laos and Siam (Thailand). The country was known as Cambodia until 1970 when its king was deposed and it became the Khmer Republic. A civil war erupted between the government and the Communist Khmer Rouge, led by a Hitler-like psychopath named Pol Pot. The situation was complicated by spillovers from the Vietnam War. The Khmer Rouge triumphed and renamed the country Kampuchea. Pol Pot, announcing a policy of radical agrarianism, declared "Year Zero" and unleashed a genocidal reign of terror designed to exterminate intellectuals, professionals (including 90 percent of the country's physicians), the middle class and anyone who wore glasses or owned a wristwatch. Cities were emptied and their inhabitants forced into rural labor camps. Even cooking pots were confiscated. As many as two million people died due to exhaustion, malnutrition and execution. Vietnam invaded the country and toppled Pol Pot in 1979. The country has since resumed its original name of Cambodia. The situation inside Cambodia remains confused and dangerous as the Khmer Rouge are still active in some areas.

The huge temple complex of Angkor Wat constructed eight hundred years ago is considered a world masterpiece of architecture and sculpture.

Temple and crest

Readings: Canby, 1984; Olson, 1988.

KIAUCHAU (Kiautschou)

> When the Germans occupied Kiowchow, they had to give all the words of command to their native soldiers in pidgin English, much to their annoyance; John Chinaman firmly declined to learn any German.
> — Viscount Northcliffe, 1923.

Area: 117 sq. miles (303 sq. km); Capital: Tsingtao
Population: 60,000 (est. 1910)

Kiauchau was a German territory on a bay in the southern part of the Shantung Promontory in northern China. Following the murder of two German missionaries in 1897 the Imperial German Navy had an excuse to occupy Kiauchau. After negotiations with China it was agreed that Germany would lease the territory and have the right to build a railway into the interior and establish a naval base. The Germans developed what had been a fishing village into the important port of Tsingtao. In World War I Japan joined the Allies and captured

Kiauchau in 1914. The Japanese were reluctant to leave and only vacated Kiauchau in 1922 after international pressure was applied. The Japanese reoccupied Kiauchau between 1938 and 1945. Since then it has been Chinese.

Readings: Dillon, 1979; Northcliffe, 1923.

KOREA (Corea) / CHOSEN

Do I think that Korea is able to rule herself? No, I don't. The Koreans strike me as being very similar to the Egyptians and Filipinos — very polite, very suave, fond of writing letters and of oratory, but very impractical.
— Viscount Northcliffe, 1923.

Area: 85,246 sq. miles (220,786 sq. km); Capital: Seoul
Population: 12,000,000 (est. 1900)

A peninsula jutting out from Manchuria between the Sea of Japan and the Yellow Sea. For centuries Korea chafed under Chinese influence and control. In the 19th century it came under increasing pressure from Russia and Japan, as well. During the Sino-Japanese War (1894-1895) Korea established itself, in theory, as an independent monarchy. In fact it became a Japanese vassal. The Japanese assumed administrative control of Korea in 1904 and in 1910, dropping all pretence, they annexed the country outright. Korea was then ruled solely for the benefit of the Japanese Empire. Japanese control lasted until 1945 when, at the end of World War II, Korea was partitioned along the 38th parallel of latitude. The area north of the line, occupied by the Soviets, became the People's Democratic Republic of Korea (North Korea) and the area to the south became the Republic of Korea (South Korea). The two Koreas fought a destructive war (1950-1953) that left the border approximately in the same place. Tension in the Korean peninsula remains high.

Readings: *Kodansha Encyclopedia of Japan*, 1983; Northcliffe, 1923.

KWANGCHOWAN (Kouang Tchéou-wan)

The decapitation of two sailors during the landing operations gave [France], belatedly, martyrs to avenge, and the subsequent murder of a missionary enlarged the scope and the importunacy of her requisitions on Peking.
— Peter Fleming, 1959

Area: 325 sq. miles (842 sq. km); Capital: Fort Bayard
Population: 250,000 (est. 1932)

A coaling station on the south China coast acquired by France in 1898 under a 99-year lease. The leased territory was on the eastern side of the Luichow Peninsula and included a defensible roadstead and two large islands in Kwangchow Bay. In 1900 Kwangchowan was placed under the authority of the governor-general of Indochina. The area was occupied by Japan during World War II. France surrendered its lease in 1946 and returned Kwangchowan to China.

Junk

Readings: *Encyclopædia Britannica*, 1926; *Statesman's Yearbook*, 1932.

LABUAN

The shooting costume here consists of a pair of shorts, singlet, and pith helmet. That by the way, is the exact costume worn by the young Scotch Bishop of Sarawak and Labuan, when up country. He very often has to carry a rifle with him to church!
— Viscount Northcliffe, 1923.

Area: 38 sq. miles (98 sq. km); Capital: Victoria
Population: 7,538 (est. 1931)

A triangular-shaped island in Brunei Bay, off the northwest coast of Borneo. The Sultan of Brunei ceded the then uninhabited island of

Labuan to Great Britain for use as a base for the suppression of piracy. A crown colony was established in 1848, which lasted until 1890. From 1890 to 1906 Labuan was administered by the British North Borneo Company and after 1906 the island was part of the Straits Settlements, as a dependency of Singapore. In 1912 Labuan became a separate Straits Settlement. Labuan was occupied by the Japanese during World War II and became part of the colony of North Borneo in 1946. The island is now a federal territory of Malaysia. The large sheltered harbor of Victoria made Labuan the entrepôt for much of Brunei, North Borneo and Sarawak.

Crown

Readings: Northcliffe, 1923; Cowan, 1961.

MACAO (Macau)

> The town is a bit of Medieval Portugal transported half the world away. People old Coimbra with Chinese and there you have it.
> — Crosbie Garstin, 1923.

Area: 7 sq. miles (17 sq. km); Capital: Macao; Population: 452,300 (est. 1990)

Macao is a territory at the mouth of the Pearl River in southern China. It comprises a peninsula, where the city of Macao is located, connected to the Chinese mainland by a narrow isthmus. There are also the islands of Taipa and Colôane linked to the peninsula by bridge and causeway. The Portuguese reached Macao in 1517 and gained the right to land cargoes there in 1535. They turned Macao into a colony in 1557 and used it as a base for commercial and missionary activities. The Chinese tolerated the presence of the Portuguese but built a wall across the isthmus in 1573 to isolate the barbarians. Until 1849 China collected rent for Macao and did not acknowledge Portuguese sovereignty until 1887. Before being eclipsed by the nearby British colony of Hong Kong, in the mid-19th century, Macao was the most important entrepôt for Chinese and Japanese trade. Macao has long had a reputation as a smugglers' and gamblers' haven. Under a 1974 agreement with China Macao is now a Chinese territory under Portuguese administration. The agreement calls for Macao's return to China in 1999 and guarantees its autonomy and way of life for fifty years thereafter. Macao is the world's most densely populated territory.

Map of Macao

Readings: Canby, 1984; Dillon, 1979.

FEDERATED MALAY STATES

The Malay Peninsula, with the climate of a perpetual Turkish bath.
— Sir Frank Swettenham, 1906.

Area: 27,585 sq. miles (71,449 sq. km); Capital: Kuala Lumpur
Population: 2,304,417 (est. 1949)

In 1874 the state of Perak on the west coast of the Malay Peninsula was placed under British protection. Before long the states of Pahang, Selangor and the Confederation of Negri Sembilan (nine small states) were in a similar relationship with the British Government. In 1896 these states formed a British-inspired federation. Apart from Japanese occupation in World War II the Federation endured until 1948 when it joined the larger Federation of Malaya. The four Federated Malay States retained their hereditary rulers and are now part of Malaysia.

Tiger

Readings: Cowan, 1961; Wallace, 1869.

FEDERATION OF MALAYA / MALAYAN UNION

I have come to believe that every country where a man cannot live
naked in all seasons, is condemned to work, to war, and to the
hampering restraint of moral codes.
— R.H. Bruce Lockhart, 1932.

Area: 50,700 sq. miles (131,312 sq. km); Capital: Kuala Lumpur
Population: 7,491,325 (est. 1962)

The Malayan Union was set up by the British after World War II
to unite all the protected states and colonies in the Malayan Peninsula.
It was succeeded in 1948 by the Federation of Malaya. The Federation
consisted of the Federated Malay States (the sultanates of Perak,
Pahang, Selangor and Negri Sembilan), the unfederated Malay states
(Johore, Kedah, Perlis, Kelantan, Trengganu) and Penang and Malacca,
formerly of the Straits Settlements. The Federation became independent
in 1957. With the addition of Singapore, Sarawak and North Borneo
(Sabah) in 1963 the name was changed to Malaysia. Singapore
withdrew in 1965 to form a republic of its own. The princely states of
Malaya continue to exist in Malaysia.

Inauguration of the first
federal parliament

Readings: Cowan, 1961; Collier's Encyclopedia 1994.

MANCHUKUO

> To my mind Manchuria is infinitely more beautiful in its leafless state
> than in summer. When the kowliang is cut the hidden undulations and
> delicate lines are revealed. It is a country of exquisite outlines.
> — Maurice Baring, 1913.

Area: 550,000 sq. miles (1,400,000 sq. km); Capital: Hsinking
Population: 43,233,954 (est. 1940)

Manchukuo, or the "Manchu State," was a Japanese puppet state established in Manchuria, the Chinese province of Jehol and parts of Inner Mongolia from 1932 to 1945. After the Chinese Revolution of 1911 the Japanese were able to demand commercial, political and military concessions in Manchuria. In 1931-1932, following a clash with Chinese troops, Japan occupied Manchuria and created Manchukuo. P'u-i, the last emperor of China, was installed as chief executive and later, emperor of Manchukuo. The state of Manchukuo was, in fact, a Japanese colony organized to support Japan's conquests in Asia. In 1945 the Japanese were ousted by the Russians and Manchukuo ceased to exist. Its territory was returned to China.

Sacred White Mountains and Black Waters

Readings: Dillon, 1979; *Kodansha Encyclopedia of Japan*, 1983.

NORTH BORNEO / BRITISH NORTH BORNEO / STATE OF NORTH BORNEO

> Then up spoke a sunburned man who had interests in North Borneo —
> he owned caves in the mountains, some of them nine hundred feet

high, so please you, and filled with the guano of ages, and had been
telling me leech-stories till my flesh crawled.
— Rudyard Kipling, 1899.

Area: 29,388 sq. miles (76,115 sq. km); Capital: Jesselton
Population: 454,121 (est. 1960)

A mountainous British colony at the northern tip of the island of
Borneo. Although the British became involved in North Borneo as early
as 1762, to suppress piracy, the territory was not occupied until 1877
when it was ceded to a syndicate by the sultan of Brunei. The British
North Borneo Company was formed in 1881 and under a royal charter
ruled the territory, apart from a brief Japanese occupation in World
War II, until 1946. In that year North Borneo became a crown colony,
a status it kept until 1963 when it joined Malaysia. North Borneo is
now known as Sabah.

Murut man

Readings: Canby, 1984; Kipling, 1899.

NORTH VIETNAM (Democratic Republic of Vietnam)

On a big billboard in the city centre, the number of US planes shot
down is revised forward almost daily in red paint — 2,818, they
claimed when I left and, the number keeps growing.
— Mary McCarthy, 1968.

Area: 63,360 sq. miles (164,102 sq. km); Capital: Hanoi
Population: 23,787,375 (est. 1974)

North Vietnam was formed from Tonkin and the northern region of Annam, protectorates in French Indochina. During World War II all of Vietnam was occupied by the Japanese. Upon their defeat the Vietminh, Communist-led Nationalists, seized the opportunity to declare the Democratic Republic of Vietnam. The returning French promised to recognize North Vietnam as an autonomous state within the Indochinese Union but did not do so. When the French navy bombarded the port of Haiphong in 1946 the First Indochina War began. From the beginning the Vietminh had broad popular support and controlled most of the countryside leaving the urban centers to the French. The war ended in 1954 when the French were decisively defeated at the Battle of Dien Bien Phu and Vietnam was partitioned at 17° north latitude between Communist and non-Communist governments. Reunification was scheduled to take place after elections but the elections were never held. Beginning almost immediately the North sponsored a guerrilla insurgency in South Vietnam and the Vietnam or Second Indochina War was underway. Despite the assistance of large numbers of American and other combat troops the South was defeated. Vietnam was finally united in 1975 as the Socialist Republic of Vietnam.

Defeating American invaders

Reading: *New Encyclopædia Britannica*, 1991; Olson, 1988.

OUTER MONGOLIA

The Great Hungry Desert.
— Harry de Windt, 1889.

Area: 604,250 sq. miles (1,565,000 sq. km); Capital: Ulan Bator
Population: 1,800,000 (est. 1932)

Outer Mongolia (as distinguished from Inner Mongolia, an

autonomous region of China), was a landlocked nation between Russia and China. Most of the country consisted of grasslands and the Gobi Desert. In the 13th century Mongolia was the home of the legendary warriors Genghis Khan and Kublai Khan. They established a Mongol empire stretching from China to the Middle East. After their time Mongolia declined in importance and was under loose Chinese control for centuries. Following the Chinese Revolution of 1911 Outer Mongolia, with the active support of Tsarist Russia, broke away from China. From 1911 to 1921 the Living Buddha of Urga was head of state and the government was dominated by Mongol princes and Buddhist clerics. When the Tsar was overthrown Outer Mongolia lost its Russian patron and returned to Chinese suzerainty. In 1920, during the Russian Civil War, Outer Mongolia was invaded by a White Russian army. The next year Mongolian revolutionaries, aided by Bolshevik troops, overthrew the conservative government and drove off the White Russians and the Chinese. Outer Mongolia became the Mongolian People's Republic in 1924 (renamed the State of Mongolia in 1992).

Readings: *Great Soviet Encyclopedia*, 1975; Ossendowski, 1922.

PORT ARTHUR / KWANTUNG LEASED TERRITORY

> The Japanese are men in armour, carrying a machine-gun; the Chinese men in undershirts, wondering when it is going to rain.
> — John Gunther, 1939.

Area: 1,438 sq. miles (3,724 sq. km); Capital: Port Arthur
Population: 1,328,011 (est. 1930)

Located at the end of the Liaotung Peninsula in Manchuria, guarding the seaward approaches to Tientsin and Beijing, the area was briefly occupied by the British in 1858 who named it Port Arthur. As a result of the Sino-Japanese War (1894-1895) Port Arthur was occupied by Japan. However Russia, supported by Britain and France, pressured Japan to accept an indemnity and withdraw. The Russians, who coveted its ice-free harbor, secured Port Arthur under a twenty-five-year lease in 1897. They developed Port Arthur into a large port, established a naval base and built a railway across Manchuria. During the Russo-Japanese War (1904-1905) Port Arthur witnessed several large battles. After the Russian defeat the Japanese took over the lease of Port Arthur and extended its duration to ninety-nine years. The Japanese changed the name to the Kwantung Leased Territory and held it until 1945. The territory was used as a staging area for the Japanese invasion of Manchuria in 1928 but remained separate from the puppet state they created there. After World War II Port Arthur was returned to China, although the Russians maintained a naval base and enjoyed extraterritorial rights until 1955.

Readings: Dillon, 1979; *Encyclopædia Britannica*, 1926.

PORTUGUESE TIMOR (Timor Portugués) / DEMOCRATIC REPUBLIC OF EAST TIMOR

> The Portuguese government in Timor is a most miserable one. Nobody seems to care the least about the improvement of the country, and at this time, after three hundred years of occupation, there has not been a mile of road made beyond the town, and there is not a solitary European resident anywhere in the interior.
> — Alfred Russel Wallace, 1869.

Area: 5,673 sq. miles (14,693 sq. km); Capital: Dili
Population: 670,000 (est. 1975)

Timor, the largest of the Lesser Sunda Islands, was intermittently fought over for centuries by Portugal and the Netherlands. The Portuguese established themselves in eastern Timor in 1520 and the Dutch, in the western portion of the island, in 1613. The Dutch part of the island was included in the Dutch East Indies. The eastern half of the island, the enclave of Oe-cusse in the western part and a few small neighboring islands became the colony of Portuguese Timor, administratively attached to Macao until 1896. The boundary between the Dutch and Portuguese parts of Timor was drawn in 1860. Apart from a brief Japanese occupation during World War II eastern Timor remained Portuguese until 1975. In that year, after the Portuguese announced their intention to withdraw, the Democratic Republic of East Timor was declared. Nine days later Indonesia invaded and forcibly annexed East Timor. The occupation, fiercely resisted, has been marked by numerous human rights abuses. East Timor now forms the Indonesian province of Timor Timur.

Carved elephant jar

Readings: *New Encyclopædia Britannica*, 1991; Wallace, 1869.

RYUKYU ISLANDS

The Ryukyu Islands, the tail to the rocket of Japan . . .
— George Woodcock, 1966.

Area: 848 sq. miles (2,176 sq. km); Capital: Naha
Population: 945,465 (est. 1970)

An archipelago between Japan and Taiwan; the main island was Okinawa. The people, although closely related to the Japanese, maintain an ethnic and linguistic distinctiveness. At times independent and at other times subjected to Chinese authority the Ryukyus became an integral part of Japan in 1879. In World War II Okinawa was the scene of intense fighting between American and Japanese forces. When Japan was defeated in 1945 the Ryukyus were occupied by the Americans who ruled them under a military government. In 1951 the islands became semiautonomous under a civil administration. The Ryukyu Islands were returned to Japan by the United States in 1972 and now form a prefecture.

Yabuchi Island

Readings: *Kodansha Encyclopedia of Japan*, 1983; *New Encyclopædia Britannica*, 1991.

SHAN STATES / FEDERATED SHAN STATE

Throughout its course [the Salween River] preserves the same appearance of a gigantic ditch or railway cutting, scooped through the hills, which everywhere rise on either bank 3,000 to 5,000 feet above the river.
— *Imperial Gazetteer of India*, 1908.

Area: 56,313 sq. miles (145,850 sq. km); Capital: Taunggyi
Population: 1,433,000 (est. 1932)

About fifty tribal states in northeastern Burma (Myanmar) bordering China, Laos and Siam (Thailand) in a feudatory arrangement with the government of British India. The Shan people ruled northern Burma from the 13th to the 16th century after which they became Burmese vassals until the British annexation of Burma in 1886. In 1922 most of the Shan States joined the Federated Shan State which enjoyed local autonomy. Since Burmese independence in 1948 the Shan States have lost their autonomy and have hosted armed separatist movements. The Shan people are major producers and exporters of illegal opium, in an area that has come to be known as the Golden Triangle.

Readings: *Encyclopædia Britannica*, 1926; *Imperial Gazetteer of India*, 1908.

SIAM

Bangkok is stuck as thick with pagodas as a duff with plums.
— Crosbie Garstin, 1928.

Area: 198,270 sq. miles (513,517 sq. km); Capital: Bangkok
Population: 17,517,742 (est. 1947)

A country in southeast Asia bordered by Cambodia, Laos, Malaya
(Malaysia) and Burma (Myanmar), that has been a unified monarchy
since 1350. Although the British and French seized Siamese territories
in Malaya, Laos and Cambodia in the 19th and early 20th centuries
Siam, unlike the other countries in the region, was never a European
colony. The word *Siam*, in use since 1592, was the name favored by
Europeans and only became official in 1856. Between 1939 and 1945
the country was known as Thailand, "Land of the Free." From 1945
to 1949 Siam was again the name used. Since 1949 the country has
been known as the Kingdom of Thailand.

Siam was ruled as an absolute kingdom until 1932 when a coup
d'état transformed the country into a constitutional monarchy. There
have been several coups since then. During World War II Siam, under
Japanese military occupation, temporarily recaptured its lost territories.
The notorious Bridge on the River Kwai, constructed at enormous cost
in human lives by the forced labor of Allied prisoners of war, was
located in Siam.

King Chulalongkorn

Readings: *New Encyclopædia Britannica*, 1991; Smith, 1976.

SIBERIA (Sibir)

I found the prisons of Siberia clean and comfortable.
— Harry de Windt, 1889.

Area: 4,950,000 sq. miles (12,800,000 sq. km); Capital: Omsk
Population: 9,366,335 (est. 1911)

Siberia, the "sleeping land," is an enormous territory stretching
from the Ural Mountains to the Pacific Ocean. After the Russian

Revolution monarchists, moderate socialists and anti-Bolsheviks set up a government at Omsk in 1919. The counterrevolutionaries, who controlled much of Siberia, invaded European Russia and for a time threatened Moscow. The Bolsheviks counterattacked, defeated their enemies and took control of Siberia in 1922.

Readings: *Great Soviet Encyclopedia*, 1975; Jackson, 1989.

SOUTH VIETNAM (Republic of Vietnam)

[Saigon]: My little party was amazed to discover that we were in a miniature Paris — wide boulevards, fine shops as in the Rue de la Paix, and a palace of tremendous size, wider than Fountainebleau.
— Alfred Viscount Northcliffe, 1923.

Area: 66,263 sq. miles (171,620 sq. km); Capital: Saigon
Population: 20,000,000 (est. 1976)

Cochin China and southern Annam in French Indochina. Following the defeat of France in 1954 Vietnam was partitioned at 17° north latitude—Communist forces to the north of that line and non-Communist forces to the south. Elections to reunify the country were never held and the North, which had felt it would win any such election, launched a guerrilla insurgency against South Vietnam. By 1965 South Vietnam was nearing collapse. A decision was taken to send in American ground troops — peaking at 500,000 — to prop up the South and reassure nervous allies in the region. The American intervention was not popular at home, and beginning in 1968 U.S. troop strength was reduced. In 1973 a cease-fire was negotiated and American forces were withdrawn completely. The peace existed nowhere but on paper. In 1975 North Vietnam launched an invasion of the South. South Vietnam was completely defeated and the two halves of Vietnam were formally reunited in 1976 as the Socialist Republic of Vietnam. It has been estimated that the war in Vietnam killed about 1,200,000 people and cost a staggering $200 trillion!

War wounded

Readings: Northcliffe, 1923; Olson, 1988.

SOUTHERN MOLUCCAS (Republik Maluku Selatan) / AMBOINA

> Amboyna sitteth as Queene between the Iles of Banda and the
> Moluccas; hee is beautified with the fruits of severall Factories, and
> dearly beloved of the Dutch: which the better to declare, they say they
> would give thirtie millions there were no Cloves but on that Iland
> onely.
> — Humphrey Fitzherbert, 1625.

Area: 28,767 sq. miles (74,506 sq. km); Capital: Ambon
Population: 579,129 (est. 1930)

The Moluccas, home of cloves and nutmeg, were once known as
the Spice Islands. As such they were a valuable prize and the original
goal of European colonizers in the East. The Portuguese were the first
to arrive and were followed by the Spanish, English and Dutch. The
last named became dominant early in the 1600s, monopolizing the spice
trade until it declined in the 18th century. The islands became part of
the Dutch East Indies until they were occupied by the Japanese in
World War II. After the expulsion of the Japanese the islands were part
of the Dutch-sponsored state of East Indonesia until 1949 when they
were incorporated into Indonesia. The Moluccans were Christians and
had loyally served the Dutch as soldiers and civil servants. They felt
uncomfortable about joining an independent, Muslim-dominated
Indonesia. In 1950 the Southern Moluccas revolted and established a
republic. The republic was suppressed by Indonesia but sporadic

terrorism and guerrilla warfare have resulted ever since. In the 1970s Southern Moluccans living in the Netherlands hijacked trains to bring attention to their grievances.

Butterfly

Readings: Canby, 1984; *New Encyclopædia Britannica*, 1991.

STRAITS SETTLEMENTS

> While looking over the jungle from the embankment, the Governor pointed to a spot near by and naively said, "By the way, there is a beast of a tiger in that jungle, but he doesn't attack white men."
> — William N. Armstrong, 1903.

Area: 1,535 sq. miles (3,976 sq. km); Capital: Singapore
Population: 1,114,012 (est. 1931)

A British colony comprising the settlements of Malacca, Singapore and Penang on the west coast of the Malay Peninsula. The British came to Malaya from India and were interested in protecting their trade route to China. Penang, the oldest British settlement in Malaya, was ceded to the British East India Company in 1786, Malacca in 1825 and Singapore in 1826. The settlements were placed under a single government and administered from India, becoming the Straits Settlements Colony in 1867. The Cocos Islands and Christmas Island, southwest of Java, became dependencies of the Settlement of Singapore in 1900 and 1903, respectively. Labuan Island, off the northwest coast of Borneo became a dependency of Singapore in 1903 and a Settlement in 1912. After being occupied by the Japanese in World War II the colony was dissolved in 1946. Singapore became a crown colony while Malacca and Penang joined the Malayan Union, renamed the

Federation of Malaya in 1948. Labuan became part of North Borneo (Sabah). Singapore joined the Federation of Malaysia in 1963 but withdrew in 1965 to become the Republic of Singapore. The other Settlements remain part of Malaysia. The dependencies of the Cocos Islands and Christmas Island were transferred to Australia in 1955 and 1958.

Coronation of
King George VI

Readings: Armstrong, 1903; Cowan, 1961.

SUNGEI UJONG (Sungai Ujong)

> Murders, plundering and burning are the order of the day, and the bad ones are beginning to believe the popular cry that "nothing will induce the Government to interfere."
> — Harry Ord, 1872, q. by C.D. Cowan.

Area: 1,860 sq. miles (4,820 sq. km); Capital: Seremban
Population: 3,600 (est. 1835)

A tiny nonfederated native state on the west coast of Malaya. The British intervened in Sungei Ujong, "River's End," to stop a civil war and placed the state under suzerainty in 1876. The state was amalgamated with the Confederation of Negri Sembilan in 1895 and became an important source of tin.

Readings: Cowan, 1961; *Encyclopædia Britannica*, 1926.

TANNU TUVA / URIANGHAI (Urianhai)

> The inhabitants of Urianhai, the Soyots, are proud of being the genuine Buddhists and of retaining the pure doctrine of holy Rama and the deep wisdom of Sakkia-Mouni. They are the eternal enemies of war and of the shedding of blood.
> — Ferdinand Ossendowski, 1922.

Area: 65,810 sq. miles (170,500 sq. km); Capital: Kyzyl
Population: 65,000 (est. 1944)

A remote country of Buddhist reindeer herders and hunters between Outer Mongolia and Siberia, known originally as Urianghai. From 1757 to 1911 the country was a vassal of Mongolian princes who were themselves subject to the Manchus. Tribute was given in the form of furs, and the fur trade attracted the Russians. After the Sino-Russian Treaty of 1860 Urianghai came increasingly under Russian sway. During the Chinese Revolution (1911) Urianghai declared its independence but was soon occupied by Russian troops who set up a protectorate. Power passed to the Communists after the Russian Revolution and the People's Republic of Tannu Tuva was created in 1921. Unlike the other Soviet satellite states in central Asia, which were short-lived, Tannu Tuva existed for more than twenty years. Tannu Tuva was absorbed by the U.S.S.R. in 1944 becoming an autonomous oblast, or province. The former Tannu Tuva is now part of Russia, although it renamed itself the Republic of Tuva in 1991.

Rapids

Readings: *Great Soviet Encyclopedia*, 1975; Ossendowski, 1922.

TIBET / BODYUL / PÖ

> [Sherlock Holmes]: I travelled for two years in Tibet . . . and amused
> myself by visiting Lhassa and spending some days with the head
> Lama.
> — Sir Arthur Conan Doyle, 1903.

Area: 469,294 sq. miles (1,215,466 sq. km); Capital: Lhasa
Population: 2,775,622 (est. 1953)

A remote country in the high tablelands of central Asia, north of
the Himalayas. Tibet has often been called "the roof of the world."
Ruled as a theocracy by Buddhist monks Tibet became an independent
country in the 7th century. For many centuries thereafter Tibet's rulers
took advantage of their land's physical remoteness to adopt a deliberate
policy of isolation from the rest of the world. The Chinese established
a suzerainty over Tibet in the 18th century but as time passed it became
increasingly nominal. Following the Chinese Revolution (1911) Tibet
expelled the Chinese and reasserted its independence. In 1950 Chinese
troops invaded Tibet making it an autonomous province. Chinese
attempts to suppress Tibetan culture, language and worship were
bitterly resented and resulted in a bloody uprising in 1959. After this
was harshly put down the Dalai Lama, Tibet's spiritual and temporal
ruler, fled to India with his followers. There have been numerous
demonstrations and revolts against Chinese domination since. Although
Chinese rule has grown less repressive it still remains unpopular among
the Tibetans.

Readings: Dillon, 1979; Harrer, 1955.

TONKIN (Tongking; Tonking)

> Tonquin does not nearly pay her way. . . . Where is one to see trade
> being carried on? Not at Hanoi, for that is a town of "fonctionnaires."
> — C.W. Leamington, 1891.

Area: 40,530 sq. miles (104,972 sq. km); Capital: Hanoi
Population: 8,132,962 (est. 1930)

In northern Vietnam bordering China. After military interventions
in 1873-1874 and 1882 the French established a protectorate over

Tonkin in 1883. The territory was grouped with Annam, Cochin China and Cambodia to form Indochina in 1887. Tonkin was occupied by Japanese troops during World War II. The French returned in 1946 but were only able to control Hanoi and the port of Haiphong. The rest of Tonkin was in the hands of the Vietminh (Communist-led) insurgents and their leader, Ho Chi Minh. After the French suffered a crushing defeat at Dien Bien Phu peace was declared in 1954. Tonkin then formed the nucleus of the Democratic Republic of Vietnam (North Vietnam).

Readings: Leamington, 1891; Olson, 1988.

TREATY PORT CONCESSIONS

There is very little Chinese about Shanghai, and we left it without any regret.
— Viscount Northcliffe, 1923.

The treaty ports — Canton, Shanghai and about fifty others along the Yangtze River and the Chinese coast — were cities in which foreigners could reside and trade. Within the treaty ports were concessions, semi-sovereign enclaves where foreigners had extraterritorial rights. Courts, police, post office, sanitation, roads, local administration and taxation were in foreign hands and independent of China. The concessions were set up after the Opium Wars of the mid-19th century and some of them lasted into the 1930s. Britain, France, Germany, Japan, Russia, Belgium, Italy, Austro-Hungary and the United States all had concessions in China. In most cases concession land was leased in perpetuity to foreigners and Chinese could not legally own land or reside there.

Readings: *Encyclopædia Britannica*, 1926; Northcliffe, 1923.

WEI-HAI-WEI (Wei-hai; Weihaiwei)

On my right was Mr. J., an Oxford man of forty-five, who had been governor of Wei-hai-wei. He has lived in China all his life, and speaks Chinese perfectly. He is tutor to the young Emperor, now aged sixteen. He not only explained to me the meaning of every Chinese dish, but Chinese etiquette too.
— Viscount Northcliffe, 1923.

Area: 285 sq. miles (738 sq. km); Capital: Port Edward
Population: 154,416 (est. 1921)

A British coaling station and naval base in northeastern China. Wei-hai-wei was captured by the Japanese during the Sino-Japanese War (1894-1895) and retained until the Chinese paid an indemnity. The British helped China pay the indemnity and in return obtained Wei-hai-wei under lease in 1898. The British wanted to keep an eye on the nearby Russian territory of Port Arthur and the terms of the lease stated that Great Britain could retain Wei-hai-wei as long as the Russians were in Port Arthur. After Port Arthur passed into Japanese hands in 1905 the terms of the British lease were altered accordingly. Wei-hai-wei was used as a summer station by the Royal Navy's China squadron until 1923. It was returned to China in 1930 but shortly after was occupied for a second time by Japan. Wei-hai-wei did not return to China until after World War II.

Readings: Dillon, 1979; Northcliffe, 1923.

CHAPTER 10

North Africa

In Africa moisture is everything.
— James Bryce, 1897.

ANGLO-EGYPTIAN SUDAN

So 'ere's to you, Fuzzy-Wuzzy, at your 'ome in the Soudan;
You're a pore benighted 'eathen but a first-class fightin' man.
— Rudyard Kipling, 1892.

Area: 967,500 sq. miles (2,500,000 sq. km); Capital: Khartoum
Population: 8,961,000 (est. 1955)

The people Kipling and a generation of British soldiers referred to as the Fuzzy-Wuzzies, because of their huge heads of matted hair, were the warriors of the nomadic tribes of the Red Sea hills. They were famous as the only people to break the British infantry square.

Located south of Egypt, bordering the Red Sea and Abyssinia (Ethiopia), Anglo-Egyptian Sudan was the largest country in Africa. It had deserts in the north, vast marshes in the south and was traversed by both the Blue and the White Nile.

In 1821 Sudan was conquered by the Khedive of Egypt. Egyptian rule was resented by the Sudanese who rose in revolt in 1881. The rebels were led by the Mahdi, a messianic religious leader, who soon drove the Egyptians and their British advisors out of the country.

During the famous siege of Khartoum (1884-1885) General Charles Gordon, who had been sent by the British to organize local resistance to the Mahdists and effect a withdrawal of Egyptian civilian and military personnel, was killed. The victorious Mahdists set up their capital at Omdurman and ruled the Sudan as a strict Islamic state. Between 1896 and 1898 the Sudan was invaded by an Anglo-Egyptian army under Lord Kitchener. The British were eager to recover lost territory, avenge the death of Gordon and prevent other colonial powers, notably France, establishing themselves on the Nile. The Mahdists were defeated and Great Britain and Egypt set up a condominium to rule the Sudan. Though the British and Egyptian flags were flown side by side the real power rested with the British. In 1956 Great Britain and Egypt granted independence to the Republic of Sudan.

Camel post rider

Readings: King, 1984; Voll, 1978.

BARBARY STATES

From the halls of Montezuma,
To the shores of Tripoli . . .
— The Marines' Hymn, 1847.

Area: 1,200,000 sq. miles (3,100,000 sq. km); Population: 10,000,000 (est. 1865)

A group of states, nominally subject to the Ottoman Empire, stretching along the Mediterranean coast of what is now Morocco,

Algeria, Tunisia and Libya. Algiers, Tunis and Tripoli were the major ports and the bases for powerful pirate fleets that arose in the 16th century and reached their greatest extent in the 17th. The Barbary Pirates were infamous for their raids in the Mediterranean Sea, the slaves they captured, and the tribute they exacted. They were so bold as to threaten the coasts of Ireland and Iceland and to raid the Newfoundland fishing fleet. In the first major action by American troops on foreign soil the United States Marine Corps defeated Tripoli in the Tripolitanian War (1801-1805). The Americans and the British attacked Algiers in 1815. Thereafter piracy continued on a nuisance level until France began the conquest of Algeria in 1830.

Salé fortress

Readings: *Encyclopædia Britannica*, 1926; Heravi, 1973.

CAPE JUBY (Cabo Juby) / SOUTHERN MOROCCO / TARFAYA

When the wind blows, the sand moves like a sea, so that . . . walls, built for defence, were in about three months all sanded up, and an Arab on his camel could fire right down into the fort.
— R.B. Cunninghame Grahame, 1898.

Area: 10,039 sq. miles (26,000 sq. km); Capital: Villa Bens (Tarfaya) Population: 21,000 (est. 1956)

Cape Juby is a feature on the northwest coast of Africa. In order to head off French incursions Spanish troops occupied Cape Juby in 1916 and quickly set up a protectorate. The protectorate, which was never completely subdued, was made up of a stretch of coastline, mostly north of the Cape, and its sparsely populated hinterland, about 250 miles (400 km) in depth. For administrative purposes the protectorate was attached to Spanish Sahara. Cape Juby was transferred to Morocco in 1958.

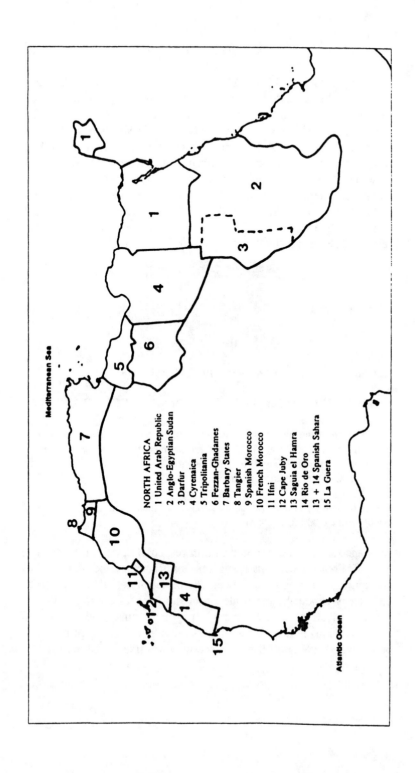

Mediterranean Sea

Atlantic Ocean

NORTH AFRICA
1 United Arab Republic
2 Anglo-Egyptian Sudan
3 Darfur
4 Cyrenaica
5 Tripolitania
6 Fezzan-Ghadames
7 Barbary States
8 Tangier
9 Spanish Morocco
10 French Morocco
11 Ifni
12 Cape Juby
13 Saguia el Hamra
14 Rio de Oro
13 + 14 Spanish Sahara
15 La Guera

Landscape

Readings: Mercer, 1976; Spencer, 1980.

CYRENAICA (Cirenaica)

For it is said that the most fatal disease in the Desert is the sword.
— Charles Wellington Furlong, 1909.

Area: 330,000 sq. miles (855,000 sq. km); Capital: Benghazi
Population: 225,000 (est. 1934)

The eastern portion of Libya bordering the Mediterranean Sea and Egypt. Settled since ancient times Cyrenaica was captured by the Arabs in A.D. 642 and Islamicized. The country became part of the Ottoman Empire in the 15th century but enjoyed a large measure of autonomy. Following the Italo-Turkish War (1911-1912) Cyrenaica became an Italian colony. The Italians faced stiff resistance during their occupation, being obliged to station one soldier per fourteen inhabitants. About one third of adult male Cyrenaicans died fighting the Italians. In 1934 Cyrenaica and Tripolitania were combined as the Colony of Libya which, in turn, became part of the Kingdom of Italy in 1939. The scene of important battles in World War II Cyrenaica came under British military administration from 1943 to 1951. In 1951 Cyrenaica became the eastern province of the Kingdom of Libya and its emir the king of Libya. When Libya was reorganized as a unitary state in 1963 Cyrenaica ceased to exist.

Allegory of victory and fascism

Readings: Furlong, 1909; Hahn, 1981.

DARFUR

Darfoor, the notoriously evil home of fanaticism . . .
— F. Sidney Ensor, 1881.

Area: 150,000 sq. miles (388,000 sq. km); Capital: El-Fasher
Population: 750,000 (est. 1926)

A sultanate in western Sudan founded in the 15th century. Egypt conquered Darfur in 1874 and incorporated it into Egyptian Sudan. Though the Egyptians were fellow Muslims their rule was not popular. When the army of the Mahdi drove the British and Egyptians out of the Sudan in the 1880s Darfur was incorporated into his domains. The Darfurians disliked the Mahdists as much as the Egyptians and were in a state of continuous revolt. Following the defeat of the Mahdists in 1898 by an Anglo-Egyptian force, Darfur regained a degree of independence and conducted frequent raids on more settled lands. That state of affairs lasted until 1916 when the last independent ruler of the area was defeated by a British military expedition. Egyptian troops, led by British officers, and a small number of British machine-gunners, marched 400 miles (650 km) into the country. After two small engagements Darfur was conquered. Darfur was incorporated into Anglo-Egyptian Sudan and is now the largest region in the Republic of Sudan.

Readings: Ensor, 1881; Voll, 1978.

FEZZAN-GHADAMES (Gadames; Rhadames)

> You can recognize the Fezzanis by their powerful frames and well-developed muscles. The shoulder attains in some of them a formidable development, fitting them to pose for statues of Hercules.
> — Francis McCullagh, 1913.

Area: 212,000 sq. miles (551,000 sq. km); Capital: Sebha
Population: 54,000 (est. 1934)

Fezzan was the broiling desert region of southwest Libya. Ghadames was an important desert oasis near the borders of Algeria and Tunisia. Officially these areas came under Italian sway after the Ottomans were supplanted in 1912. In practice it was much later. Ghadames was not occupied by the Italians until 1924. Resistance in Fezzan continued until 1932. For a time Fezzan was known as the Military Territory of South Tripolitania. After World War II Fezzan-Ghadames was placed under French military administration. With the independence of Libya in 1951 Fezzan became a province. That status was abolished in 1963 when Libya became a unitary state. Libyan leader Muammar Qaddafi was born in Fezzan in 1942.

Sebha Fort

Readings: Hahn, 1981; McCullagh, 1913.

FRENCH MOROCCO (Maroc)

> In Morocco the prevailing tone is greyish white, men's clothes and houses, towns, bushes, tall umbelliferae, nodding like ghosts in autumn, all are white; white sands upon the shore, and in the Sahara, and over all a white and saddening light, as if the sun was tired with shining down for ever on the unchanging life.
> — R.B. Cunningham Graham, 1898.

Area: 153,870 sq. miles (400,000 sq. km); Capital: Rabat
Population: 8,340,000 (est. 1954)

French Morocco, comprising most of what is now the Kingdom of
Morocco, was a French protectorate from 1912 to 1956. In the 1920s
a serious revolt, centered in the Rif Mountains, required 300,000
troops and the combined efforts of France and Spain to contain. A
Berber chieftain named Abd-el-Krim made himself the master of
Spanish Morocco and was then determined to drive out Europeans from
all of Morocco. Ably advised on modern military tactics by a German
deserter from the French Foreign Legion the Moroccans fought
tenaciously for five years. It was a brutal conflict, marked by massacre
and torture, that killed at least 100,000 people. French Morocco
became independent as the Kingdom of Morocco in March 1956.
Within a year Spanish Morocco and the international zone of Tangier
united with the former French Morocco.

Cityscape

Readings: Graham, 1898; Spencer, 1980.

LA GUERA

La Guera . . . is characterless but for the ancient and weathered fort-
cum-fishing factory on the end of a curving spit of sand-drifted rock.
— John Mercer, 1976.

Capital: La Guera; Population: 300 (est. 1920)

A remote settlement in Spanish Sahara, located at the tip of Cap
Blanc on the northwest coast of Africa. La Guera was occupied by a

detachment of Spanish troops in 1920. By 1922 it had been absorbed into the Colony of Rio de Oro as an administrative district.

Reading: Mercer, 1976.

IFNI

A visit to Morocco must be considered as an Epilogue, or preface to a tour through Spain.
— H. O'Shea, 1865.

Area: 580 sq. miles (1,500 sq. km); Capital: Sidi Ifni
Population: 53,000 (est. 1967)

Ifni was a Spanish enclave on the Atlantic coast of southern Morocco. It had a hot semidesert climate and comprised mountains and coastal plain. Sidi Ifni was the only significant town, and the population were all Berbers and Islamic. The territory was originally settled and fortified by Spaniards from the Canary Islands in 1476 and was used as a station for fishing, trading and slaving until the Spanish were forced to abandon it in 1524. The Spanish reasserted their claim in 1860 forcing Morocco to cede Ifni to them. Though Spanish sovereignty was confirmed by a Franco-Spanish agreement in 1912 the Spanish flag was not raised over the territory until 1934. The area of Ifni under effective Spanish control was never more than 5 percent of the total. In 1948 Ifni became part of Spanish West Africa and Sidi Ifni became the administrative capital. In 1958 Ifni became a separate Spanish province. After years of agitation by Morocco Spain returned Ifni to that country on June 30, 1969.

Beetle

Readings: Mercer, 1976; Spencer, 1980.

RIO DE ORO (Colonia de Rio de Oro)

> Nobody travels here without expecting some sudden attack.
> — Michel Vieuchange, 1933.

Area: 71,600 sq. miles (185,000 sq. km); Capital: Villa Cisneros; Population: 27,000 (est. 1956)

Rio de Oro, "River of Gold," was a Spanish colony in northwest Africa facing the Atlantic Ocean. In 1958 Rio de Oro was combined with the Protectorate of Saguia el Hamra to form the province of Spanish Sahara.

Readings: Mercer, 1976; Vieuchange, 1933.

SAGUIA EL HAMRA / SEGUIET EL HAMRA / SEKIA EL HAMRA

> In the opening between two hills, appeared a vast valley with yellow earth covered with bushes and thorny trees; the Seguiet.
> — Michel Vieuchange, 1933.

Area: 32,000 sq. miles (83,000 sq. km); Capital: Aaiun
Population: 13,520 (est. 1956)

A remote protectorate that occupied the northern third of Spanish Sahara. In 1958 Saquia el Hamra was combined with the Colony of Rio de Oro to form the Province of Spanish Sahara.

Readings: Mercer, 1976; Vieuchange, 1933.

SPANISH MOROCCO (Marruecos Protectorado Español)

> The Riff is swarthy and hollow-cheeked, tall and phenomenally lean, inclined to be toothy and with that fixed mesmerized look of children often. He is evidently a machine — truly "a fighting machine" in the literal sense — a murderous, child-like, clean-shaven or bearded mahogany automaton.
> — Wyndham Lewis, 1932.

Area: 7,592 sq. miles (19,663 sq. km); Capital: Tetuan
Population: 1,010,117 (est. 1950)

From 1912 to 1956 Spain controlled a strip of territory along the Mediterranean coast of northern Morocco. Spanish Morocco was divided into sovereign and protected territories. The sovereign territories were the city enclaves of Ceuta and Melilla, and the islands of Alhucemas, Chafarinas and Peñón de Vélez; 82 square miles (212 sq. km) in total.

Following an attempt by the Spanish to consolidate their hold on northern Morocco the indigenous population, centered in the Rif Mountains, rose in an armed revolt from 1919 to 1926. The war went badly for the Spanish who were nearly driven out of Morocco. It ended only after troops from French Morocco joined Spanish forces to defeat the rebels. Sporadic attacks continued until 1934. Spanish Morocco ceased to exist in April 1956 when it joined newly independent French Morocco to form the Kingdom of Morocco. The sovereign territories of Spanish Morocco are still in Spanish hands.

View of Xauen

Readings: Lewis, 1932; Spencer, 1980.

SPANISH SAHARA / WESTERN SAHARA (Sahara Español)

The helpless traveller with wild surprise,
Sees the dry desert all around him rise,
And, smothered in the dusty whirlwind, dies.
— Joseph Addison, 1713.

Area: 102,680 sq. miles (266,000 sq. km); Capital: Aaiun
Population: 76,425 (est. 1970)

Spanish Sahara was the most sparsely populated territory in Africa. It occupied an arid region in the northwest of the continent bordered by the Atlantic Ocean, Morocco, Algeria and Mauritania. Originally a subdivision of Spanish West Africa, Spanish Sahara was formed in 1958 when the Colony of Rio de Oro and the Protectorate of Saguia el Hamra were united. The Spanish arrived in 1884 and soon proclaimed a protectorate over the coastal region. The interior was brought under Spanish control between 1916 and 1934. Claimed by both Morocco and Mauritania, immense deposits of phosphate and rich fishing grounds made Spanish Sahara a valuable prize. Beginning in the early 1970s a guerrilla war was launched by the indigenous population, backed by Algeria, to establish the Saharawi Arab Democratic Republic. The Spanish abandoned the territory in 1976, the northern two-thirds being annexed by Morocco and the southern one-third by Mauritania. Faced with guerrilla attacks Mauritania soon dropped out and the entire territory of Spanish Sahara was annexed by Morocco. The guerrilla war continues.

Ostrich

Readings: Mercer, 1976; Vieuchange, 1933.

SPANISH WEST AFRICA (Territorios del Africa Occidental Española)

> As I left, I found the stairway leading to the minaret. From that height the prayers went to the four corners of the Sahara, towards the tent-strewn desert.
> — Michel Vieuchange, 1933.

Area: 117,000 sq. miles (300,000 sq. km.); Capital: Sidi Ifni
Population: 95,000 (est. 1950)

Until 1958 Spanish West Africa was the political unit comprising all Spanish territories in west Africa — Rio de Oro, Saguia el Hamra,

Ifni and Cape Juby. In that year Cape Juby was ceded to Morocco and Ifni became a separate province. Rio de Oro and Saguia el Hamra were combined into the Province of Spanish Sahara.

Readings: Mercer, 1976; Vieuchange, 1933.

TANGIER

The movies could not have done it better than Tangier did it.
— Cedric Belfrage, 1936.

Area: 144 sq. miles (373 sq. km); Capital: Tangier
Population: 172,000 (est. 1952)

Tangier was a city-state, created in 1923, occupying a strategic spot near the Strait of Gibraltar. Aside from the years 1940 to 1945, when it was occupied by Spain, Tangier was a demilitarized, neutralized international zone. France, Spain, Britain, Italy, the United States, Belgium, the Netherlands, Sweden and Portugal were all represented on the committee that controlled Tangier. The administrator was always a national of Portugal, Sweden, Italy, Belgium or the Netherlands. The sultan of Morocco also had a representative in the zone. In 1956 Tangier was absorbed by the newly independent Kingdom of Morocco. During its years as an international zone Tangier became famous as a haven for political refugees, and its name a byword for intrigue.

View of Tangier

Readings: Heravi, 1973; Spencer, 1980.

TRIPOLITANIA

> Transformed and magnified under the magic sunlight of Africa,
> Tripoli, the white-burnoosed city, lies in an oasis on the edge of the
> desert, dipping her feet in the swash and ripple of the sea.
> — Charles Wellington Furlong, 1909.

Area: 350,000 sq. miles (900,000 sq. km); Capital: Tripoli
Population: 572,700 (est. 1931)

In western Libya bordering on the Mediterranean Sea, Tunisia and
Algeria. Though officially part of the Ottoman Empire since the 16th
century, Tripolitania was one of the semi-independent Barbary States.
Between 1801 and 1805 Tripolitania was at war with the United States.
In 1835 the Ottomans took direct control of Libya, administering it as
a province, until ousted by the Italians in 1911. The Italians governed
Tripolitania as a colony until it was united with Cyrenaica in 1934 as
the Colony of Libya. Resistance to their rule required the Italians to
station one soldier in Cyrenaica for every twenty-eight inhabitants. In
1939 Libya was incorporated into the Kingdom of Italy. During World
War II Tripolitania was captured by the British and governed by a
military administration from 1943 to 1951. From 1951 to 1963
Tripolitania was the western province of the Kingdom of Libya. When
Libya became a unitary state in 1963 Tripolitania ceased to be a
political entity.

Arab horseman (Overprint commemorates flight from Rome to Buenos
Aires)

Readings: Furlong, 1909; Hahn, 1981.

UNITED ARAB REPUBLIC \ UNITED ARAB STATES

This country is a palimpsest, in which the Bible is written over
Herodotus, and the Koran over that.
— Lady Duff Gordon, 1865.

Northern Region (Syria) — Area: 72,234 sq. miles (187,000 sq. km); Capital:
Damascus; Population: 4,420,587 (est. 1958)

Southern Region (Egypt) — Area: 386,198 sq. miles (1,000,000 sq. km)
Capital: Cairo; Population: 25,625,000 (est. 1959)

Yemen — Area: 75,000 sq. miles (194,000 sq. km); Capital: San'a
Population: 4,500,000 (est. 1959)

In February 1958 Egypt and Syria combined to form the United
Arab Republic. Gamel Abdel Nasser of Egypt was the president and
Nureddin Kuhala of Syria the vice president. Syria and Egypt were
declared to be the northern and southern regions of the new republic.
Plebiscites were held which claimed that 99.99 percent of Egyptians
and 99.98 percent of Syrians were in favor of the merger. Be that as
it may, the Syrians quickly became disenchanted at what they perceived
to be Egyptian domination. On September 28, 1961, Syrian troops
seized Damascus with the intent of seceding from the United Arab
Republic. President Nasser chose not to resist and the republic
collapsed in December 1961. Egypt continued to call itself the United
Arab Republic until 1971.

In March 1958 Yemen joined with the United Arab Republic to
form the United Arab States. Yemen never fully integrated with the
republic. Its participation was more in the nature of a federation with
Egypt as Yemen retained its flag, diplomatic representatives and king
as head of state.

Weight lifter

Readings: Heravi, 1973; King, 1984.

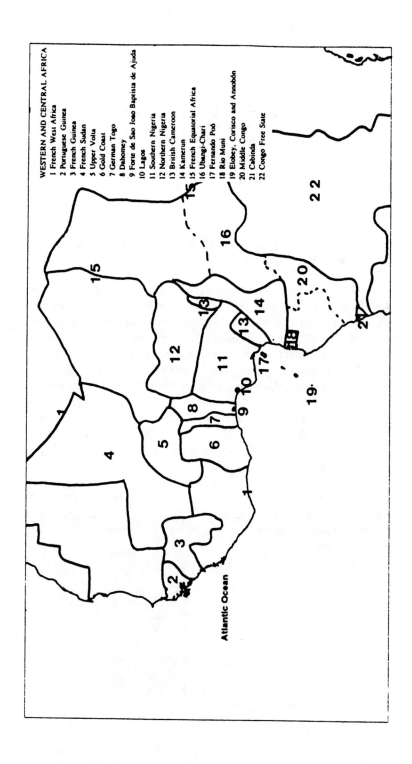

WESTERN AND CENTRAL AFRICA
1 French West Africa
2 Portuguese Guinea
3 French Guinea
4 French Sudan
5 Upper Volta
6 Gold Coast
7 German Togo
8 Dahomey
9 Forte de Sao Joao Baptista de Ajuda
10 Lagos
11 Southern Nigeria
12 Northern Nigeria
13 British Cameroon
14 Kamerun
15 French Equatorial Africa
16 Ubangi-Chari
17 Fernando Poó
18 Rio Muni
19 Elobey, Corisco and Annobón
20 Middle Congo
21 Cabinda
22 Congo Free State

Atlantic Ocean

CHAPTER 11

West Africa

I inquired of all my friends as a beginning what they knew of West Africa. The majority knew nothing. A percentage said, "Oh, you can't possibly go there . . . the white man's grave, you know."
— Mary Kingsley, 1897.

ASHANTI / ASANTE

Their capital was a charnel house; their religion a combination of cruelty and treachery; their policy the natural outcome of their religion.
— Lord Wolseley, 1873-1874.

Area: 23,000 sq. miles (60,000 sq. km); Capital: Kumasi
Population: 500,000 (est. 1907)

Founded in 1697 the Ashante Union was a strong African kingdom in what is now central Ghana. During the 18th century Ashanti steadily increased in size, at the expense of its neighbors, and wealth as it traded slaves, ivory, spices and gold with Europeans on the Gulf of Guinea. In 1807 Ashanti began to expand toward the coast. Conflict with the British, who had established a sphere of influence in the area, was inevitable. An Ashanti army was defeated by the British and their tribal allies in 1826. The Ashanti capital was captured by the British in 1874 and again in 1896, the year a protectorate was proclaimed.

Ashanti was incorporated into the Gold Coast Colony in 1901.

In 1935 the British permitted the Ashanti Union to be revived but not as a sovereign state. Ashanti is now the name of the central region of Ghana.

Readings: *Encyclopædia Britannica*, 1926; McFarland, 1985.

BIAFRA

> In every sense it is the most developed country in the continent, with more industry, the highest per capita income, the highest purchasing power, the greatest density of roads, schools, hospitals, business houses and factories in Africa.
> — Frederick Forsyth, 1969

Area: 29,484 sq. miles (76,363 sq. km); Capital: Enugu
Population: 12,388,646 (est. 1963)

In the 1960s Nigeria was racked by internecine conflicts, principally between the Hausa people of the north and the Igbo (Ibo) of the southeast. As a result the Igbo-dominated Eastern Region seceded from Nigeria on May 30, 1967, declaring itself to be the Republic of Biafra. A bloody civil war erupted that raged until 1970, when Biafran forces were defeated by federal Nigerian troops and the Eastern Region reabsorbed into Nigeria. Several million people perished in the war, most from starvation and disease. Only Tanzania, Ivory Coast, Zambia, Gabon and Haiti had recognized the breakaway state.

Visit of Pope Paul VI to Africa

Readings: Forsyth, 1969; Oyewole, 1987.

DAHOMEY (République du Dahomey)

Beware and take heed of the Bight of Benin
Where few come out though many go in.
— Anon.

Area: 43,484 sq. miles (122,622 sq. km); Capital: Cotonou
Population: 3,110,000 (est. 1975)

Dahomey was an important African kingdom on the Gulf of Benin
that reached its zenith in the 19th century. The country was involved
in ceaseless warfare with its neighbors to provide human sacrifices and
slaves. It was estimated that 20,000 slaves a year were exported to the
New World. Dahomey had the largest and best-organized army in West
Africa. Perhaps 10 percent of its army consisted of Amazons, a force
of women organized into separate regiments with distinctive uniforms
and badges. The Amazons, who were technically married to the king
and personally loyal to him, constituted the royal guard and formed the
elite of the army. The French, who already had commercial interests
in the area, established a protectorate over the Dahomian coast in 1863.
After defeating the King of Dahomey's Amazon regiments the French
conquered the kingdom between 1890 and 1894. Direct French rule
was instituted in 1900, and in 1904 Dahomey was incorporated into the
federation of French West Africa. The country became the Republic of
Dahomey in 1960. In 1975 a Marxist-Leninist state was founded and
the name changed to the People's Republic of Benin. Dahomey's post-
independence period was marked by political instability and coups.

Panther and man

Readings: Burton, 1864; Mercer, 1965.

FORTE DE SAO JOAO BAPTISTA DE AJUDA

> The Portuguese Fort is surrounded by a moat, whose depth is
> concealed by a mass of vegetation: the people of the country prefer for
> safety a ditch in this state. The defences, a square compound bastioned
> at the angles, and the battery of rusty guns, are here purposely
> neglected.
> — Sir Richard Burton, 1864.

A Portuguese enclave in Dahomey, on the Gulf of Guinea. Though
Dahomey had long been under French administration the Portuguese
occupied a fort in the town of Ouidah continuously from 1865 to 1961.
Under pressure from newly independent Dahomey the tiny Portuguese
garrison withdrew on July 31, 1961, setting fire to the fort as they did
so.

Fort in ruins

Readings: Burton, 1864; Decalo, 1976.

FRENCH GUINEA (Guinée Française) / RIVIERES DU SUD

> Even in 1935, there was in Guinea only one hospital, which had been
> built at Conakry in 1901. . . . . after sixty years of colonization the
> campaigns against epidemics and trypanosomiasis as well as a native
> medical service, had not moved beyond the stage of projects.
> — Claude Rivière, 1977.

Area: 94,925 sq. miles (245,857 sq. km); Capital: Conakry
Population: 2,492,000 (est. 1957)

French and Portuguese slave and ivory traders were at work on the
Guinea coast from the 17th century. After the prohibition of the slave

trade Guinea's indented coastline made it one of slavery's last strongholds. The French founded a settlement in the early 19th century and established the Rivières du Sud protectorate over the coastal area in 1849. The protectorate was administered from Senegal until it became a separate colony in 1890. Five years later it was renamed French Guinea and became part of the governor-generalship of French West Africa. Gradually the colony of Guinea expanded as the French subdued the hinterland. French Guinea became a French overseas territory in 1946 and the independent Republic of Guinea in 1958.

Village scene

Readings: *Encyclopædia Britannica*, 1926; Rivière, 1977.

FRENCH SUDAN (Soudan Français) / HAUT-FLEUVE / UPPER SENEGAL AND MIDDLE NIGER / SÉNÉGAMBIA AND NIGER / UPPER SENEGAL AND NIGER

To that impracticable place Timbuctoo,
Where Geography finds no one to oblige her
With such a chart as may be safely stuck to.
— Lord Byron, 1819.

Area: 464,873 sq. miles (1,204,021 sq. km); Capital: Bamako
Population: 3,708,000 (est. 1957)

French Sudan was annexed by France between 1881 and 1895 becoming part of the governor-generalship of French West Africa. The territory had one of the most convoluted political histories in colonial Africa. It was known as Haut-Fleuve (1880-1890), French Sudan (1890-1899), Upper Senegal and Middle Niger (1899-1902), Sénégambia and Niger (1902-1904), Upper Senegal and Niger (1904-1920), and French Sudan again (1920-1958). French Sudan achieved independence in 1960, with Senegal, as part of the Mali Federation.

The federation lasted less than a year when the former French Sudan became the Republic of Mali. Timbuktu, a name associated with extreme remoteness, is a town in the center of the country.

Sudanese woman

Readings: *Encyclopædia Britannica*, 1926; Imperato, 1986.

FRENCH WEST AFRICA (Afrique Occidentale Française)

Nothing is more impressive about French authority in this land than the way in which they have made conditions just, livable and humane.
— David Prescott Barrows, 1927.

Area: 1,789,182 sq. miles (4,633,985 sq. km); Capital: Dakar
Population: 19,032,000 (est. 1957)

French West Africa was established in 1904 as a federation of all the French colonies and protectorates in west Africa — Senegal, Mauritania, French Sudan, French Guinea, Ivory Coast, Togo, Dahomey, Upper Volta and Niger. Each colony had its own governor and administration under the authority of the governor of Senegal, who adopted the title of governor-general. The boundaries and names of territories in French West Africa were often revised. During World War II French West Africa was briefly controlled by the Vichy government before joining the cause of Free France in 1942. Between 1958 and 1960 nine independent republics were carved out of French West Africa.

Boat in Niger River

Readings: Barrows, 1927; *Encyclopœdia Britannica*, 1926.

FULANI EMPIRE / SOKOTO CALIPHATE

The soft hoof-beats of a drove of cattle could be heard passing along
the road, guided southward to market by their Fula herdsmen.
Immediately in front of me lay the belt of thick tropical forest, and
beyond, the sea.
— David Prescott Barrows, 1927.

Area: 125,000 sq. miles (325,000 sq. km); Capital: Sokoto
Population: 10,000,000 (est. 1900)

The Fulani are a martial people who live in a huge area of west
Africa from Senegal to Sudan. Devoutly Muslim since the 11th
century, the Fulani conducted a successful jihad (holy war) against the
Hausa Confederation of northern Nigeria between 1804 and 1810.
Other states to the south and southeast were subsequently conquered by
the Fulani who made Islam the dominant religion of west Africa. Their
empire survived until the British conquest of northern Nigeria, 1903-
1906.

King George VI and
Fulani cattle

Readings: Barrows, 1927; Oyewole, 1987.

GERMAN TOGO (Schutzgebiet Togo)

> Togo was an unusual part of the German colonial empire . . . . Since
> Togo was usually self-supporting, it was held up as a fiscal model to
> officials elsewhere.
> — Arthur J. Knoll, 1978.

Area: 33,700 sq. miles (87,282 sq. km); Capital: Lomé
Population: 1,000,000 (est. 1910)

A German colony on the Gulf of Guinea. German missionaries and traders arrived in Togo in the 1840s and exerted a powerful influence. A protectorate, which was accepted by coastal chiefs in 1884, was expanded northward between 1897 and 1899. The Germans, who aimed to turn Togo into a model colony, ran an efficient, if authoritarian, regime. They built roads, railways, harbors and schools and developed the economy. The period of German rule was generally peaceful and prosperous and is fondly remembered by many Togolese. In 1914, at the outbreak of World War I, Togo was occupied by British and French troops and then partitioned under League of Nations mandates. The British portion of Togo became part of the Gold Coast, now Ghana. The French portion became a unit of French West Africa until it achieved independence as the Republic of Togo in 1960.

Anglo-French occupation

Readings: Decalo, 1976; Knoll, 1978.

GOLD COAST

> Accra is one of the five West Coast towns that look well from the sea.
> The others don't look well from anywhere.
> — Mary Kingsley, 1897.

Area: 91,843 sq. miles (237,872 sq. km); Capital: Accra
Population: 4,676,000 (est. 1955)

On the Gulf of Guinea, the name being derived from the gold once found there. The Gold Coast, governed by the British, was composed of four divisions — the Colony, Ashanti, the Northern Territories and Togoland. In 1482 the Portuguese established themselves on the Gold Coast to trade in ivory, spices, gold and slaves. Before long the English and other European powers were also active. After a series of wars with the Ashanti kingdom the British became dominant, establishing the Gold Coast Colony in 1874 (which until 1886 included Lagos in Nigeria). Conflicts with the warlike Ashanti continued until 1900, after which their lands and the Northern Territories were annexed by the British. In 1919 a portion of German Togoland was added to the Gold Coast under a League of Nations (later, United Nations) mandate. On March 6, 1957, the Gold Coast changed its name to Ghana and became an independent dominion in the British Commonwealth. The country became a republic in 1960. The Gold Coast was the first state in sub-Saharan Africa to gain its independence.

Queen Elizabeth II and map of the Gold Coast

Readings: Kingsley, 1897; McFarland, 1985.

HAUSALAND / HAUSA CONFEDERATION

The only Central African people who value a book.
— Henry M. Stanley, q. by Sir George Goldie, 1898.

Area: 500,000 sq. miles (1,295,000 sq. km); Capital: Kano
Population: 5,000,000 (est. 1910)

The Hausa are a large ethnic group of Niger and northern Nigeria. By the 14th century Hausaland was a prosperous confederation of seven independent states. In 1819 the Hausa Confederation was conquered by the Fulani who imposed their government and aristocracy on the Hausa social structure. The Hausa have been Islamic since the 14th century and their language is the lingua franca of west Africa. The British conquered most of Hausaland in 1903.

Readings: *Encyclopædia Britannica*, 1926; Oyewole, 1987.

LAGOS

> The British Consulate . . . a corrugated iron coffin or plank-lined morgue, containing a dead consul once a year.
> — Sir Richard Burton, 1863.

Area: 3,460 sq. miles (8,961 sq. km); Capital: Lagos
Population: 1,500,000 (est. 1901)

Lagos was a British crown colony in southwestern Nigeria. Lagos Island was purchased by the British in 1861, to be used as a base for the suppression of the slave trade. Between 1866 and 1874 it was placed under the governor of Sierra Leone and between 1874 and 1886 was part of the Gold Coast colony. Lagos became a separate colony chartered to the Royal Niger Company in 1886. It was united with the Protectorate of Southern Nigeria in 1906 and became the capital of all of Nigeria in 1914. Lagos has become the principal city of Nigeria and one of the largest in Africa. Recently the Nigerian capital has been moved to the planned city of Abuja in the center of the country. Most government departments, however, remain in Lagos.

Queen Victoria

Readings: *Encyclopædia Britannica*, 1926; Oyewole, 1987.

MALI FEDERATION (Fédération du Mali)

I particularly liked the scrawl on the wall of a back street in Dakar:
"Défense de stationner et d'uriner."
— Richard West, 1965.

Area: 540,997 sq. miles (1,401,182 sq. km); Capitals: Dakar, Bamako
Population: 6,904,000 (est. 1960)

A short-lived federation of former colonies in French West Africa.
The federation was founded in 1959 by Senegal, the Sudanese Republic
(former French Sudan), Dahomey and Upper Volta. The latter two
states dropped out before the federation achieved independence from
France in 1960. Within a year the federation collapsed as the republics
of Senegal and Mali were created.

Woman and view
of Saint Louis,
Senegal

Readings: Imperato, 1986; *Statesman's Yearbook*, 1960.

NORTHERN NIGERIA

It is to British interest to maintain the prestige and, up to a certain
point, the authority of the emir, to satisfy the native population that
their princes are respected and treated with consideration.
— David Prescott Barrows, 1927.

Area: 281,703 sq. miles (729,607 sq. km); Capital: Zungeru
Population: 11,866,250 (est. 1914)

British interests in the Niger River area had been established by the
National African Company, which obtained a charter in 1886 as the
Royal Niger Company. The charter was revoked in 1900 and most of

the Company's lands became the British Protectorate of Northern Nigeria. In 1914 Northern Nigeria was united with Southern Nigeria to form the Colony and Protectorate of Nigeria. A new theory of imperial government using traditional leaders and political structures — indirect rule — was developed in Northern Nigeria. Indirect rule was soon in use throughout Nigeria and in other places in the British Empire.

Readings: *Encyclopædia Britannica*, 1926; Oyewole, 1987.

OIL RIVERS PROTECTORATE / NIGER COAST PROTECTORATE / COLONY AND PROTECTORATE OF SOUTHERN NIGERIA

. . . abstain from exposing yourself to the direct rays of the sun, take 4 grains of quinine every day for a fortnight before you reach the Rivers, and get some introductions to the Weslayans; they are the only people on the Coast who have got a hearse with feathers.
— Mary Kingsley, 1897.

Area: 90,896 sq. miles (235,000 sq. km); Capital: Lagos
Population: 8,590,545 (est. 1914)

With the abolition of the slave trade in the early 19th century the production of palm oil, used in the manufacture of soap, became the chief product of the vast Niger River delta. As a result, the area came to be known as the Oil Rivers. In the 19th century the Oil Rivers Protectorate was considered to be one of the most unhealthy and pestilential places in Africa. Today the region produces another type of oil. Most of Nigeria's petroleum production is centered there.

In 1885 the Royal Niger Company gained title over the coastline of the Gulf of Guinea, between the British Colony of Lagos in the west and German Cameroon in the east. From 1893 the Oil Rivers Protectorate began to expand into the interior. The enlarged dependency was called the Niger Coast Protectorate. The new protectorate was administered by the Royal Niger Company until 1900. At that date the Company's charter was revoked and the Niger Coast came under direct British control. The protectorate was amalgamated with other territories in Nigeria to form the Protectorate of Southern Nigeria. In 1906 Southern Nigeria was joined to the Colony of Lagos to form the Colony and Protectorate of Southern Nigeria. Southern Nigeria was united with Northern Nigeria in 1914 to form the Colony and Protectorate of Nigeria. The union was effected primarily to unify Nigeria's rail system and offset the North's budgetary deficit with the South's surplus.

Queen Victoria

Readings: Kingsley, 1897; Oyewole, 1987.

PORTUGUESE GUINEA (Guiné Portuguesa)

But the time has arrived where colonialism has to finish. Portugal is making many efforts, using all kinds of help in order to maintain our peoples under colonial domination. But we are sure we are going to win, and we have until now liberated more than two-thirds of our country.
— Amilcar Cabral, 1970.

Area: 13,944 sq. miles (36,115 sq. km); Capital: Bissau
Population: 530,000 (est. 1975)

A Portuguese navigator discovered Guinea in 1446. Despite encroachments by the Spanish, French, Dutch and British; and continual resistance from the indigenous population; the Portuguese established themselves in the coastal region turning it into a major center for the slave trade. The interior was not occupied before 1920. Portuguese Guinea became a separate colony in 1879. Before then the territory was administered from the Portuguese colony of the Cape Verde Islands. Beginning in 1963 a war of liberation was waged. The Portuguese had to maintain an army of 30,000 men in the colony. By 1973 the insurgents controlled most of the territory and declared it to be the Republic of Guinea-Bissau. The Portuguese withdrew their forces from Guinea-Bissau in 1974 and recognized its independence.

Beetle

Readings: Lobban, 1979; *New Encyclopædia Britannica*, 1991.

SAMORY'S STATE / WASSULU

A bold strategist as well as a clever and tenacious politician.
— Claude Rivière, 1977.

Area: 100,000 sq. miles (250,000 sq. km); Capital: Bissandugu

Samory Touré was a brilliant Mandingo leader who, by 1879, had established an Islamic state in parts of what is now Guinea, Mali, Sierra Leone and Ivory Coast. With an army of armed horsemen Touré fiercely resisted encroachments by both the French and the British. At other times Touré used negotiation to skillfully play the two European powers off against each other. On one occasion British and French troops mistakenly fought each other. Touré signed treaties with the French and accepted protection from the British when it suited him and ignored those arrangements when it did not. Heavy fighting lasted until 1898 when Samory Touré was finally captured by the French and exiled to Gabon.

Readings: Foray, 1977; Rivière, 1977.

SÉGOU - KAARTA / TUKULOR EMPIRE

I saw with infinite pleasure the great object of my mission — the long sought for majestic Niger, glittering to the morning sun . . . and flowing slowly *to the eastward*.
— Mungo Park, q. by David Prescott Barrows, 1927.

Area: 200,000 sq. miles (500,000 sq. km); Capital: Ségou

The Bambara are the most important ethnolinguistic group in Mali.

In the 17th century two large Bambara kingdoms — Ségou and Kaarta — were founded along the banks of the upper Niger River, reaching their greatest extent around 1830. After a series of jihads (holy wars) Kaarta was conquered in the late 1850s by an Islamic cleric determined to eradicate the "pagan" kingdoms. Ségou fell to the onslaught in 1862. The two kingdoms were reorganized along strict Islamic lines and became known as the Tukulor Empire. The Tukulor Empire lasted until 1892 when it was absorbed by French West Africa.

Readings: Barrows, 1927; Imperato, 1986.

UPPER VOLTA (République de Haute-Volta)

> The footprints of the elephant and the buffalo were very numerous.
> — Heinrich Barth, 1857.

Area: 105,870 sq. miles (274,000 sq. km); Capital: Ouagadougou
Population: 6,695,000 (est. 1984)

A poor landlocked country north of Ghana and Ivory Coast. The French annexed Upper Volta in the 1890s and made it part of the governor-generalship of French West Africa. In 1904 Upper Volta was part of the Colony of Upper Senegal and Niger, becoming a separate colony in 1919. As an economy measure, brought on by the world depression, Upper Volta was abolished in 1932 and its territory apportioned to neighboring colonies. The French reconstituted Upper Volta in 1947 and it achieved independence in 1960. The country was renamed Burkina Faso, "land of honest people," in 1984.

Elephant

Readings: Barth, 1857; *New Encyclopædia Britannica*, 1991.

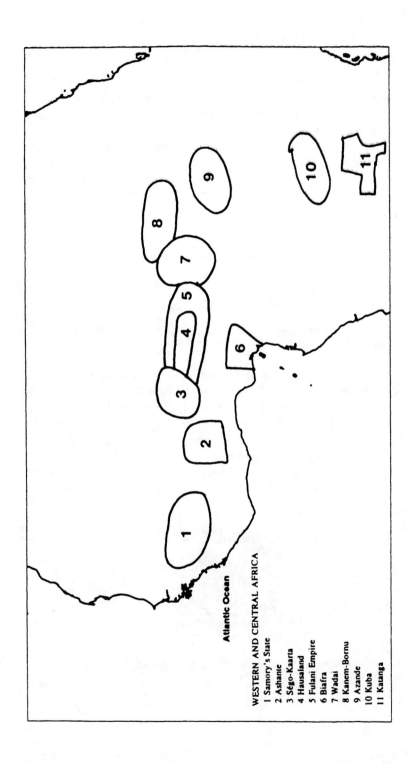

WESTERN AND CENTRAL AFRICA

1 Samory's State
2 Ashante
3 Ségo-Kaarta
4 Hausaland
5 Fulani Empire
6 Biafra
7 Wadai
8 Kanem-Bornu
9 Azande
10 Kuba
11 Katanga

Atlantic Ocean

CHAPTER 12

Central Africa

Fatal Africa! One after another, travellers drop away.
— Sir Henry Morton Stanley, 1909.

AZANDE (Asande, Zande, Niam-Niam)

The Niam-niam . . . string the teeth of their victims around their necks, adorning the stakes erected beside their dwellings . . . with the skulls of the men whom they have devoured.
— Georg Schweinfurth, 1873.

Area: 48,000 sq. miles (125,000 sq. km); Population: 2,000,000 (est. 1870)

A loosely structured empire in the northeastern corner of the Belgian Congo (Zaïre) and adjacent districts of Sudan and Ubangi-Shari (Central African Republic). Azande arose in the 18th century conquering and absorbing many different peoples. The inhabitants were prone to cannibalism and it is that custom which probably explains the old name for Azande, Niam-Niam, "Great Eaters." The empire was weakened by Arab slave traders and eventually destroyed by the forces of Anglo-Egyptian Sudan and the Congo Free State. Azande was partitioned between France, Belgium and Great Britain.

Readings: *Encyclopædia Britannica*, 1926; Kalck, 1980.

BRITISH CAMEROON

> One feels here, as if one were constantly dropping, unasked and
> unregarded, among painful and violent discussions between the
> elemental powers of the Universe.
> — Mary Kingsley, 1897.

Area: 34,136 sq. miles (88,412 sq. km); Capital: Buéa
Population: 1,430,000 (est. 1953)

Two noncontiguous territories, approximately equal in area and
population, sandwiched between Nigeria and Cameroon. British
Cameroon, formerly part of the German protectorate of Kamerun, was
a League of Nations mandated territory awarded to Great Britain at the
end of World War I. For administrative reasons it was integrated with
Nigeria. As a result of plebiscites the northern division of British
Cameroon chose to join independent Nigeria in 1960. The southern
division briefly became a separate United Nations trust territory before
uniting with the Federal Republic of Cameroon in 1961.

Cameroons U.K.T.T. (United Kingdom Trust Territory)

Readings: Kingsley, 1897; Le Vine, 1974.

CABINDA (Kabinda) / PORTUGUESE CONGO (Congo)

> Gabenda was a pretty place, the few houses being built on the Old
> Portuguese style were cool and artistic.
> — Alfred "Trader" Horn, 1927.

Area: 2,807 sq. miles (7,270 sq. km); Capital: Cabinda
Population: 10,000 (est. 1910)

An enclave 25 miles (40 km) north of the mouth of the Congo
River. The Portuguese reached Cabinda in 1470 and its possession by

them was the result of an attempt to control both banks of the Congo estuary. The Portuguese managed to gain sovereignty over the southern bank but the opposite shore was controlled by the Belgians. When Angola became independent in 1975 Cabinda was included. It now forms the northernmost district of Angola and is separated from the rest of that country by a narrow strip of Zaïre. The discovery of a vast offshore oil field in Cabinda has spurred a secessionist movement.

King Carlos of Portugal

Readings: Lewis, 1927; Martin, 1980.

CONGO FREE STATE (État Indépendant du Congo) / BELGIAN CONGO (Congo Belge; Belgisch Congo) / REPUBLIC OF CONGO (Republique du Congo) / ZAIRE

> My rights over the Congo are to be shared with none; they are the fruits of my own struggle and expenditure.
> — Léopold II, q. by Peter Forbath, 1978.

Area: 895,348 sq. miles (2,319,000 sq. km); Capital: Léopoldville
Population: 14,000,000 (est. 1959)

In 1877, after his famous meeting with Dr. Livingstone, Henry Morton Stanley traveled through the Congo Basin, becoming the first European to do so. Léopold II, King of Belgium, commissioned Stanley to undertake further explorations in the Congo and sign treaties with local chieftains on his behalf. Léopold's astute diplomacy at the 1884-1885 Congress of Berlin resulted in his claims to the Congo being accepted by all the major world powers. Léopold arranged things so that he personally owned the Congo! The Congo Free State was established as an absolute monarchy with Léopold as its sovereign. The Free State existed solely to enrich Léopold and a handful of large companies to which he had granted charters. Léopold's administration was harsh in the extreme. Chain gangs and flogging were sanctioned by decree. Laborers needed a special pass to leave their villages and were liable to have a hand chopped off if they did not work hard enough. After an international storm of protest and revulsion the Belgian government annexed the Congo Free State in 1908, renaming it the Belgian Congo. Though the worst abuses were ended and some measures were taken to improve living standards and provide basic services, the African population of the Belgian Congo continued to be regarded as little more than cheap labor. About 100,000 Belgian settlers and bureaucrats ran the country's commerce and administration. The Belgians made no attempt to prepare their huge African possession for self-rule. When independence came in 1960 there were only seventeen Congolese university graduates. The Europeans fled as the new nation sank into civil war and anarchy almost immediately. The country was called the Republic of Congo from 1960 to 1964 and the Democratic Republic of Congo from 1964 to 1971 and from 1997. It was commonly referred to as Congo (Léopoldville) and Congo (Kinshasa) to distinguish it from the former French Congo, Congo (Brazzaville). The name was changed to Zaïre between 1971 and 1997.

Léopold II,
King of the Congo Free State

Readings: *Encyclopædia Britannica*, 1926; Hallet, 1967.

ELOBEY, CORISCO AND ANNOBÓN

> The great rollers of the South Atlantic, meeting here their first check since they left Cape Horn and the Americas, fly up in sheets of foam with a never-ending thunder.
> — Mary Kingsley, 1897.

Area: Elobey Grande-1.3 sq. miles (3.453 sq. km), Elobey Chico-0.35 sq. miles (0.9 sq. km), Annobón-7 sq. miles (18 sq. km); Capital: Elobey Chico
Population: 1,403 (est. 1950)

A group of islands that formed administrative districts of Spanish Guinea. Elobey Grande, Elobey Chico and Corisco are low sandy islands close to the coast of Gabon. Discovered by the Portuguese in 1472 the Spanish obtained slaving rights there in 1778. Spain annexed the islands in 1846 establishing a trading station on Elobey Chico.

Annobón is a volcanic island 220 miles (355 km) off the coast of Gabon. Discovered by the Portuguese on January 1, 1473, the island was named Anno Bon (New Year) as a result. Ceded to Spain in 1778, effective occupation did not take place until 1843. From 1907 to 1942 Annobón was an administrative district. It was then integrated with Rio Muni.

Between 1960 and 1968 Elobey Grande, Elobey Chico and Corisco were part of the Spanish overseas province of Rio Muni, Annobón was integrated with Fernando Póo. The islands have been part of the republic of Equatorial Guinea since 1968. Gabon lays claim to Elobey Grande, Elobey Chico and Corisco. Annobón has been renamed Pagalu. Though Equatorial Guinea is a Spanish-speaking country the people of Annobón continue to speak a Portuguese patois.

Readings: *Encyclopædia Britannica*, 1926; Liniger-Goumaz, 1979

FERNANDO PÓO (Fernando Po)

Anything more perfect than Fernando Póo when you sight it . . . in the sunset, floating like a fairy island made of gold or amethyst, I cannot conceive.
— Mary Kingsley, 1897.

Area: 779 sq. miles (2,017 sq. km); Capital: Santa Isabel
Population: 62,612 (est. 1960)

An island with several extinct volcanoes and crater lakes, in the Bight of Bonny about 20 miles (50 km) off the coast of Cameroon. The Portuguese came to the island in 1471, naming it after the navigator who discovered it, and made some attempt to exploit it commercially. In 1778 Fernando Póo was transferred to the Spanish but the danger of yellow fever prevented an occupation for many years. Though the Spanish retained sovereignty it was the British who established trading posts and administered the island from 1827 to 1858. The British used Fernando Póo as a base for the suppression of the slave trade. Coffee and tobacco plantations were established using imported Nigerian laborers. After rejecting two British offers to buy the island the Spanish finally occupied Fernando Póo in 1858. Fernando Póo was part of Spanish Guinea until 1960 when it and Annobón island became a Spanish overseas province. In 1968 Fernando Póo and the province of Rio Muni united to form the Republic of Equatorial Guinea. Between 1973 and 1979 the island was renamed Macías Nguema Biyogo after the president of Equatorial Guinea. It is now called Bioko.

Nuns

Readings: Kingsley, 1897; Liniger-Goumaz, 1979.

FRENCH CONGO (Congo Français) / FRENCH EQUATORIAL AFRICA (Afrique Équatoriale Française)

> French Equatorial is the most under-paid, under-staffed . . . and has the most abominable climate . . . of any territory in Africa.
> — Negley Farson, 1940.

Area: 969,112 sq. miles (2,510,000 sq. km); Capital: Brazzaville
Population: 4,875,000 (est. 1957)

A region extending from the Atlantic Ocean to the southern Sahara Desert, between Cameroon and the Belgian Congo. The French established themselves on the coast of Gabon in 1839 and gradually expanded inland until by 1891 they had annexed all of Gabon and Middle Congo. The Colony of French Congo was created in 1888 by joining Gabon and Middle Congo. Ubangi-Shari was added to French Congo in 1894 and the Chad military protectorate in 1900, though neither of those was completely conquered until 1913.

French Congo was renamed French Equatorial Africa in 1910 and was originally federated into three autonomous colonies; Gabon, Middle Congo and Ubangi-Shari-Chad. Chad became a separate colony in

1920. Four administrations were maintained until 1936 when French Equatorial Africa became a single colony. In World War II French Equatorial Africa became the first French colonial territory to renounce the Vichy regime and declare for Free France. It was divided into the autonomous republics of Gabon, Congo, Chad and Central Africa in 1958; each of which proceeded to full independence in 1960.

Centenary of colonial troops

Readings: *Encyclopædia Britannica*, 1926; Thompson, 1984.

KAMERUN (Schutzgebeit Kamerun)

Farewell, Camaroons! Farewell, beautiful heights! where so many calm and quiet days have sped without sandflies or mosquitoes, or prickly heat.
— Sir Richard Burton, 1863.

Area: 190,000 sq. miles (492,000 sq. km); Capital: Yaoundé
Population: 3,500,000 (est. 1908)

Kamerun was a German protectorate occupying what is now the Republic of Cameroon and parts of Nigeria and Congo. During the scramble for colonies in the late 19th century Kamerun was the last unappropriated territory on the west coast of Africa. The Germans raised their flag and proclaimed a protectorate on July 15, 1884, five days before the British arrived to do the same thing, and eleven days before the arrival of a French gunboat. German rule is remembered as being authoritarian but relatively progressive. The Germans created a basic infrastructure that exists today.

In 1914, in what was one of the least-known campaigns of World War I, Kamerun was invaded by French troops from Chad and Gabon, and British troops from Nigeria. The Germans put up a stubborn resistance until 1916. Surviving German forces were gradually pushed southward and into internment in Spanish Guinea.

After World War I Kamerun was divided between France and Britain as League of Nations mandated territories. The French territory, about 85 percent of the total, became independent in 1960 as the Republic of Cameroon. The southern half of the British mandated territory became part of the renamed Cameroon Federal Republic. The northern portion joined Nigeria. Between 1972 and 1984 the country was called the United Republic of Cameroon. It is now known by its original post-independence name, Republic of Cameroon.

French occupation

Readings: *Encyclopædia Britannica*, 1926; Le Vine, 1974.

KANEM-BORNU

I laid me down by one of the distant wells . . . and these moments of tranquility, the freshness of the air, with the melody of the hundred songsters that were perched amongst the creeping plants, whose flowers threw an aromatic odour all around, were a relief scarcely to be described.
— Dixon Denham, 1826.

Area: 50,000 sq. miles (130,000 sq. km); Capital: Kukawa
Population: 500,000+ (est. 1910)

An important and long-surviving Islamic sultanate, which was centered around Lake Chad and occupied parts of what is now Nigeria, Niger, Chad and Cameroon. Kanem-Bornu was founded around 800 and became Islamic in the 11th century. The sultanate reached its peak about 1600 subjugating neighboring states. Kanem-Bornu began to decline in the 17th century but it lasted until 1893 when it was conquered by Rabah Zulayr, a former Sudanese slave. Rabah Zubayr's well-drilled army was soon defeated by the French and Kanem-Bornu was partitioned between Britain, France and Germany in 1898.

Readings: Decalo, 1977; Oyewole, 1987.

KATANGA (État du Katanga; Inchi ya Katanga)

> Every nation has a right to its own War of the Roses.
> — Anon., q. by A.M. Schlesinger, 1965.

Area: 191,878 sq. miles (496,965 sq. km); Capital: Elisabethville
Population: 1,687,000 (est. 1959)

Immediately after the independence of the Belgian Congo in 1960, as the Republic of Congo, the southern province of Katanga, now Shaba, declared its secession. Katanga was the richest region of the Congo. It produced two-thirds of the world's cobalt and had large deposits of copper, diamonds and other minerals. The secession of Katanga was backed by Belgium and the large mining companies operating in the province. It took a major United Nations military intervention to end the rebellion in 1963. After the reabsorption of Katanga into the Congo trouble continued. Former Katangan troops, who had fled to nearby Angola, launched an invasion of Shaba in 1977. The invasion was defeated with the help of French and Belgian troops.

Carvings

Readings: *New Encyclopædia Britannica*, 1991; Canby, 1984.

KUBA

Only the eyes tell the truth, not the stories one hears.
— Kuba Proverb, q. by Jean-Pierre Hallet, 1967.

Area: 7,720 sq. miles (20,000 sq. km); Capital: Nsheng
Population: 120,000 - 160,000 (est. 1880)

A kingdom of Bantu-speaking people in the center of the Belgian
Congo (Zaïre) founded around 1600. It comprised a number of
autonomous subkingdoms. In the 19th century rebellions and invasions
began to seriously weaken Kuba. Forces of the Belgian Congo took
control of the region about 1910 and ended the disorders, as well as the
independence of Kuba.

Readings: Hallet, 1967; *New Encyclopædia Britannica*, 1991..

MIDDLE CONGO (Moyen-Congo) / AUTONOMOUS REPUBLIC OF THE CONGO (Republique Autonome du Congo)

Then I saw the Congo, creeping through the black,
Cutting through the jungle with a golden track.
— Vachel Lindsay, 1914.

Area: 132,000 sq. miles (342,000 sq. km); Capital: Pointe Noire
Population: 794,577 (est. 1959)

A former French colony occupying approximately the same territory
as what is now the Republic of the Congo (Congo-Brazzaville).
Explorations by an Italian-born French explorer, de Brazza, between
1875 and 1883, established French claims to the Congo, which received
international recognition in 1885. In its early days Middle Congo was
virtually turned over to concessionary companies until scandals erupted
over the use of forced labor. Although an estimated 17,000 workers
died during the building of a railway the concession system was not
completely extinguished until 1930. In 1888 Middle Congo was
federated with Gabon to form French Congo. By 1910 Ubangi-Shari
and Chad were added and the name of the federation changed to French
Equatorial Africa. Middle Congo soon came to dominate the federation
as its principal town, Brazzaville, was the administrative capital of all
French Equatorial Africa. During World War II Middle Congo became

a bastion of the Free French and the site of a historic declaration by General de Gaulle on the political evolution of the French colonial empire. The colony became the Autonomous Republic of the Congo in 1958 and fully independent in 1960. Since 1970 the country has been called the People's Republic of the Congo. It has often been referred to as Congo (Brazzaville) to distinguish it from its neighbor, Congo (Kinshasa).

Mindouli viaduct

Readings: *Encyclopædia Britannica*, 1926; Thompson, 1984.

RIO MUNI

> Aye, the natives there were melodious singers. A beautiful language theirs. More words to it than you'll find in Anglo-Saxon.
> — Alfred "Trader" Horn, 1927.

Area: 10,045 sq. miles (26,016 sq. km); Capital: Bata
Population: 183,377 (est. 1960)

A rectangular territory on the Gulf of Guinea between Gabon and Cameroon. Though ceded by the Portuguese to the Spanish in 1778 Rio Muni was all but ignored by Spain for the next century and a half. Apart from a few trading posts on the coast Rio Muni was not effectively occupied by the Spanish until 1926. The territory was part of Spanish Guinea until 1960 when it became an overseas province of Spain. In 1968 Rio Muni, along with Fernando Póo, formed the Republic of Equatorial Guinea. Rio Muni is now known as Mbini. The rare goliath frog, three feet (91 cm) from nose to tail, the largest-known frog in the world, inhabits the mountain streams of Rio Muni.

Croton plant

Readings: Lewis, 1927; Liniger-Goumaz, 1979.

SPANISH GUINEA (Territorios Españoles del Golfo de Guinea; Guinea Española)

The Foreign Office grave.
— Sir Richard Burton, 1863.

Area: 10,852 sq. miles (28,107 sq. km); Capital: Santa Isabel
Population: 212,000 (est. 1957)

On the west coast of Africa near the Equator. Spanish Guinea comprised a large continental territory called Rio Muni and the small islands of Fernando Póo, Elobey, Corisco and Annobón. Even though the area was ceded by the Portuguese to the Spanish in the late 18th century the Spanish never occupied Fernando Póo until 1858 and Rio Muni until 1926. The Spanish administration of their equatorial territories was marked by neglect. There were sixty-five governors-general appointed between 1865 and 1910. Postage stamps were issued before it was realized that there was no post office in the colony. From the beginning Spanish Guinea was a colony of exploitation not of settlement. The colony ceased to exist in 1960 when the Spanish overseas provinces of Rio Muni (including the islands of Elobey and Corisco) and Fernando Póo (including Annobón) were created. Rio Muni and Fernando Póo were gradually given a measure of internal self-government and in 1968 they achieved independence as the Republic of Equatorial Guinea. The new state was Africa's only Spanish-speaking nation and one of the world's poorest. A dictator,

Francisco Macías Nguema, seized power and unleashed a reign of terror in which 20 percent of the population was killed. Nguema was overthrown and executed in 1979.

General Franco and river scene

Readings: Lewis, 1927; Liniger-Goumaz, 1979.

UBANGI-SHARI (Oubangui-Chari) / CENTRAL AFRICAN EMPIRE (Empire Centrafricain)

> It was the only place in the world where I have seen almost the entire French community drunk at 10 o'clock in the morning.
> — Negley Farson, 1940.

Area: 240,324 sq. miles (626,436 sq. km); Capital: Bangui
Population: 2,000,000 (est. 1979)

Ubangi-Shari, between the Belgian Congo (Zaïre), Sudan and Chad was one of the last blanks on the map of Africa. Depopulated by Arab slave raiders it was one of the least desirable places to establish a colony, earning a reputation as the Cinderella of the French Empire. The French penetrated the area in 1889 and soon annexed it to the French Congo. At the turn of the century Ubangi was established as a colony, one of the four territories of French Equatorial Africa. Complete control of Ubangi-Shari was not realized until 1911. The colony progressed to self-government in 1958 and independence in 1960 as the Central African Republic.

In 1965 the army chief of staff, a psychotic former colonial army sergeant, Jean Bedel Bokassa, staged a coup and made himself president-for-life. The Bokassa regime was to become one of Africa's worst dictatorships. The country was transformed into the Central African Empire in 1976. The next year, in an extravagant ceremony modeled after Napoleon's coronation, Bokassa crowned himself emperor. After it was revealed that Bokassa I had taken part in the massacre of one hundred children, the French intervened and overthrew him. The Central African Republic was reestablished in 1979. The ex-emperor was convicted of crimes ranging from embezzlement to murder and sentenced to life imprisonment in solitary confinement.

Rhinoceros

Readings: *Encyclopædia Britannica*, 1926; Kalck, 1980.

UBANGI-SHARI-CHAD (Ubangi-Chari-Tchad)

> The banks [of the Shari River] were thickly scattered with trees rich in foliage, and all hung over with creeping plants, bearing various coloured and aromatic blossoms, amongst which the purple convolvulus flourished in great beauty.
> — Denham Dixon, 1826.

Area: 730,000 sq. miles (1,900,000 sq. km); Capital: Bangui
Population: 3,000,000 (est. 1906)

The Circumscription of Ubangi-Shari and the Circumscription of Chad were the divisions that formed the colony of Ubangi-Shari-Chad. Together or apart Ubangi-Shari and Chad were under the administrative control of the governor-general of French Equatorial Africa until 1958. The divisions now comprise the Central African Republic and the Republic of Chad. Ubangi-Shari-Chad was a French colony from 1906 to 1916.

Leopard

Readings: *Encyclopædia Britannica*, 1926; Kalck, 1980.

WADAI (Waday; Ouddaï)

> The horses are said to be excellent; and exposed as they are to storm
> and heat, never enjoying the protection of a roof or shade, they are
> able to support the greatest fatigue, while at the same time, those of
> the great men at least are said to be fed sumptuously with rice and
> milk.
> — Heinrich Barth, 1857.

Area: 150,000 sq. miles (388,000 sq, km); Capital: Abeshr
Population: 3,000,000 - 4,000,000 (est. 1910)

A warlike sultanate in eastern Chad. Established in the 16th century
Wadai was a major slave-trading state until it was conquered by the
French between 1906 and 1914. Areas of the Central African Republic
are still underpopulated as a result of the Wadai slavers. Originally
subordinate to Darfur the sultanate became independent in the 1790s
and began a rapid expansion to the west at the expense of Kanem-
Bornu. Although Wadai sat astride the major north-south and east-west
trade routes it remained remote and suspicious of outsiders. It was not
visited by a European until 1850. Though officially annexed to French
Congo in 1909 Wadai was under direct military rule until 1935. Since
1960 Wadai has been part of the Republic of Chad. Chad has, since its
independence, been plagued by nearly continuous civil war in which the
Wadai region has figured. Wadai has resisted being integrated into
Chad, refusing to be ruled by the southern regions, which until recently
were considered merely a source of slaves.

Readings: Barth, 1857; Decalo, 1977.

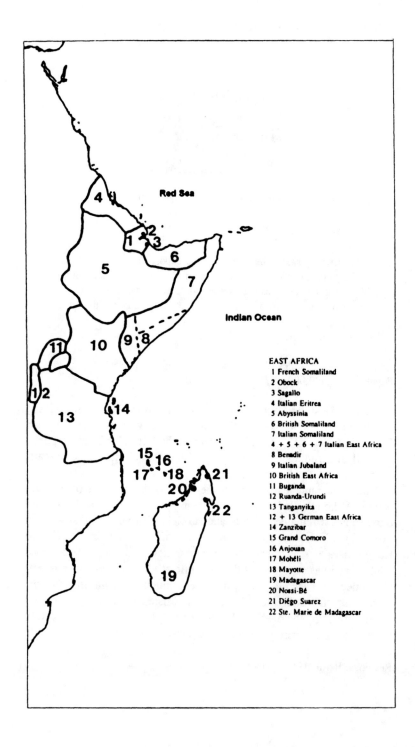

Red Sea

Indian Ocean

EAST AFRICA
1 French Somaliland
2 Obock
3 Sagallo
4 Italian Eritrea
5 Abyssinia
6 British Somaliland
7 Italian Somaliland
4 + 5 + 6 + 7 Italian East Africa
8 Benadir
9 Italian Jubaland
10 British East Africa
11 Buganda
12 Ruanda-Urundi
13 Tanganyika
12 + 13 German East Africa
14 Zanzibar
15 Grand Comoro
16 Anjouan
17 Mohéli
18 Mayotte
19 Madagascar
20 Nossi-Bé
21 Diégo Suarez
22 Ste. Marie de Madagascar

CHAPTER 13

East Africa

Never take a cold bath in Africa, unless ordered to do so by a doctor.
— William Henry Cross, 1906.

ABYSSINIA

. . . the Abyssinians . . . look down with genuine contempt on every human being who has not had the good fortune to be born Abyssinian.
— Gerald H. Portal, 1892.

Area: 395,000 sq. miles (1,023,000 sq. km); Capital: Addis Ababa
Population: 16,000,000 (est. 1953)

Bounded by the Red Sea, Sudan and Somaliland. Abyssinia was converted to Christianity in the fourth century but its origins go back many centuries before that. The country's emperors claimed direct descent from King Solomon and the Queen of Sheba. In the late 1800s, after centuries of virtual isolation, Abyssinia found itself under increasing pressure from Egypt, France, Great Britain and Italy. Fortunately, Abyssinia was ruled by a dynamic and resourceful emperor, Menelik II. The Italians, who had established the Colony of Eritrea on the Red Sea coast, were the most eager to dominate the rest of Abyssinia. In 1896 Italy invaded the empire but suffered a crushing defeat at the hands of Menelik's well-armed Abyssinian army. Italy and the other colonial powers were forced to recognize Abyssinia's continued independence.

After Menelik's death Abyssinia entered into a period of weakness and internecine conflict. Abyssinia would probably have been carved up at that time except that the European powers were preoccupied with World War I. The new emperor, Haile Selassie I, who ascended the throne in 1928, stabilized his country and tried to modernize it.

In 1935, without a declaration of war, Italy, using the excuse of a trumped-up border incident, launched a second invasion of Abyssinia from bases in Eritrea and Italian Somaliland. Despite an eloquent plea by Haile Selassie at the League of Nations no country came to Abyssinia's aid. Unlike their army of forty years before the Abyssinians of 1935 were poorly equipped and no match for Italy's modern war machine. After a campaign that included the deliberate terror-bombing of civilian targets and the use of poison gas Abyssinia surrendered in 1936. Italy's king, Victor Emmanuel, was declared Emperor of Abyssinia and the country became the major part of Italian East Africa. Though the Italians did create some much-needed infrastructure and material improvements they faced continuous resistance from the Abyssinian population. British, Commonwealth and Abyssinian forces cleared the Italians out of the country in 1941 and its independence was restored. Since the end of World War II Abyssinia has been known as Ethiopia. Haile Selassie was deposed in 1974 and strangled to death in 1975.

Coronation of Emperor Haile Selassie

Readings: *New Encyclopædia Britannica*, 1991; Prouty, 1981.

ANJOUAN / JOHANNA

The inhabitants are very civil, but are said to be the greatest thieves in existence.
— Eliza Fay, 1815.

Area: 164 sq. miles (425 sq. km); Capital: Mossammondu
Population: 12,000 (est. 1910)

The second-largest island in the Comoro archipelago. Long a base for pirates, Anjouan was a sultanate under French protection from 1886 until 1914. Between 1914 and 1946 the island was administered from Madagascar (Malagasy) and from then until 1975 Anjouan was a constituent part of the French colony of the Comoro Islands. It is now part of the Federal Islamic Republic of the Comoros.

Anjouan Bay

Readings: *New Encyclopædia Britannica*, 1991; Newitt, 1984.

BENADIR

The eye is at first attracted by four minarets of considerable height, towering above the town, and giving it an air of silly grandeur but a nearer approach soon convinces the spectator that these massive buildings are principally the residences of the dead, while the living inhabit the low thatched huts by which these costly sepulchres are surrounded.
— William Fitz William Owen, 1833.

Area: 15,000 sq. miles (40,000 sq. km); Capital: Chisimayu

The southern coast of Italian Somaliland east of the Juba River. In 1889 Italy sublet the Benadir coast from the Imperial British East Africa Company, which in turn had leased it from the sultan of

Zanzibar. The territory was exploited by concessionary firms until 1905 when the Italian government purchased Benadir outright from Zanzibar and incorporated it into Italian Somaliland. Italian influence in Benadir never went far beyond the coastal fringe.

Readings: Castagno, 1975; Owen, 1833.

BRITISH EAST AFRICA / IBEA

> Come to Kenya where the Zoo looks at you, and not you at the Zoo!
> — Tourist poster, q. by James Agate, 1946.

Area: 220,624 sq. miles (571,416 sq. km); Capital: Nairobi
Population: 2-4,000,000 (est. 1910)

Although *British East Africa* was the term used for all British possessions in eastern Africa, strictly speaking, it was only applied to what is now Kenya.

Though the Portuguese reached the coast of Kenya in 1498 European explorers and missionaries did not begin to penetrate the interior until the 1850s. British East Africa was created in 1895 when a protectorate was declared between the coast and Uganda. A 10-mile (16 km)-wide coastal strip had been leased from the sultan of Zanzibar in 1887 by the Imperial British East Africa Company. When the Company folded in 1895 its territory, known as IBEA from the Company's initials, was transferred to the British government.

In its early days British East Africa was the scene of revolts by the Arabs of the coast and the Kikuyu and other powerful tribes of the interior. The Masai was the only important tribe that cooperated with the British administration. A railway constructed before World War I linking Mombasa, Nairobi and Lake Victoria facilitated an influx of white settlers. The highlands, with their rich farmlands and pleasant climate — later known as the White Highlands — were reserved for white settlement. That policy became a source of conflict with the indigenous population, most notably in the form of the Mau Mau Rebellion in the 1950s. British East Africa was renamed Kenya in 1920, after the country's highest mountain. The interior became the Crown Colony of Kenya and the coast, over which the sultan of Zanzibar continued to exert nominal control, became the Kenya

Protectorate. Kenya became independent in 1963. In practice the colony and the protectorate had been administered as a single territory.

Sun and crown symbolizing light and liberty

Readings: *Encyclopædia Britannica*, 1926; Ogot, 1981.

BRITISH SOMALILAND / SOMALILAND PROTECTORATE / STATE OF SOMALILAND

British Somaliland is the only country I know where you see camels walking in the sky and goats climbing trees. This of course, is the effect of the mirage, and not exposing your head to the sun.
— Geoffrey Harmsworth, 1935.

Area: 68,000 sq. miles (176,000 sq. km); Capital: Hargeisa
Population: 640,000 (est. 1960)

Located in the Horn of Africa on the Gulf of Aden. Despite its being a legendary source of frankincense and myrrh the British never had much interest in their Somali protectorate. They saw it merely as a source of supply for the garrison in Aden and as part of the outer defenses of India. After an attack by Somali tribesmen on the famous explorers Burton and Speke, a British Resident was established in Somaliland in 1855. A series of treaties were signed and a protectorate created in 1884.

Between 1899 and 1920 the interior of British Somaliland was in a state of revolt and civil war. Fanatical dervishes, under Mohamed bin Abdullah Hassan, the "Mad Mullah," declared a holy war against Europeans, Ethiopians and any Somalis who opposed them. After repeated military expeditions in arid wastelands, and the creation of a special camel constabulary, the British, under a policy termed "strict coast concentration," essentially abandoned the interior. Friendly tribes were armed by the government and told to fend for themselves. It was only after World War I that the British, with the aid of bombing raids by the Royal Air Force, were able to pacify the interior of the Protectorate.

In 1940 the Italians invaded British Somaliland and briefly added it to Italian East Africa. The next year British and Commonwealth forces ousted the Italians from all of east Africa. British Somaliland was ruled by a military administration until 1948 and then by a civilian government until it became independent as the State of Somaliland on June 26, 1960. Five days later the State of Somaliland merged with Italian Somaliland to create the Somali Republic.

King George VI and goat

Readings: Castagno, 1975; *Encyclopædia Britannica*, 1926.

BUGANDA

Kampala is a Buganda cosmopolis — in which the English are shop or bank employees.
— Negley Farson, 1940.

Area: 10,000 sq. miles (25,000 sq. km); Capital: Kampala
Population: 840,000 (est. 1930)

Buganda was a sophisticated Bantu kingdom north of Lake Victoria. It existed as an independent country from about 1400 until the British created the Protectorate of Uganda in 1884. The British were obliged to make Buganda a separate province in Uganda and rule through its traditional kings. A similar situation has existed since Uganda's independence in 1962. The Kingdom of Buganda enjoys a considerable degree of autonomy within Uganda.

Readings: Canby, 1984: *Encyclopædia Britannica*, 1926.

DIÉGO-SUAREZ (Établissements Français de Diégo-Suarez) /
ANTSIRANE

> The Bay of Diégo-Suarez is beginning to be known as one of the finest
> harbours in the world. It comprises five large harbours, and is
> completely sheltered from the Indian Ocean. The scenery around is
> extremely beautiful, the climate is healthy, and the soil black, rich,
> and fertile, and at the same time well watered.
> — Henry W. Little, 1884.

Capital: Diégo-Suarez; Population: 12,237 (est. 1900)

A town at the northern tip of Madagascar (Malagasy), which was
established as a French colony in 1885. Upon the formation of the
French colony of Madagascar in 1896 Diégo-Suarez ceased to be a
separate territory. The town was situated on one of the world's greatest
deepwater ports and became the site of a French naval base. Diégo-
Suarez was named after the Portuguese explorer who discovered it in
1543.

Readings: Brown, 1979; Little, 1884.

FRENCH SOMALILAND (Côte Française des Somalis) / FRENCH
TERRITORY OF THE AFARS AND ISSAS (Territoire Français des
Afars et des Issas)

> Jibuti, white and neat and empty, looked as if it had just been washed
> and dumped out in the sun to dry.
> — Rosita Forbes, 1925.

Area: 8,958 sq. miles (23,200 sq. km); Capital: Djibouti
Population: 300,000 (est. 1977)

Extremely hot and dry, with less than 1 percent of its land arable,
the value of French Somaliland was in its location. It was on the Bab
al Mandab, the narrow southern entrance to the Red Sea, and was the
terminus of the Imperial Ethiopian Railway, that country's principal
access to the outside world. The protectorate of French Somaliland was
created around the port of Djibouti, which became a major transshipment center and coaling station. Most of the population lived in
Djibouti. Because of its strategic location the French territory became

more prosperous than neighboring British and Italian Somaliland.

Between 1883 and 1887 treaties with local rulers allowed the French to establish their protectorate. French Somaliland was officially founded in 1888 with a governor residing in Djibouti from 1896. The protectorate was controlled by Vichy from 1940 to 1943 and then by the Free French.

Recognizing the two largest ethnic groups, the name was changed to the French Territory of the Afars and Issas in 1967. The Issas are a Somali clan and the Afars, also called the Danakil, a non-Somali people. The two groups have a history of enmity. Despite two referenda, in which the population voted to remain French, the country became independent in 1977 as the Republic of Djibouti.

Outpost at Khor-Angar

Readings: Castagno, 1975; Treat, 1931.

GERMAN EAST AFRICA (Deutsch Ostafrika)

Far away in the distance the august mountain Kilimanjaro shone in the upper air like a vast celestial mould of Christmas pudding streaked with frozen rivers of brandy-butter.
— Edward Marsh, 1939.

Area: 384,180 sq. miles (995,000 sq. km); Capital: Dar es Salaam
Population: 7,680,132 (est. 1913)

In east-central Africa bounded by British East Africa (Kenya), the Belgian Congo (Zaïre), Portuguese East Africa (Mozambique) and the Indian Ocean. The highest mountain in Africa, Mount Kilimanjaro (19,340 ft., 5,894 m) was located in German East Africa. When missionaries returned to the coast with stories of a snowcapped mountain on the equator no one would believe them.

German missionaries and explorers had been at work in the country for about forty years before the German East Africa Company began negotiating treaties with local chieftains in the 1880s. When the Company leased a coastal strip from the sultan of Zanzibar in 1888 trouble erupted. The Arabs of the coast rose in a revolt that was beyond the means of the Company to contain. The imperial German government was forced to send troops and take over the territory itself. German East Africa was born in 1890. Further revolts occurred in 1891-1892 and 1905-1906. The last revolt inflamed the entire southern portion of the territory and killed at least 120,000 people. The Germans had to raise large African levees, bring soldiers from Germany, and even transport native troops from their Pacific island colony of New Guinea to end the disturbance.

During World War I the Royal Navy blockaded German East Africa, cutting it off from Europe. British and Indian troops invaded the territory in 1914 but were repulsed. In 1915 a German battleship, the Königsberg, was sunk by British ships and aircraft in the delta of the Rufiji River. British and imperial forces invaded German East Africa again in 1916 winning an important battle within sight of Mount Kilimanjaro. Faced with superior numbers, and cut off from all means of supply, the German commander, General Von Lettow-Vorbeck, fought a brilliant guerrilla action tying down large numbers of Allied troops. He was never defeated and surrendered only when the war in Europe came to an end.

After the war the British received a League of Nations mandate over most of German East Africa, renaming it the Tanganyika Territory. The Belgians were given Ruanda-Urundi in the northwest of the country, and the Kionga triangle, in the southeast, was added to Portuguese East Africa (Mozambique).

Kaiser's yacht Hohenzollern

Readings: *Encyclopædia Britannica*, 1926; Kurtz, 1978.

GRAND COMORO (Grande Comore)

> Comoro is a huge, highe, massie peece of land; but our Shipps never
> touched there, by reason of the treacherie of the Inhabitants.
> — Peter Mundy, 1628.

Area: 443 sq. miles (1,147 sq. km); Capital: Moroni
Population: 50,000 (est. 1910)

The most westerly and the largest of the Comoro Islands, at the
northern entrance of the Mozambique Channel between Madagascar
(Malagasy) and the southeastern coast of Africa. The population was
mostly Muslim of mixed African, Malay, Arab and Malagasy origins.
Though French was the official language most people spoke Comoran,
an Arabized dialect of Swahili. The French, partly to keep the Germans
out, established a protectorate over Grand Comoro between 1886 and
1914. The island then became a dependency of Madagascar and after
1946 part of the colony of the Comoro Islands. Since 1975 Grand
Comoro Island has been included in the Federal Islamic Republic of the
Comoros. Living specimens of the coelacanth, a fish thought to have
been extinct for seventy million years, have been caught near Grand
Comoro.

Grand Comoro canoe

Readings: *New Encyclopædia Britannica*, 1991; Newitt, 1984.

ITALIAN EAST AFRICA (Africa Orientale Italiana)

> There was a press bureau which you visited, as a sort of conventional
> rite, each morning. You waited for an hour or so in a bare room with

a large map of Switzerland and a few Italian shipping posters on the walls. One day a wit marked Addis Ababa and Harar on the Swiss map, and you saw newcomers studying it with earnest, puzzled expressions, wondering why they had never noticed all those lakes before.
— Patrick Balfour, 1936.

Area: 665,977 sq. miles (1,7725,000 sq. km); Capital: Asmara
Population: 12,100,000

The Italians had long had designs on the ancient empire of Abyssinia (Ethiopia). From their colony of Eritrea on the Red Sea they invaded Abyssinia in 1896 and suffered a crushing defeat at the battle of Adawa. In 1935-1936 the Italians launched a second invasion of Abyssinia from Eritrea in the north and Italian Somaliland in the south. This time they were successful. King Victor Emmanuel was declared emperor of Abyssinia and all Italian territories in the Horn of Africa were amalgamated under the name, Italian East Africa. In 1940 the Italians seized British Somaliland and added it to Italian East Africa. The Italian conquests were to be short-lived, however. In 1941 British and Commonwealth forces defeated the Italians and put an end to Italian East Africa.

Adolf Hitler and Benito Mussolini "Two peoples, one war"

Readings: Castagno, 1975; Prouty, 1981.

ITALIAN ERITREA (Colonia Eritrea)

Asmara was founded by the Italians seventy years ago and looks like a lost suburb of Milan.
— Dervla Murphy, 1968.

Area: 45,754 sq. miles (118,500 sq. km); Capital: Asmara
Population: 510,000 (est. 1931)

On the Red Sea, bounded by Sudan and Abyssinia (Ethiopia).
Though its history has been linked with that of Abyssinia for more than
a thousand years Eritrea had usually enjoyed a measure of autonomy.
Between the 17th and 19th centuries Eritrea was claimed by Egypt, the
Ottoman Empire, Abyssinia and Italy. The Italians began their
occupation of the Eritrean coast in 1869 when an Italian steamship
company purchased a coaling station on the Red Sea. By force of arms
— a military post was established in 1879 — and a series of unequal
treaties the Italians gained the upper hand. They founded the Colony of
Eritrea in 1890 giving it a name reminiscent of the Roman Mare
Erythraeum; Red Sea. From their bases in Eritrea the Italians invaded
Abyssinia in 1896 and were soundly defeated. Licking their wounds
and nursing their pride the Italians allowed their Eritrean colony to
stagnate until the Italian dictator, Mussolini, launched a second invasion
of Abyssinia in 1935-1936. This time the Abyssinians were defeated
and Eritrea became a province of the newly constituted Italian East
Africa. After the 1941 defeat of Italian forces in east Africa Eritrea was
administered by the British. The British stayed until 1952 when Eritrea
was federated with Ethiopia as an autonomous region. Eritrea lost its
autonomy in 1962 when it was fully integrated into the Empire of
Ethiopia. This touched off a thirty-year guerrilla war. The
independence of Eritrea was finally achieved in 1993.

Camel

Readings: *New Encyclopædia Britannica*, 1991; Prouty, 1981.

ITALIAN JUBALAND (Oltre Giuba; Trans-Juba)

Just back from the mangrove-lined, or coral-bound seashore of the
southern coast line there is generally a thick bush belt, wherever the
country has not been cleared to make way for plantations.
— C.H. Stigand, 1913.

Area 33,000 sq. miles (85,470 sq. km); Capital: Kismayu
Population: 12,000 (est. 1926)

A strip of land in southern Somalia, 50 to 100 miles (80 to 160 km) wide, west of the Juba River. The British had acquired Jubaland from Zanzibar in 1888 and made it part of British East Africa. A World War I treaty between Great Britain and Italy called for the transferral of Jubaland to Italy should Britain expand her African dominions at the expense of Germany. When this occurred Jubaland was ceded to Italy in 1925. For one year Jubaland was the separate Italian colony of Oltre Giuba. It was absorbed into Italian Somaliland in 1926.

Map of Oltre Giuba

Readings: Castagno, 1975; *Encyclopædia Britannica*, 1926.

ITALIAN SOMALILAND (Somalia Italiana) / TRUST TERRITORY OF SOMALIA

The legend is that this is the place to which Mussolini sent Italians whom he *really* wanted to get rid of.
— John Gunther, 1955.

Area: 178,201 sq. miles (461,541 sq. km); Capital: Mogadishu
Population: 1,263,584 (est. 1958)

On the eastern seaboard of the Horn of Africa. In 1905 Italy purchased the coastal district around Mogadishu from Zanzibar and established the Colony of Italian Somaliland. Land to the south, the Benadir coast, had been acquired in 1889. Gradually Italian Somaliland was expanded until it reached its maximum area in 1927. The Italians

were drawn to Somaliland by its possibilities for commerce and as a
site for Italian emigration. The Italians did develop the country
economically but Somaliland never became a popular place for settlers.
In the 1920s and 1930s the Italians (often using forced labor)
established plantations, built roads, ports, hospitals and a railroad but
did nothing to bring the territory toward self-government. In 1935
Italian Somaliland and Eritrea were the launching pads for an invasion
of Abyssinia (Ethiopia). The British drove the Italians out of east
Africa in 1941 and governed Italian Somaliland under a military
administration until 1950. In that year Italy returned to Somaliland
when it was given responsibility for the newly formed United Nations
Trust Territory of Somalia. Independence came in 1960 when Italian
and British Somaliland were merged to form the Republic of Somalia.

Mother and child

Readings: Castagno, 1975; *Encyclopædia Britannica*, 1926.

MADAGASCAR

> To such as believe that the quaint product called French civilization
> would be an improvement . . . the snatching of Madagascar, and the
> laying on of French civilization there will be fully justified.
> — Mark Twain, 1897.

Area: 226,658 sq. miles (587,042 sq. km); Capital: Tananarive
Population: 5,065,372 (est. 1957)

Madagascar, 250 miles (400 km) off the coast of southwestern

Africa, is the fourth-largest island in the world. The island, which was settled around the first century by people of Malayo-Polynesian origin, was visited by the Portuguese in 1500. The French established their first outpost in 1643. The Merina Kingdom, founded in the 16th century, unified Madagascar between 1797 and 1861. The French, from their bases in Nossi-Bé, Ste. Marie and Diégo-Suarez, steadily increased their power and influence in the island at the expense of the Merina. They fought a war with the Merina (1882-1884) to establish French sovereignty to the northwest coast. The last native resistance was quelled in 1895 the year all of Madagascar became a French protectorate. By 1897 the Merina monarchy was abolished and Madagascar was a French colony. The next serious revolt against French rule occurred in 1947 when as many as 80,000 people were killed. After a referendum Madagascar became the autonomous Malagasy Republic in 1958 and fully independent in 1960.

Madagascar's dwindling forests provide the habitat for a huge number of unique animal and plant species including most of the world's lemurs, half of its chameleon species and 6,000 varieties of flowering plants.

Sakalava chief

Readings: Brown, 1979; Little, 1884.

MAYOTTE

> In the twentieth century the French administration had maintained the capital of the islands on the tiny waterless rock of Dzaoudzi, which had originally been chosen because its guns could dominate the lagoon. The inappropriateness of having a capital on Dzaoudzi must be emphasized.
> — Malyn Newitt, 1984.

Area: 144 sq. miles (373 sq. km); Capital: Dzaoudzi
Population: 13,500 (est. 1915)

The southernmost island in the Comoro archipelago. Mayotte was the first of the Comoro Islands to come under French control and the only one never to have been a protectorate. It became a colony in 1843. By a decree of 1914 Mayotte was united with the islands of Grand Comoro, Anjouan and Mohéli as the French colony of the Comoro Islands, a dependency of French-ruled Madagascar (Malagasy). In 1946 Mayotte and the other islands were created a French overseas territory, becoming self-governing in 1961. In a 1974 referendum Grand Comoro, Anjouan and Mohéli voted for independence and the Federal Islamic Republic of the Comoros came into being the next year. Mayotte rejected independence and opted to retain its links with France. The island is now a territorial collectivity, a status similar to a department of France. French currency and postage stamps are in use and the islanders vote in French elections, being represented in Paris by a deputy and a senator. Mayotte is claimed by the Comoros Republic.

150th anniversary of Mayotte's attachment to France

Readings: *New Encyclopædia Britannica*, 1991; Newitt, 1984.

MOHÉLI (Mohilla)

In my opinion it is a very prettie pleasant and fruitefull Island, as
well for necessetye as delighte, full of shadie woods of strange Trees,
Springs and Rilletts of Water.
— Peter Mundy, 1628.

Area: 112 sq. miles (290 sq. km); Capital: Fomboni
Population: 9,000 (est. 1910)

The smallest and least populous of the Comoro Islands, Mohéli was
a sultanate under French protection from 1886 to 1914. From 1914
until the island was grouped with the other Comoro Islands, as a
French overseas territory, it was a dependency of Madagascar
(Malagasy). In 1975 Mohéli, along with Anjouan and Grand Comoro,
became independent as the Federal Islamic Republic of the Comoros.

Symbols of navigation and commerce

Readings: *New Encyclopædia Britannica*, 1991; Newitt, 1984.

NOSSI-BÉ

I do believe by God's blessing, that not any part of the world is more
advantageous for a plantation, being every way as well for pleasure as
well as profit, in my estimation.
— Robert Hunt, 1650.

Area: 130 sq. miles (337 sq. km); Capital: Hell-Ville
Population: 9,000 (est. 1900)

An island 5 miles (8 km) off the northwest coast of Madagascar (Malagasy). Nossi-Bé, which became a protectorate in 1840, was one of the bases from which France established its control of Madagascar. When the colony of Madagascar was created in 1896 Nossi-Bé was incorporated into it. The name meant "Big Island."

Readings: Brown, 1979; *Encyclopædia Britannica*, 1926.

OBOCK (Obok)

> . . . a bare white cube that shelters a French sergeant and a handful of Somali soldiers, sole representatives of colonial France.
> — Ida Treat, 1931.

Area: 6,000 sq. miles (15,500 sq. km); Capital: Obock
Population: 22,400 (est. 1890)

In order to counterbalance the British occupation of the strategic island of Perim at the southern entrance to the Red Sea, the French consul at Aden purchased the town and territory of Obock on the African side of the strait. Though the French occupation was ratified by treaties with Afar chiefs in 1862 France did not formally take possession until 1883. Obock was absorbed by French Somaliland in 1888 and became the capital of that protectorate. When the French transferred their administration to Djibouti in 1896 Obock went into a steep decline. Obock was on the caravan routes to Abyssinia (Ethiopia) and was the site of a cable station.

Somali warriors

Readings: *Encyclopædia Britannica*, 1926; Treat, 1931.

REUNION / ILE DE BONAPARTE / ILE BOURBON

Passing Isle de Bourbon. Broken-up skyline of volcanic mountains in the middle. Surely it would not cost much to repair them, and it seems inexcusable neglect to leave them as they are.
— Mark Twain, 1897.

Area: 970 sq. miles (2,512 sq. km); Capital: St. Dennis
Population: 242,062 (est. 1946)

One of the Mascarene Islands about 420 miles (676 km) east of Madagascar (Malagasy). Réunion, apart from a period of British occupation during the Napoleonic Wars, was a French colony from 1638 to 1946. Since 1946 the island has been an overseas department of France, an integral part of the French Republic. The population, mostly Creole, have full French citizenship. Discovered early in the 16th century Réunion was uninhabited until annexed by France in 1638 as Bourbon Island. The first settlers were mutineers. Later, Africans were imported as slaves. After slavery was abolished indentured laborers were brought in from India, China and Malaya. The island's name was changed to Réunion during the French Revolution and for a short time to Bonaparte's Island. After the Restoration of the Bourbon kings in France the colony again became Bourbon Island. The name Réunion was restored in 1848.

After Madagascar achieved its independence from France in 1960 the uninhabited islands of Bassas da India, Europa, Juan de Nova, Tromelin and Iles Glorieuses were transferred to Réunion. Tromelin is claimed by Mauritius and Seychelles. Madagascar claims all the islands.

Salazie falls

Readings: *New Encyclopædia Britannica*, 1991; Canby, 1984.

RUANDA-URUNDI / BELGIAN EAST AFRICA

That African Switzerland.
— Negley Farson, 1940.

Area: 21,234 sq. miles (54,996 sq. km); Capital: Usumbura
Population: 4,700,000 (est. 1958)

A Belgian mandated territory bounded by Uganda, the Belgian Congo (Zaïre) and Tanganyika (Tanzania). The territory was made up of two Tutsi kingdoms; Ruanda in the north and Urundi in the south. The Tutsi people had migrated to Ruanda-Urundi in the 14th century and though they numbered no more than 15 percent of the population they were able to dominate the Hutu majority in a feudal system.

German explorers and missionaries had reached Ruanda-Urundi by the middle of the 19th century. Although the German presence was never very strong the territory was officially part of German East Africa by 1890. The first German resident in Urundi did not arrive until 1906.

Ruanda-Urundi was occupied by Belgian troops from the Congo in 1916. After World War I Belgium was awarded the territory as a League of Nations mandate. The Belgians administered Ruanda-Urundi as part of the Congo but maintained a separate budget for it. A resident was stationed in each kingdom of the mandate and the Belgians adopted a policy of ruling through traditional kings and chiefs. Urundi was in turmoil until the Belgians pacified the kingdom in 1921. In 1959 war erupted between the Hutu and Tutsu in Ruanda and the Tutsi king was deposed. Ruanda-Urundi became independent in 1962 as the Republic of Rwanda and the Kingdom of Burundi. Burundi has since become a republic. Conflict between the Hutu and the Tutsi continues to plague both countries.

Buffaloes

Readings: *New Encyclopædia Britannica*, 1991; Weinstein, 1976.

SAGALLO

> . . . the French commander, wishing to avoid a hand-to-hand combat
> with the Russians, having an insufficient landing-force, fired shells into
> the fort, killing five persons and wounding as many more. Some one
> inside then displayed a white flag, and the Russian colors were hauled
> down.
> — *American Cyclopædia*, 1889.

Capital: Sagallo; Population: 146

Sagallo was a town on the Gulf of Tajura in French Somaliland and
the site of a short-lived Russian colony in Africa. Between 1875 and
1884 the town was occupied by the Egyptians, who built a fort there.
In 1889 a Cossack soldier of fortune, by the name of Nicholas
Achinov, arrived with settlers, a detachment of infantry and the
Archimandrite Païsi. The Metropolitan of Novgorod had enlisted Païsi
to undertake an evangelical mission for the Abyssinian Orthodox
Church. Achinov, who had aided the Abyssinians in their conflicts with
the Italians and who claimed to have fought with the Mahdi against
Gordon at Khartoum, brought arms and ammunition, occupied the
deserted Egyptian fort and hoisted the Russian flag. The French
considered the presence of Russians in Sagallo a violation of their
territorial rights and dispatched two gunboats. The fort was bombarded
and the Russians, after some loss of life that included women and
children, surrendered. The would-be colonists were deported to Odessa
by way of Suez and their colony came to an abrupt end.

Readings: *American Cyclopædia*, 1889; *Encyclopædia Britannica*, 1926.

STE. MARIE DE MADAGASCAR

> The first foreign settlers in Madagascar were swept off in such
> numbers by the malaria, that the Isle of S. Marie was called the
> "Grave of the French," and "the Churchyard," and the "Dead Island,"
> by the Dutch and other sailors who visited the harbours of the east
> coast.
> — Henry W. Little, 1884.

Area: 64 sq. miles (166 sq. km); Capital: Ste. Marie
Population: 8,000 (est. 1900)

An island on Madagascar's east coast. In the 17th century Ste. Marie de Madagascar was the most powerful pirate port in the world playing host to the likes of Captain Kidd. The French established themselves in Ste. Marie and it became one of the bases from which they carried out a conquest of all of Madagascar. The island of Ste. Marie became part of Madagascar colony in 1896.

Readings: Brown, 1979; Little, 1884.

TANGANYIKA TERRITORY

> A man in a Mandate is like a mule — he has no pride of ancestry and no hope for posterity.
> — Negley Farson, 1940.

Area: 362,688 sq. miles (939,358 sq. km); Capital: Dar es Salaam
Population: 9,404,000 (est. 1961)

Tanganyika comprised most of the former German East Africa and was held by the British under a League of Nations (later, United Nations) mandate granted in 1919. The name *Tanganyika* was first used for the territory in 1920. It meant "mixing place" and was derived from Lake Tanganyika, a body of water about 400 miles (650 km) in length on the border with the Belgian Congo (Zaïre).

The British repatriated all German settlers from Tanganyika and set about repairing the damage done during fighting in World War I. The British ran a benevolent regime developing Tanganyika's economy and gradually bringing the country toward self-government. Tanganyika became independent in 1961 and a republic the next year. In 1964 Tanganyika united with Zanzibar to form the United Republic of Tanganyika and Zanzibar (later renamed Tanzania). Dar es Salaam, the capital, means "Harbor of Peace."

Flag of Tanganyika

Readings: Kurtz, 1978; *New Encyclopædia Britannica*, 1991.

UNITED REPUBLIC OF TANGANYIKA AND ZANZIBAR

When a flute plays in Zanzibar all of Africa east of the Lakes must dance.
— Arab proverb.

Area: 364,881 sq. miles (945,037 sq. km); Capital: Dar es Salaam
Population: 9,700,000 (est. 1962)

Tanganyika became independent in 1961 and Zanzibar in 1963. On April 26, 1964, the two countries merged to form the United Republic of Tanganyika and Zanzibar. The republic was renamed Tanzania on October 29, 1964.

Readings: Kurtz, 1978; *New Encyclopædia Britannica*, 1991.

ZANZIBAR / PEOPLE'S REPUBLIC OF ZANZIBAR

I am surprised at the combined folly and brutality of civilized husbands, who anxious to be widowers, poison, cut the throats, or smash the skulls of their better halves. The thing can be done as neatly and quietly, safely and respectably effected by a few months of African air at Zanzibar.
— Sir Richard Burton, 1857.

Area: 1,044 sq. miles (2,704 sq. km); Capital: Zanzibar
Population: 354,360 (est. 1967)

The Sultanate of Zanzibar consisted of the coral islands of Zanzibar and Pemba off the east African coast. Pemba was the world's major producer of cloves. Zanzibar's history was shaped by its proximity to the African mainland — 22½ miles (36 km) away — and the annual monsoon winds. The first made Zanzibar the natural starting point for explorers, missionaries, traders and slavers; the second put the island on the major trade routes to India and Arabia making it the entrepôt for all of East Africa.

Vasco da Gama, the Portuguese navigator, came ashore in 1498, and his countrymen remained in Zanzibar for about two hundred years, until displaced by Arabs from Oman. By 1830 Zanzibar had its own resident sultan and controlled a large area of the African mainland. The British, in order to keep out the French and Germans and to end the slave trade, established a protectorate in 1890. Zanzibar had internal autonomy, the British being responsible for foreign affairs. Over time the British assumed more and more authority, reducing the sultan to a figurehead.

Zanzibar became independent in 1963. A month later, in a bloody revolt, the sultan was overthrown and the People's Republic of Zanzibar was created. Zanzibar united with Tanganyika in 1964 to form the United Republic of Tanganyika and Zanzibar (renamed Tanzania).

Zanzibar was the site of the Anglo-Zanzibari War, the shortest war in history. It lasted for 38 minutes on the morning of August 27, 1896. Unhappy with a self-appointed sultan, Sa'id Khalid, the British bombarded him into submission. As a token of gratitude the new sultan, Hamud ibn Muhammad, awarded Rear-Admiral Harry Rawson, commander of the British battle squadron, the Brilliant Star of Zanzibar (first class).

Sultan Khalifa bin Harub

Readings: Kurtz, 1978; *New Encyclopædia Britannica*, 1991.

CHAPTER 14

Southern Africa

There is one feature of the high veld which has not had the attention it deserves — I mean the wind — and with the wind go all manner of tin cans, trundling from one skyline to another with a most purposeful determination. Somewhere . . . there must be a Land of Tin Cans, where in some sheltered valley all the *debris* of the veld has come to anchor.
— John Buchan, 1903.

BASUTOLAND

Basutoland is the Switzerland of South Africa, and very appropriately, is the part of South Africa where the old inhabitants, defended by their hills, have retained the largest measure of freedom.
— James Bryce, 1897.

Area: 11,716 sq. miles (30,340 sq. km); Capital: Maseru
Population: 976,000 (est. 1966)

A small mountainous country, surrounded entirely by South Africa, named after its principal ethnic group, the Basuto (or Sotho). From the middle of the 19th century the Basutos were in constant conflict with the Boers of the Orange Free State over land and cattle. At the request of its king, Basutoland became a native state under British protection in 1843. When the British abandoned the protectorate in 1854 trouble with the Boers continued. War broke out in 1858 and 1865-1868. The

Basutos won the first but lost the second. In 1868 Basutoland was again placed under British protection but in 1871, without consulting the Basutos, the country was handed over to the Cape Colony. Basuto traditions were ignored and when an attempt was made to disarm the warriors, rebellion was the result. The turmoil was more than the Cape Colony could handle and in 1884 Basutoland came under British rule for the third time, as a crown colony. Wisely, the British respected Basuto customs and traditional rulers.

South Africa, after its formation in 1910, wanted to annex Basutoland, but the Basutos were strongly opposed to annexation, as well as South Africa's racial policies. Even though Basutoland preserved its national identity, becoming independent as the Kingdom of Lesotho in 1966, it became completely integrated into the South African economy.

Herd boy and Queen Elizabeth II

Readings: Haliburton, 1977; *Standard Encyclopedia of Southern Africa*, 1971.

BECHUANALAND

We travelled over hundreds of miles of dreary wilderness, not a soul appearing in sight.
— David Livingstone, 1841.

Area: 222,000 sq. miles (712,250 sq. km); Capital: Mafeking
Population: 543,105 (est. 1964)

A landlocked country, dominated by the Kalahari Desert, bordered by South Africa, South-West Africa (Namibia) and Rhodesia (Zimbabwe). Threatened by Boer expansion the Tswana, the country's largest ethnic group, asked Great Britain for protection in 1885. Bechuanaland was included in the British South Africa Company's sphere of influence but never administered by them. The British wanted to transfer Bechuanaland to the Company but a delegation of chiefs, accompanied by missionaries, traveled to London to plead for their country's continued protection. This was granted and over the next decade the borders of the Bechuanaland Protectorate were expanded northward.

In the 20th century South Africa wanted to annex Bechuanaland but the introduction of apartheid in that country made annexation unacceptable. Until 1961 Bechuanaland was administered by a resident commissioner, under the direction of the British High Commissioner in South Africa, and advised by a council of chiefs. After that date there was a steady progression toward independence, which was achieved as the Republic of Botswana in 1966.

Bechuanaland was the only country in the world to have its capital located in another country. Mafeking, which was Bechuanaland's seat of government, was situated on South African soil.

Queen Elizabeth II and golden oriole

Readings: *Standard Encyclopedia of Southern Africa*, 1971; Stevens, 1975.

BOPHUTHATSWANA

I don't know if you have ever unrolled a map of Bophuta-Tswana? Even cartographically that independent State shows signs of mental strain. It looks less like a country than it does like a colony of bacilli under the microscope: a cluster of disconnected blobs of assorted sizes.
— Conor Cruise O'Brien, 1979.

Area: 16,988 sq. miles (44,000 sq. km); Capital: Mmabatho
Population: 1,740,600 (est. 1991)

Seven widely separated parcels of land in Transvaal, Cape Province and the Orange Free State. Bophuthatswana, "that which binds the

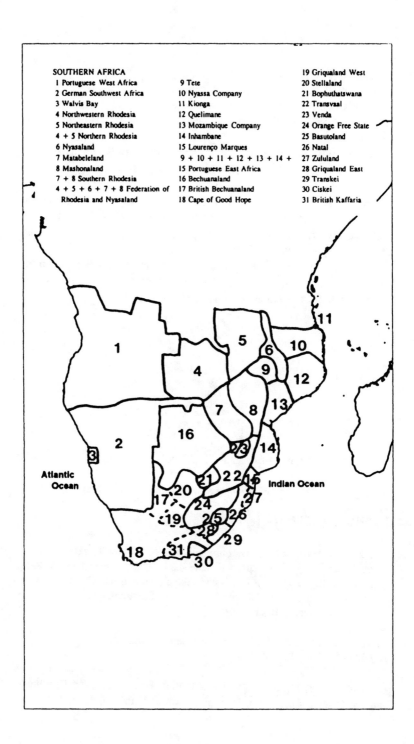

SOUTHERN AFRICA
1 Portuguese West Africa
2 German Southwest Africa
3 Walvis Bay
4 Northwestern Rhodesia
5 Northeastern Rhodesia
4 + 5 Northern Rhodesia
6 Nyasaland
7 Matabeleland
8 Mashonaland
7 + 8 Southern Rhodesia
4 + 5 + 6 + 7 + 8 Federation of
   Rhodesia and Nyasaland

9 Tete
10 Nyassa Company
11 Kionga
12 Quelimane
13 Mozambique Company
14 Inhambane
15 Lourenço Marques
9 + 10 + 11 + 12 + 13 + 14 +
15 Portuguese East Africa
16 Bechuanaland
17 British Bechuanaland
18 Cape of Good Hope

19 Griqualand West
20 Stellaland
21 Bophuthatswana
22 Transvaal
23 Venda
24 Orange Free State
25 Basutoland
26 Natal
27 Zululand
28 Griqualand East
29 Transkei
30 Ciskei
31 British Kaffaria

Atlantic
Ocean

Indian Ocean

Tswana," was a homeland, or Bantustan, set up for the Tswana people by the government of South Africa. The homeland was granted self-government in 1972 and independence in 1977. Only South Africa recognized Bophuthatswana's independence. The one million Tswana living outside of the homeland, in South Africa, became citizens of Bophuthatswana whether they wanted to or not. Although Bophuthatswana produced 30 percent of the world's supply of platinum and had rich deposits of chromium, manganese and vanadium it was highly dependent upon South Africa. The country was reintegrated with South Africa in 1994.

Brickworks

Readings: *New Encyclopædia Britannica*, 1991; Saunders, 1983.

BRITISH BECHUANALAND

[The heat was so intense that] the very flies sought the shade and the enormous centipedes coming out by mistake from their holes were roasted to death on the burning sand.
— David Livingstone, 1841.

Area: 51,424 sq. miles (133,000 sq. km); Capital: Mafeking
Population: 84,219 (est. 1904)

A territory located south of the Bechuanaland Protectorate. Though the London Missionary Society had established a station in what was to become British Bechuanaland in 1818 it was the Boers from Transvaal who had designs on the country. This upset both the indigenous population and the British in the Cape Colony to the south. The British, who were worried about Boer expansion, had little interest in the territory for its own sake. In order to stop the Boers the area south of the Molopo River was declared to be a crown colony in 1885. British

Bechuanaland lasted until 1895 when it was merged with the Cape Colony.

Readings: *Standard Encyclopedia of Southern Africa*, 1971; Stevens, 1975.

BRITISH CHINDE / BRITISH CONCESSION

> At Chinde, I remember, there seemed nothing but sand. I remember nothing else save a harmonium and hymns at the boarding-house, which disturbed me when I wanted to sleep, and a cheery English Consul, who invited me to the Consulate and took me out in his boat to the tug.
> — Charlotte Mansfield, 1911.

Area: 25 acres; Capital: Chinde; Population: 2,790 (est. 1907)

Chinde was a town in Portuguese East Africa (Mozambique), on the only navigable outlet of the Zambezi River. It became the main port for the Zambezi valley and the landlocked British territories of Nyasaland (Malawi) and Northern Rhodesia (Zambia). The British leased a five-acre tract of land (later increased to twenty-five acres) in 1891. This enclave was used as a duty-free zone for goods in transit to or from the British possessions in the interior. The town declined after 1907, with the development of port and rail facilities at Beira. Chinde was nearly destroyed by a cyclone in 1922.

Readings: Mansfield, 1911; *Standard Encyclopedia of Southern Africa*, 1971.

BRITISH KAFFARIA / KAFFARIA

> There have never been any traditions of violence, still less of crime in South Africa, except as against the natives.
> — James Bryce, 1897.

Area: 2,000 sq. miles (5,000 sq. km); Capital: King William's Town
Population: 59,000 (est. 1859)

A territory annexed by the British in 1847 as a result of a war between white settlers and the Xhosa people. Kaffaria was ruled by a high commissioner until 1860 when it became a separate colony. That status lasted until 1866 when Kaffaria was transferred to the Cape

Colony. The name Kaffaria comes from *kaffir*, a term for blacks in South Africa now seen as pejorative.

Readings: Saunders, 1983; *Standard Encyclopedia of Southern Africa*, 1971.

CAPE OF GOOD HOPE (Kaap die Goeie Hoop) / CAPE COLONY

> It is apt to be forgotten that the Cape was not occupied with a view to the establishment of a European colony in our present sense of the word. The Dutch took it that they might plant a cabbage-garden: the English took it that they might have a naval station and half-way house to India.
> — James Bryce, 1897.

Area: 247,637 sq. miles (641,377 sq. km); Capital: Cape Town
Population: 2,564,965 (est. 1911)

The Cape of Good Hope is a rocky promontory at the southern tip of Africa. It was discovered by the Portuguese in 1488 and named by them, in anticipation of the riches they hoped to acquire in the Orient. Subsequently, the Cape of Good Hope was the name given to a self-governing British colony and the largest province of South Africa.

The Dutch began settling the Cape in 1652 and soon spread to the east and north. Recognizing its strategic importance on the sea route to India, the British occupied the Cape between 1795 and 1803. After briefly being restored to the Dutch, the British returned in 1806 and the Cape of Good Hope was formally ceded to them in 1814. Large-scale British settlement began in 1820 and the language of schooling, commerce and administration rapidly changed from Dutch to English. Many of the Boers (Afrikaners), descendants of Dutch farmers, were unwilling to live under British rule. They began their Great Trek into the interior in 1836, where they established their own free republics. The Cape of Good Hope achieved representative government in 1853, and became self-governing in 1872.

For most of the 19th century the eastern frontier of the Cape was the scene of fierce African resistance. The last area was not pacified and annexed until 1895.

During the Boer War (1899-1902) Afrikaners from the Cape joined those of the Orange Free State and Transvaal in an unsuccessful attempt to force the British out of South Africa. The Cape of Good Hope joined Natal, the Orange Free State and Transvaal in 1910 to form the Union of South Africa. Since 1961 the Cape of Good Hope has been a province of the Republic of South Africa.

King Edward VII

Readings: Saunders, 1983; *Standard Encyclopedia of Southern Africa*, 1971.

CISKEI (Xhosa-Ciskei)

Pictorially the Ciskei was grand; agriculturally it was a tragedy.
— H.V. Morton, 1948.

Area: 3,475 sq. miles (9,000 sq. km); Capital: Bisho
Population: 847,000 (est. 1991)

Located in the eastern part of South Africa's Cape Province. Ciskei, "this side of the Kei River," was annexed by the Cape Colony in the late 19th century. It became an administrative territory in 1961, self-governing in 1972 and was declared by South Africa to be an independent republic for Xhosa-speaking people in 1981. Although Ciskei's independence was not generally recognized, at least 1,500,000 people living outside the republic, in South Africa, were given Ciskeian citizenship. The bantustan was reintegrated into South Africa in 1994. Throughout its existence Ciskei was poverty-stricken and totally dependent upon South Africa. About two-thirds of Ciskei's income was provided by migrant workers.

Folklore: The five heads

Readings: Morton, 1948; *New Encyclopædia Britannica*, 1991.

GERMAN SOUTH-WEST AFRICA (Deutsch Südwestafrika) /
SOUTH-WEST AFRICA (Suidwes-Afrika)

There are only five miles of paved road in all South-West Africa. And
Windhoek has all of them.
— Negley Farson, 1940.

Area: 318,261 sq. miles (824,292 sq. km); Capital: Windhoek
Population: 1,288,000 (est. 1988)

Although the Portuguese sailed along the coast of South-West Africa
in 1487, the place was basically forgotten by Europeans until the arrival
of German missionaries in 1805. The British considered the country to
be in their sphere of influence but, aside from their occupation of
Walvis Bay, did little to confirm possession. German South-West
Africa became a political entity in 1884, after boundary agreements
with Great Britain and Portugal gave Germany a free hand to establish
a colony. A narrow geographical oddity known as the Caprivi Strip,
about 300 miles (480 km) long and 20 miles (32 km) wide, was ceded
by Great Britain in 1890 to provide a link via the Zambezi River to
German East Africa (Tanganyika). Unfortunately, no one seemed to
notice the massive Victoria Falls that made the Zambezi unnavigable.
   Fierce African resistance to the Germans culminated in the Herero
War (1904-1907). As many as 100,000 Africans perished and the
Germans were forced to keep an army of 20,000 in the field. In World
War I German South-West Africa was invaded by South Africa and
German military forces surrendered in 1915. The territory, renamed
South-West Africa, was under South African military administration
until 1921, at which time it was awarded to South Africa under a
League of Nations mandate. After World War II the United Nations
refused to sanction South Africa's presence in the territory. South
Africa defied the United Nations and continued to occupy South-West
Africa. The United Nations began using the term *Namibia* for the
territory in 1968 and most of the world followed suit. Beginning in
1966 a twenty-year guerrilla war was fought against South Africa. The
country became the Republic of Namibia in 1990.

Lion

Readings: Rosenthal, 1964; *Standard Encyclopedia of Southern Africa*, 1971.

GOSHEN (Het Land Goosen)

The frontier Dutchman prefers the Old to the New Testament. He is at home among the wars of the Israelites and the doomed inhabitants of the Promised Land.
— John Mackenzie, 1871.

Area: 4,000 sq. miles (10,000 sq. km); Capital: Rooigrond

Goshen was a republic, centered around 140 farms, established by Boers from Transvaal in 1882. The land was ceded to Boer mercenaries by a Bechuana chief as a reward for their help in an intertribal war. The name derives from the Biblical "Land of Goshen," a place of refuge. The British did not recognize the existence of the Republic of Goshen and dispatched an expeditionary force to end it in 1885. Goshen then became part of British Bechuanaland and later, the Cape Colony

Readings: Rosenthal, 1964; *Standard Encyclopedia of Southern Africa*, 1971.

GRIQUALAND EAST

Fortunate is it for the inhabitants of that remote region that it is under British rule, as neither native nor Dutch chieftains could keep order among the lawless multitudes who are now flocking there.
— Thomas Morgan Thomas, 1872.

Area: 7,594 sq. miles (19,668 sq, km); Capital: Kokstad
Population: 40,000 (est. 1878)

In South Africa, south of Basutoland (Lesotho) and west of Natal.

Beginning in the 1840s groups of Griqua, a people of mixed race, were displaced from their home in the Orange Free State by the Boers. In an epic trek, 1861-1863, the Griqua migrated to a depopulated area known as No Man's Land and organized themselves as a republic. The Griquas, who had been semi-nomads, with the help of missionaries, became farmers and small traders. But in the face of continued Boer land-hunger, the Griqua, though they resisted, were soon forced from their new homes. Disturbances caused the Cape Colony to annex Griqualand East in 1874. With the introduction of apartheid in South Africa the Griqua were classed as a subgroup within the Coloureds.

Readings: Rosenthal, 1964; *Standard Encyclopedia of Southern Africa*, 1971.

GRIQUALAND WEST

> I must add also that a visitor to Kimberley should, if possible, take an opportunity of looking down upon the mine by moonlight. It is a weird and wonderful sight, and may almost be called sublime in its peculiar strangeness.
> — Anthony Trollope, 1878.

Area: 15,197 sq. miles (39,000 sq. km); Capital: Kimberley
Population: 83,375 (est. 1891)

Located in South Africa, between the Orange River and Bechuanaland (Botswana). The Griquas were a people of mixed African-European origin who, in response to discrimination, migrated from the Cape Colony about 1800. They were originally proud to call themselves "The Bastards" but missionaries in 1813 convinced them to rename themselves after a former leader. Encouraged by missionaries the settlements along the Orange River became the Republic of Griqualand West. The discovery of the Kimberley diamond field in 1867 was the beginning of the end for Griqualand West. The republic became British territory in 1871 and a crown colony in 1873. In 1879 Griqualand West was merged with the Cape Colony.

Readings: Rosenthal, 1964; *Standard Encyclopedia of Southern Africa*, 1971.

INHAMBANE

> The soldiers are picked out of those who misbehave themselves at
> Mozambique; and as the garrison of that place consists of the refuse of
> the convict regiments at Goa, who are sent to Mozambique as a further
> punishment, it may be imagined what a thorough set of scoundrels the
> Inhambane company are.
> — Lyons McLeod, 1860.

Area: 21,000 sq. miles (54,390 sq. km); Capital: Inhambane
Population: 308,000 (est. 1940)

Inhambane was a town and district in Portuguese East Africa
(Mozambique). The Portuguese arrived in Inhambane in the person of
Vasco da Gama at the end of the 15th century. Founded in the 16th
century, the town became a major center for the export of ivory, and
slaves to Brazil. The Portuguese hold on Inhambane was often tenuous.
They were driven out and massacred by the Zulus in 1834. The
Portuguese returned, however and stayed until the independence of
Mozambique in 1975. Inhambane is now a province of Mozambique.

Ceres

Readings: *Encyclopædia Britannica*, 1926; *Standard Encyclopedia of Southern
Africa*, 1971.

KIONGA (Quionga)

Area: 245 sq. miles (635 sq. km); Capital: Kionga
Population: 2,456 (est. 1990)

Kionga was a village on the Indian Ocean near the southern bank of
the Ruvuma River. In 1886 Germany and Portugal agreed that
everything north of the river would be German East Africa

(Tanganyika) and everything to the south would be Portuguese East Africa (Mozambique). However in 1892 the Germans announced that the boundary was at Cape Delgado, 20 miles (32 km) south of the Ruvuma's mouth. The German navy captured the village in 1894 and soldiers occupied the hinterland, known as the Kionga Triangle. In 1916, during World War I, Portuguese troops seized the disputed area. Kionga was awarded to Portugal "as the original and rightful owner" by the Treaty of Versailles in 1919 and absorbed into Portuguese East Africa. Kionga was Portugal's only territorial acquisition from World War I.

Reading: *New Encyclopædia Britannica*, 1991.

KLEIN VRYSTAAT (Little Free State)

In their prayers the language of the heroes of the Old Testament is freely appropriated: they are God's people, and their enemies are His enemies.
— John Mackenzie, 1871.

Area: 50 sq. miles (129 sq. km); Population: 72 (est. 1891)

A minuscule Boer republic that came into being in 1886, on territory granted to two hunters by the paramount chief of Swaziland in 1877. The independent Republic of Klein Vrystaat was governed by a triumvirate and incorporated into South Africa in 1891.

Readings: Rosenthal, 1964; *Standard Encyclopedia of Southern Africa*, 1971.

KLIP RIVER REPUBLIC (Kliprivier)

Dutchmen will tell you that in a certain engagement the "heathen" loss was so many, and there were so many Christians *murdered*.
— John Mackenzie, 1871.

Area: 5,000 sq. miles (13,000 sq. km); Capital: Utrecht

An independent Boer republic founded in 1846 in the north of Natal, South Africa. Klip River joined Transvaal in 1860 and was transferred to Natal in 1902.

Readings: Rosenthal, 1964; *Standard Encyclopedia of Southern Africa*, 1971.

LOURENÇO MARQUES

Steaming slowly in the stupendous Delgoa Bay; its dim arms stretching far away and disappearing on both sides. It could furnish plenty of room for all the ships in the world, but it is shoal.
— Mark Twain, 1897.

Area: 28,800 sq. miles (74,600 sq. km); Capital: Lourenço Marques
Population: 474,000 (est. 1940)

Located in the extreme south of Portuguese East Africa (Mozambique), on Delgoa Bay. Lourenço Marques was named after the Portuguese trader who explored Delgoa Bay in 1544, and the colony developed around a fort the Portuguese constructed in 1787. Lourenço Marques replaced the town of Moçambique as the capital of Portuguese East Africa in 1907. Its pleasant climate and fine beaches made it a popular resort for white South Africans and Rhodesians, before the independence of Mozambique in 1975. Beginning in the late 19th century Lourenço Marques became an important transshipment point. Roads and railways linked it with South Africa, Rhodesia (Zimbabwe) and Swaziland. The name was changed to Maputo in 1976. Lourenço Marques was considered by many to be the most beautiful city in eastern Africa.

Ceres

Readings: *Encyclopædia Britannica*, 1926; Twain, 1897.

LYDENBURG REPUBLIC (Republiek Lijdenburg in Zuid-Afrika)

All the hedges are of sweet-briar, and there are many very well-stocked gardens. Altogether it is a pretty little town, and strikes a traveller as

very homely and cheerful after the miles of wild solitude he has passed
through to reach it.
— E.F. Sandeman, 1880.

Area: 3,491 sq. miles (9,042 sq. km); Capital: Lydenburg

A Boer republic in eastern Transvaal. Lydenburg was established in
1846 and after briefly uniting with the Republic of Zoutpansberg
merged with Transvaal in 1860.

Readings: Sandeman, 1880; *Standard Encyclopedia of Southern Africa*, 1971.

MASHONALAND

The rifle and the hoe went in together.
— Isaac F. Marcosson, 1921.

Area: 75,000 sq. miles (195,000 sq. km); Capital: Salisbury
Population: 370,000 (est. 1900)

Mashonaland was the name given by Europeans, in the 19th century,
to the eastern portion of Southern Rhodesia (Zimbabwe) inhabited
principally by the Shona people. The British South Africa Company
arrived in Mashonaland in 1890 and encouraged settlement by European
farmers. After Rhodesia was formally organized in 1895 Mashonaland
became the eastern province. The Shona's unsuccessful rebellion
against the Company's rule (1896-1897) marked the end of Shona
independence.

Readings: Grotpeter, 1979; Marcosson, 1921.

MATABELELAND

It is well to protect the aborigine; but when he is armed with a dozen
assegais and earnestly desires your blood it is safer to shoot him or
drive him further afield.
— John Buchan, 1903.

Area: 75,000 sq. miles (195,000 sq. km); Capital: Bulawayo
Population: c. 100,000 (est. 1890)

Matabeleland was the country of the Matabele (Ndebele) people in western Southern Rhodesia (Zimbabwe). From a base in Mashonaland, to the east, the British South Africa Company invaded Matabeleland in 1893. Briefly the territory had a separate political identity. After Southern Rhodesia was formally created in 1895 Matabeleland became the western province. The Matabele's rebellion in 1896 ended in defeat and ended their independence.

Pioneer in Matabeleland

Readings: Rasmussen, 1979; *Standard Encyclopedia of Southern Africa*, 1971.

MOZAMBIQUE COMPANY (Companhia de Moçambique)

And *Sofala* thought Ophir.
— John Milton, 1667.

Area: 52,056 sq. miles (135,000 sq. km); Capital: Beira
Population: 368,447 (est. 1939)

The Mozambique Company, backed mostly by British capital, administered the Manica and Sofala region of Portuguese East Africa (Mozambique), under a royal charter. The Company was granted full sovereign rights to govern, develop and exploit its territory for fifty years, from 1891. When the Mozambique Company's charter expired its territory reverted to direct Portuguese rule in 1942.

Sofala, a port on the Indian Ocean, was visited by the Portuguese in 1500 and at one time was the most important town in east Africa. The first governors of Portuguese East Africa were titled captains-general of Sofala. It was believed that Sofala was the Biblical Ophir, home of the Queen of Sheba, and the place from where King Solomon obtained sandlewood, ivory, apes, peacocks and gold. Sofala went into steep decline after the Mozambique Company developed rail and port facilities at nearby Beira.

Giraffe

Readings: *Encyclopædia Britannica*, 1926; *Standard Encyclopedia of Southern Africa*, 1971.

NATAL

> I should distrust Durban as, if I were a man, I should distrust a woman who was so beautiful that she cast a spell over my senses and drained my manhood.
> — Gertrude Page, 1910.

Area: 35,284 sq. miles (91,385 sq. km); Capital: Pietermaritzburg
Population: 1,200,386 (est. 1908)

On the southeastern coast of South Africa. The location of present-day Durban, the principal city of Natal was sighted by the Portuguese navigator Vasco da Gama on Christmas Day 1497 and named Terra Natalis as a result. After 1824, when the British began settling Natal, the colonists had to contest the land with the powerful Zulu Kingdom and encroaching Boers from the Cape of Good Hope. When Natalia, a Boer republic, was set up in part of Natal the British refused to accept it. The British annexed Natal in 1843. The next year, when it was transferred to the Cape of Good Hope, many of the Boers trekked into the interior to escape British rule. Natal became a separate colony in 1856 and was given responsible government in 1893. Natal was the scene of the Zulu War in 1879. After the British defeated the Zulu their land was annexed in 1887 and added to Natal in 1897. During the Boer War (1899-1902) Natal was the scene of major military operations and guerrilla raids. In 1910 Natal became part of the Union of South

Africa. Since 1961 it has been a province of the Republic of South Africa.

Queen Victoria

Readings: Rosenthal, 1964; *Standard Encyclopedia of Southern Africa*, 1971.

NATALIA (Republiek Natalia)

> The little town is so well planted with trees, and has so many gardens both in it and around, that the view from the hill, driving down towards it, quite unprepares a stranger for the well-built continuous streets he may presently drive through, and makes the town look far smaller than it actually is.
> — E.F. Sandeman, 1880.

Area: 15,000 sq. miles (39,000 sq. km); Capital: Pietermaritzburg

Natalia comprised a large part of present-day Natal and the Orange Free State. The Republic of Natalia, with its own flag and elected assembly, was founded in 1836, the first independent Boer republic in South Africa. Warfare with the Zulus and the British marked its short history. When the Boers were defeated in 1842 Natalia was incorporated into Natal in 1843.

City hall, Pietermaritzburg

Readings: Saunders, 1983; *Standard Encyclopedia of Southern Africa*, 1971.

NEW REPUBLIC (Nieuwe Republiek)

And no one who has freely and for years mingled with this people can doubt that they have persuaded themselves by some wonderful mental process that they are God's chosen people, and that the blacks are the wicked and condemned Canaanites over whose heads the Divine anger lowers continually.
— John Mackenzie, 1871.

Area: 4,700 sq. miles (12,000 sq. km); Capital: Vryheid

In 1884 land was awarded in Natal to Boer freebooters from Transvaal who had helped the winning side in a war between different Zulu groups. The New Republic was proclaimed and for a time it exercised a protectorate over Zululand. The British recognized the independence of the New Republic and excluded it when they annexed Zululand in 1887. The New Republic merged with Transvaal in 1888.

Readings: Saunders, 1983; *Standard Encyclopedia of Southern Africa*, 1971.

NORTHEASTERN RHODESIA

When I saw the henna-plastered heads of North-Eastern Rhodesia, I thought, after all women are strangely alike.
— Charlotte Mansfield, 1911.

Area: 100,000 sq. miles (259,000 sq. km); Capital: Fort Jameson
Population: 346,000 (est. 1900)

A British protectorate, created in 1900, in the eastern portion of what is now Zambia. Governed by the British South Africa Company, Northeastern Rhodesia was merged with Northwestern Rhodesia in 1911 to create the Protectorate of Northern Rhodesia.

Readings: Grotpeter, 1979; Mansfield, 1911.

NORTHWESTERN RHODESIA / BAROTSELAND

They wore flat, round plaques at their necks, special tribal charms, the
kind of jewellery which since my return has come into fashion — dear,
dear! to think that in such matters North-Western Rhodesia should lead
the way.
— Charlotte Mansfield, 1911.

Area: 182,000 sq. miles (471,000 sq. km); Capital: Livingstone
Population: 400,000 (est. 1900)

Barotseland occupied the western portion of what is now Zambia.
The name was derived from the Barotse (or Lotzi), the paramount,
although far from the most numerous, tribe in the region. Aside from
a few hunters, explorers and missionaries (most notably, David
Livingstone), the first Europeans to reach Barotseland were the
emissaries of the British South Africa Company in 1890. Treaties were
signed, orders-in-council issued, and in 1899 Barotseland was reborn
as the Company-administered protectorate of Northwestern Rhodesia.
Northwestern and Northeastern Rhodesia were amalgamated in 1911 to
form Northern Rhodesia. The British South Africa Company continued
its role of administration until 1924.

Readings: Grotpeter, 1979; Mansfield, 1911.

NORTHERN RHODESIA

Northern Rhodesia, which lives mostly on copper, is like a Texas
millionaire — somewhat dull and perhaps uncouth, but rich.
— John Gunther, 1955.

Area: 290,323 sq. miles (752,000 sq. km); Capital: Lusaka
Population: 3,545,000 (est. 1964)

The protectorates of Northwestern and Northeastern Rhodesia were
merged in 1911 to form Northern Rhodesia. The new protectorate was
administered by the British South Africa Company until 1924. After
1900 railways were built and rich mines, mostly copper, were
developed. Large numbers of white settlers came to Northern Rhodesia
and the protectorate became prosperous, by African standards. In 1953
Northern Rhodesia, along with Southern Rhodesia (Zimbabwe) and

Nyasaland (Malawi), formed the Federation of Rhodesia and Nyasaland. Such a union had long been advocated by whites but it was strongly opposed by most Africans. Northern Rhodesia withdrew from the Federation in 1963 and became independent in 1964 as the Republic of Zambia.

Queen Elizabeth II, Cecil Rhodes and Victoria Falls

Readings: Grotpeter, 1979; *Standard Encyclopedia of Southern Africa*, 1971.

NYASALAND / NYASALAND DISTRICTS PROTECTORATE / BRITISH CENTRAL AFRICA

What did we Africans do to deserve such a poor place to live?
— Paul Theroux, 1971.

Area: 36,686 sq. miles (95,000 sq. km); Capital: Zomba
Population: 2,980,000 (est. 1962)

A narrow landlocked country on the western shore of Lake Nyasa. It was known as the Nyasaland Districts Protectorate from 1891 to 1893, British Central Africa from 1893 to 1907, and Nyasaland from 1907 to 1964. Between 1953 and 1963 Nyasaland was part of the Federation of Rhodesia and Nyasaland.

Missionaries, such as David Livingstone, paved the way for British occupation of the Nyasaland highlands in the 1880s. Although slavery was abolished, and roads, railways and plantations were created,

Nyasaland was never a prosperous colony. The administration was run by and for the benefit of a small class of white plantation owners. Low pay and harsh working conditions among African laborers sparked a serious uprising in 1915. From World War II the country felt the effects of African nationalism. The British adopted a policy of self-determination and Nyasaland became independent as the Republic of Malawi in 1964.

Boatman on Lake Nyassa

Readings: Rosenthal, 1964; *Standard Encyclopedia of Southern Africa*, 1971.

NYASSA COMPANY (Companhia do Nyassa)

> . . . the healthy shores of Lake Nyassa . . .
> — David Livingstone, 1865.

Area: 73,292 sq. miles (190,000 sq. km); Capital: Porto Amelia
Population: 1,914,000 (est. 1940)

By royal charter in 1894 the Nyassa Company, financed mostly by foreign capital, was granted sovereign rights to govern and develop the northern portion of Portuguese East Africa (Mozambique) from the Indian Ocean to Lake Nyasa. The level of development was a disappointment and when its charter expired in 1929 the Nyassa Company's territory became the districts of Cabo Delgado and Nyassa in Portuguese East Africa.

King Carlos of Portugal
and giraffe

Readings: Rosenthal, 1964; *Standard Encyclopedia of Southern Africa*, 1971.

ORANGE FREE STATE (Oranje-Vrystaat) / ORANGE RIVER SOVEREIGNTY / ORANGE RIVER COLONY

[Bloemfontein]: As it is one of the smallest, so it is one of the neatest, and, in a modest way, best appointed capitals in the world. . . . It looks, and one is told it is, the most idyllic community in Africa. — James Bryce, 1897.

Area: 49,418 sq. miles (127,993 sq. km); Capital: Bloemfontein
Population: 528,174 (est. 1911)

In east-central South Africa between the Orange and Vaal Rivers. Settled originally by Bantu, the area came under the increasing influence of the Boers (Afrikaners), descendants of Dutch farmers in the Cape of Good Hope. Beginning in 1836 Boers migrated to the Orange Free State to escape British domination in the Cape Colony. The British annexed the country between the Orange and Vaal Rivers in 1848 calling it the Orange River Sovereignty. By 1854 the British withdrew and recognized Boer independence in the Orange Free State. The state endured until the Boer War (1899-1902) when, at enormous cost to the British, the Boers were defeated. The Orange Free State, which was the scene of major battles in the war, was officially annexed by the British as the Orange River Colony in 1900. The crown colony lasted until 1907 when self-government was reintroduced. In 1910 the Orange Free State became part of the Union of South Africa. Since 1961 it has been a province of the Republic of South Africa.

Orange tree

Readings: Saunders, 1983; *Standard Encyclopedia of Southern Africa*, 1971.

PORTUGUESE EAST AFRICA (Provincia de Moçambique)

> Mozambique is a curious mixture — Shangri La with a bullwhip behind
> the door.
> — John Gunther, 1955.

Area: 308,642 sq. miles (799,380 sq. km); Capital: Lourenço Marques
Population: 9,680,000 (est. 1977)

On the Indian Ocean, bordered by South Africa, Rhodesia
(Zimbabwe), Nyasaland (Malawi) and Tanganyika (Tanzania). Vasco
da Gama visited the coast of Mozambique in 1498 and the Portuguese
began an occupation that would last nearly five centuries. At first
Mozambique was seen merely as a way station to India. Until 1752 it
was a dependency of Goa. Gradually the Portuguese spread their
influence along the coast of Mozambique and up the Zambezi River in
search of gold, ivory and slaves. On a map the Portuguese territory
seemed large, but effective control was restricted to a small area. In the
19th century most of Portuguese East Africa was in the hands of
African tribes and renegade settlers who threatened to make the country
independent. Pacification of the interior was begun in earnest in the
1890s and was not completed until 1912.

About half of Portuguese East Africa was administered by
concessionary companies, with full sovereign rights to develop and
exploit their holdings. It was not until 1942 that all of Mozambique
came under direct Portuguese rule. In the 20th century railways, roads
and ports were constructed as Portuguese East Africa became the major
transit point for South Africa and Rhodesia, as well as a source for

cheap contract labor. Although the territory was designated a Portuguese overseas province in 1951, political development was slow. The African population had virtually no rights or political voice. Legally they were wards of the state. Reforms were made but they were too little and too late. Beginning in 1962 a bloody war of liberation was fought against the Portuguese. Following a coup in Portugal the People's Republic of Mozambique came into being in 1975. Armed factions have kept the country in turmoil since then. Mozambique today is the world's poorest country with a per capita income of about $80.

Spotted triggerfish

Readings: Rosenthal, 1964; *Standard Encyclopedia of Southern Africa*, 1971.

PORTUGUESE WEST AFRICA (Provincia de Angola)

As for the interior of Angola if Eden sent up so quickly such a rush of rank vegetation our progenitor must have found sufficient occupation in dressing it.
— David Livingstone, 1855.

Area: 481,351 sq. miles (1,246,700 sq. km); Capital: Luanda
Population: 5,800,000 (est. 1972)

Bordered by the Belgian Congo (Zaïre), Northern Rhodesia (Zambia), South-West Africa (Namibia) and the Atlantic Ocean. The Portuguese arrived in this part of Africa in 1483 in search of gold, silver and the mythical kingdom of Prester John. They found few precious metals and no mythical kingdom but they did discover the slave trade. An estimated three to four million slaves were exported from Portuguese West Africa to the plantations of Brazil from 1500 onward. Slavery was officially abolished in 1836 but continued much later; compulsory labor was legal until 1962!

Though Luanda was founded in 1576 the Portuguese were slow to occupy the whole country. By 1680 they held only a few coastal enclaves and half a dozen forts in the interior. Two hundred years after that the area of effective Portuguese control was no more than 100 miles (160 km) deep. It was not until the last quarter of the 19th century that Portugal dispatched military expeditions and signed treaties with local rulers to confirm its centuries-old claim to the interior.

Despite their long presence in west Africa there was little permanent Portuguese settlement, other than convicts, before 1900. Missionaries, soldiers and administrators were usually temporary residents. After 1900, especially after World War II, large numbers of poor whites from Portugal were encouraged to settle in Portuguese West Africa. The white population rose from 9,000 in 1900 to 335,000 in 1974, as the Portuguese adopted a policy of tight political and economic control that favored the settlers. Africans, in both Portuguese West and East Africa, were classified as *assimilados* or *indígenas*. *Assimilados* (less than 1 percent of the population) were full Portuguese citizens. Those classified as *indígenas* had virtually no rights at all.

Beginning in 1961, after an uprising in Luanda was brutally put down, a war of liberation was waged against the Portuguese. The Portuguese were forced to maintain an army of 70,000 troops (40 percent African) to control their colony. By 1974 the war was stalemated with the Portuguese in firm control of the east and central regions and the guerrillas the rest. Following a military coup in Portugal in 1974 the People's Democratic Republic of Angola came into being in 1975. The major political factions that fought the Portuguese have continued to fight each other since independence.

Vasco da Gama

Readings: Martin, 1980; *Standard Encyclopedia of Southern Africa*, 1971.

QUELIMANE (Kilmane) / ZAMBEZIA

Quillimane must have been built solely for the sake of carrying on the slave-trade, for no man in his senses would ever have dreamed of placing a village on such a low, muddy, fever-haunted, and mosquito-swarming site, had it not been for the facilities it afforded for slaving.
— David Livingstone, 1865.

Area: 39,800 sq. miles (103,000 sq. km); Capital: Quelimane
Population: 1,006,000 (est. 1940)

Quelimane was a district, with its own governor, in north-central Portuguese East Africa (Mozambique). Visited by Vasco da Gama in 1498 the present town of Quelimane was founded by the Portuguese in 1544. During the 18th and 19th centuries the Portuguese made Quelimane one of the greatest slave markets in east Africa. Until about 1875 most of the Europeans in Quelimane were Portuguese convicts. Today Quelimane is a province of Mozambique.

Readings: Rosenthal, 1964; *Standard Encyclopedia of Southern Africa*, 1971.

FEDERATION OF RHODESIA AND NYASALAND / CENTRAL AFRICAN FEDERATION

[Victoria Falls]: A single glance into the abyss cut my breath with the sheer awe of the sight. "God Almighty!" I breathed in amazement to myself.
— J.H. Morrison, 1919.

Area: 486,722 sq. miles (1,261,000 sq. km); Capital: Salisbury
Population: 9,400,000 (est. 1962)

The federation of the British territories of Southern Rhodesia (Zimbabwe), Northern Rhodesia (Zambia) and Nyasaland (Malawi) was created on August 1, 1953, and dissolved on December 31, 1963. An amalgamation of the two Rhodesias was proposed in 1916 but the white settlers of Southern Rhodesia rejected the idea, believing such a union would delay responsible government. After Southern Rhodesia achieved self-rule in 1923 federation began to be seen as a possible route to dominion status. Discussions concerning federation were held between 1948 and 1953. Nyasaland, the poor cousin in the federation, was only included because of British insistence. The final agreement was ratified by a two-thirds majority in a referendum (whites only) in Southern Rhodesia, and by the legislative councils of Northern Rhodesia and Nyasaland. Most Africans were opposed to the federation but few had an opportunity to express an opinion. The federation was dominated by white Southern Rhodesians from the start. That, and the British policy of African self-determination in Northern Rhodesia and Nyasaland, was the cause of its collapse. The famous Victoria Falls was located in the center of the Federation.

Grave of Cecil Rhodes

Readings: Grotpeter, 1979; Rasmussen, 1979.

SOUTHERN RHODESIA / RHODESIA / RHODESIA-ZIMBABWE

They can't take it away from me, can they? You never heard of a country's name being changed?
— Cecil Rhodes, c. 1896.

Area: 150,820 sq. miles (390,622 sq. km); Capital: Salisbury
Population: 7,500,000 (est. 1980)

In 1889 British administrator and financier Cecil Rhodes received a charter to form the British South Africa Company. Its purpose was to encourage settlement and commerce north to the Zambezi River and beyond. In 1890 a column of pioneers embarked from Bechuanaland reaching the site of Salisbury, the future capital of Rhodesia. The African population resisted the invaders in 1893 and 1896 but were defeated. Their lands were claimed by the Company and were formally organized as Rhodesia in 1895. The territory south of the Zambezi became Southern Rhodesia in 1897.

The country was rich, fertile and had a climate ideal for European settlement. With the extension of a railway from South Africa the number of settlers increased rapidly. From the beginning the colony was run by and for the settlers. In a whites-only referendum, held in 1922, Southern Rhodesia chose self-government over entry into South Africa. Between 1953 and 1963 Southern Rhodesia was the dominant partner in the Federation of Rhodesia and Nyasaland. The white Southern Rhodesians saw the Federation as a route to full dominion status in the Commonwealth. But in the face of growing African nationalism the Federation became unworkable. When Northern Rhodesia became independent as Zambia in 1964 Southern Rhodesia became Rhodesia. The next year the white regime unilaterally declared Rhodesia to be independent. Only South Africa recognized the new state. A guerrilla war erupted in Rhodesia and the United Nations imposed sanctions. The war dragged on until 1979. After many attempts at negotiation a power-sharing formula was finally agreed upon and the country was briefly known as Rhodesia-Zimbabwe. The Republic of Zimbabwe came into being in 1980.

Rhodesia was named after Cecil Rhodes. One of the other names considered was Cecilia.

Seal of the British South Africa Company

Readings: *New Encyclopædia Britannica*, 1991; Rasmussen, 1979.

STELLALAND (Land of the Star)

> Vryburg is an urban community in its infancy, which may some day grow into a large and thriving town. At present it consists of a number of low buildings of somewhat mean and squalid appearance, constructed of the inevitable corrugated iron.
> — Lord Randolph Churchill, 1893.

Area: 5,000 sq. miles (12,750 sq. km); Capital: Vryburg

A short-lived republic established by Transvaal Boer adventurers on the Bechuanaland border. Stellaland, named after a comet visible at the time, was established in 1882 on land ceded to the Boers by a Bechuana chief grateful for help in an intertribal war. Stellaland wanted to unite with Transvaal but the British would not permit it. In a bloodless military action Stellaland was invaded in 1885 and annexed to British Bechuanaland.

Readings: Churchill, 1893; Rosenthal, 1964.

TETE

The number of white inhabitants is small, and rather select, many of them having been considerably sent out from Portugal "for their country's good." The military element preponderates in society; the convict and "incorrigible" class of soldiers, receiving very little pay.
— David Livingstone, 1865.

Area: 46,600 sq. miles (120,700 sq. km); Capital: Tete
Population: 400-450,000 (est. 1940)

Tete was a remote district in the interior of Portuguese East Africa (Mozambique) surrounded on the north, east and west by British territories. The colony stretched along both banks of the Zambezi River and became an important center for gold and ivory. Tete was founded in the 16th century and marked the limit of Portuguese penetration up the Zambezi River, as well as an unsuccessful attempt to link Portuguese East Africa with Portuguese West Africa (Mozambique). Tete fell into decline in the 17th and 18th centuries and was, at times, lost to Portuguese control. The development of the transit trade with Rhodesia (Zimbabwe) and British Central Africa (Malawi) restored Tete's fortunes in the 19th century. Tete is now a province of Mozambique. During that country's war of independence (1962-1975) Tete was one of the most contested areas.

Readings: Livingstone, 1865; *Standard Encyclopedia of Southern Africa*, 1971.

TRANSKEI

The birth of apartheid's first child.
— Anon.

Area: 16,910 sq. miles (43,797 sq. km); Capital: Umtata
Population: 3,458,000 (est. 1991)

Transkei, "the land across the Kei River," was an independent
homeland, or bantustan, for South Africa's Xhosa-speaking people.
Transkei was annexed by Great Britain in 1848 and merged with the
Cape Colony between 1879 and 1894. Comprising three blocks of land
in eastern Cape Province Transkei was granted self-government in 1963
and independence in 1976. All South Africans with language ties to
Transkei — about 1,500,000 — lost their South African citizenship and
became citizens of Transkei. The Republic of Transkei was not
recognized by the international community and throughout its existence
was poor and completely dependent upon South Africa. It was
readmitted into South Africa in 1994.

Preparation of a meal

Readings: *New Encyclopædia Britannica*, 1991; Saunders, 1983.

TRANSVAAL / SOUTH AFRICAN REPUBLIC (Zuid Afrikansche Republiek)

[Johannesburg]: An extended brickfield is the first impression: a
prosperous powder-factory is the last.
— John Buchan, 1903.

Area: 101,351 sq. miles (262,498 sq. km); Capital: Pretoria
Population: 1,269,951 (est. 1904)

Settled earlier by Bantus, Transvaal — the land beyond the Vaal River — was colonized by Boers (Afrikaners) who migrated from the Cape Colony, beginning in the 1830s, to escape what they considered to be oppressive British rule. In its early years the Transvaal Boers overcame determined resistance from the Zulus. The British signed a treaty whereby they recognized the independence of Transvaal in 1853 and the next year the country was renamed the South African Republic. The British annexation of the republic in 1877 caused the Boers to fight. A peace was made in 1881 by which the Transvaal was allowed internal self-government under British suzerainty. By 1884 the Transvaal, again known as the South African Republic, was independent in everything but foreign affairs. When gold was discovered, an influx of people the Boers scornfully referred to as aliens — Uitlanders — increased tension to the breaking point. Transvaal was the principal battleground of the Boer War (1899-1902). The British won the war but at the cost of fielding an army of 500,000. Transvaal was administered as a British crown colony until 1907 when self-government was restored. In 1910 Transvaal joined the Orange Free State, Natal and the Cape of Good Hope to form the Union of South Africa. Transvaal has been a province of the Republic of South Africa since 1961.

Readings: Rosenthal, 1964; *Standard Encyclopedia of Southern Africa*, 1971.

VENDA

The BaVenda were most antagonistic to European settlement, and until 1872 no missionary was allowed to settle among them. Yet even prior to this date, they made use of the white man for their own ends, in spite of their hatred of him.
— Hugh A. Stayt, 1931.

Area: 2,880 sq. miles (7,460 sq. km); Capital: Thohoyandou
Population: 558,797 (est. 1991)

Located in northern Transvaal, just south of Zimbabwe, Venda was created by South Africa to be the homeland, or bantustan, of the Vhavenda (Bavenda) people. It was granted self-government in 1973 and independence in 1979. Only South Africa recognized Venda's independence. At least 200,000 Vhavenda living outside the new state were declared to be Venda citizens. Venda had few natural resources and most of its population worked as migrant laborers in South Africa. Venda was readmitted to South Africa in 1994.

Readings: Saunders, 1983; Stayt, 1931.

WALVIS BAY

> On my first evening, when a port official had led me to the edge of the desert, and asked me to look at it, I asked him what lay above, below, and out beyond us. "Nothing!" he said, with a note of hysteria in his voice. "It's just miles and miles and miles — and MILES! — of Sweet Fanny Adams!"
> - Negley Farson, 1940.

Area: 434 sq. miles (1,124 sq. km); Capital: Walvis Bay
Population: 25,000 (est. 1978)

A territory and port on the Atlantic coast of South-West Africa (Namibia), under South African control. A deepwater anchorage and valuable guano deposits on nearby islands led the British to occupy Walvis Bay in 1878. In 1884 the territory was transferred to the Cape Colony. Although part of South Africa from 1910 Walvis Bay was administered as an integral part of South-West Africa from 1922 to 1977. During World War I the territory was briefly occupied by German troops. In 1992 Walvis Bay was placed under a joint South African-Namibian administration prior to its absorbtion by Namibia in 1994.

View of Walvis Bay

Readings: Saunders, 1983; *Standard Encyclopedia of Southern Africa*, 1971.

ZOUTPANSBERG REPUBLIC (Soutpansberg)

Deep in the wilderness, on the edge of beyond, lies a mysterious and far away range of mountains. For a length of eighty miles the Zoutpansberg rears its gaunt head from the sea of brush and a more superstition-ridden range of mountains it would be hard to find.
— T.V. Bulpin, 1950.

Area: 50,000 sq. miles (130,000 sq. km); Capital: Schoemansdal

An independent Boer state in the extreme north of Transvaal that existed from 1848 to 1858.

Readings: Bulpin, 1950; *Standard Encyclopedia of Southern Africa*, 1971.

ZULULAND

The King of the Zulus, a fine fellow of thirty, was banished six years ago, for a term of seven years. He is occupying Napoleon's old stand — St. Helena. The people are a little nervous about having him back, and they may well be, for Zulu kings have been terrible people sometimes.
— Mark Twain, 1897.

Area: 10,427 sq. miles (27,000 sq. km); Capital: Eshowe
Population: 230,000 (est. 1904)

In the 18th century the Zulu Kingdom transformed itself from a minor state into a highly warlike, centralized and absolutist nation. By 1800 their superior military organization and discipline made the Zulus the masters of southeastern Africa. Inevitably they came into conflict with the Boer republics and the British. The history of Zululand in the 19th century was one of almost constant warfare and revolt until the British were able to establish a protectorate in 1887. Mindful of the Zulu's military prowess the British respected traditional Zulu customs and limited white settlement. In 1897 Zululand became part of the colony of Natal and was incorporated into the Union of South Africa in 1910.

Readings: *Encyclopædia Britannica*, 1926; *Standard Encyclopedia of Southern Africa*, 1971.

CHAPTER 15

Australasia

The Pacific is even a nastier ocean than I had imagined, very much
nastier than the Atlantic.
— The Marchioness of Dufferin and Ava, 1891.

BRITISH NEW GUINEA / PAPUA

The name Papua, it should be said, comes from the Malay word
papuwah, meaning "wooly" or "fuzzy," and was first applied to the
natives on account of their mops of hair; later the name was applied
to the island itself.
— A.F.R. Wollaston, 1912.

Area: 90,540 sq. miles (234,500 sq. km); Capital: Port Moresby
Population: 374,217 (est. 1952)

The southeastern quarter of the island of New Guinea, bordered on
the north by German New Guinea and on the west by Dutch New
Guinea; separated from the Australian state of Queensland by the
Torres Strait. In the 19th century Queensland, worried about foreign
powers encroaching on its domain, urged the British government to
annex New Guinea before anyone else did. Faced with continued
refusal by the British to act the Queensland government annexed
southeastern New Guinea on its own authority in 1883. The imperial
government wanted to cancel the annexation but finally relented. The
Protectorate of British New Guinea was reluctantly established in 1884

345

and changed to a colony in 1888. The British, having little interest in
the place, transferred it to the Australians in 1905 who renamed it the
Territory of Papua in 1906. In 1949 Papua was unified administratively
with the former German New Guinea (since 1920 the Australian
mandated Territory of New Guinea). As Papua New Guinea the unified
territories progressed to self-government in 1973 and full independence
in 1975.

Lakatoi boat

Readings: *Encyclopedia of Papua and New Guinea*, 1972; Snow, 1989.

CAROLINE ISLANDS (Karolinen)

Though the natives had not till now made . . . birds an article of food,
yet when they went into the woods, they frequently eat their eggs; but
they did not admire them for being newly laid; the luxury to them
was, when they could swallow an imperfect chicken in the bargain.
— George Keate, 1788.

Area: 452 sq. miles (1,171 sq. km); Capital: Ponape
Population: 37,000 (est. 1951)

An archipelago of about six hundred coral atolls and volcanic
islands in the western Pacific. Inhabited by Micronesians the principal
islands were Ponape, Truk, Yap, Kosrae and Pelau.

Although the islands were visited and claimed by Spanish navigators
in the 16th century they were rarely visited except by whalers. Spain,
motivated by German counterclaims, did not colonize the Caroline
Islands until 1866. In 1899, after Spain had lost the Spanish-American
War, the Spanish withdrew from the Pacific and the Caroline Islands
were sold to Germany for $4,500,000. The Germans were ousted by
the Japanese navy in 1914, two months after the beginning of World
War I. The Japanese at first ruled the Caroline Islands as a League of
Nations mandated territory, but when Japan withdrew from the League

in 1933 it defiantly remained in the islands and fortified them. During World War II the Caroline Islands saw major battles until they were liberated by the United States in 1944. The islands became part of the U.S.-administered Trust Territory of the Pacific Islands in 1947. With the exception of the Palau group the Caroline Islands proceeded to independence in 1991 as the Federated States of Micronesia. Pelau became the independent Republic of Belau in 1994.

Yap islanders used the world's most unusual money — stone discs 6 to 12 feet (2 to 4 m) in diameter.

Readings: Craig, 1981; *New Encyclopædia Britannica*, 1991.

ELLICE ISLANDS

. . . no race in that ocean of sea-princes ever produced a more superb breed of surf-riders than theirs.
— Arthur Grimble, 1952.

Area: 10 sq. miles (26 sq. km); Capital: Funafuti
Population: 5,817 (est. 1973)

The Ellice Islands, in the central Pacific, had been part of the British colony of the Gilbert and Ellice Islands since 1892. After a referendum the Ellice Islands were split off and became a separate colony in 1975. Independence was granted in 1978 as the Republic of Tuvalu, one of the world's smallest sovereign states. Tuvalu means "eight standing together," an allusion to the tiny country's eight principal islands.

Readings: Craig, 1981; Grimble, 1952.

FRENCH OCEANIA (Établissements Française de L'Oceanie)

Man somehow got here, I think about a thousand years ago, and made a society which was on the whole the most successful the world ever saw, because it rested on the solidest possible foundation of no morals at all.
— Henry Adams, 1891.

Area: 1,544 sq. miles (4,000 sq, km); Capital: Papeete
Population: 73,201 (est. 1956)

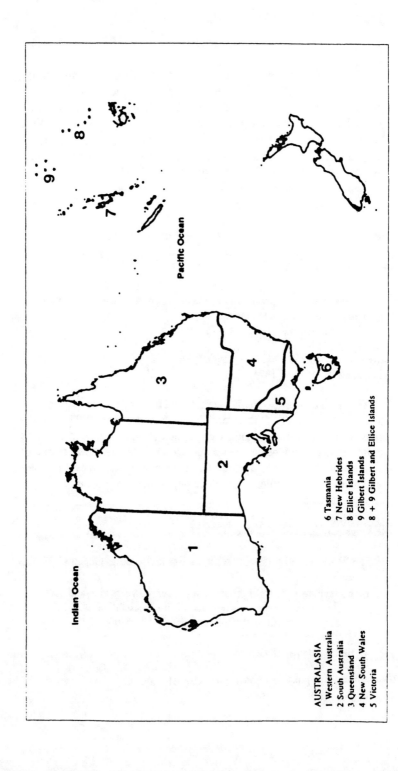

AUSTRALASIA

1 Western Australia
2 South Australia
3 Queensland
4 New South Wales
5 Victoria

6 Tasmania
7 New Hebrides
8 Ellice Islands
9 Gilbert Islands
8 + 9 Gilbert and Ellice Islands

Indian Ocean

Pacific Ocean

Famed for its languid beauty French Oceania comprised the Society Islands (including Tahiti and Bora-Bora), the Austral Islands, the Gambier Islands, the Marquesas Islands and the Tuamotu Archipelago; all in the southwestern Pacific. Tahiti was discovered by the British in 1767 and British Protestant missionaries began the mass conversion of the islands about thirty years later. It was not until 1836 that French Catholics arrived. After six years of intrigue the French established a protectorate. But a civil war erupted and French rule was not confirmed until 1847. From 1847 to 1880 Tahiti was a monarchy under French protection. By 1880 the monarchy had lost its influence and Tahiti became a French colony. The other island groups passed from protected to colonial status between 1881 and 1901. French Oceania became a French overseas territory in 1958 and its name was changed to French Polynesia. The famous mutiny on HMS *Bounty* (1789) took place in the waters of what would become French Oceania.

Kanaka men

Readings: Craig, 1981; *New Encyclopædia Britannica*, 1991.

GERMAN NEW GUINEA (Deutsch Neuguinea) / TERRITORY OF NEW GUINEA

. . . the settlements on the New Guinea mainland are few and far between, and it cannot be pretended that the country is German except in name.
— A.F.R. Wollaston, 1912.

Area: 93,000 sq. miles (241,000 sq. km); Capital: Herbertshöhe (on Neu Pommern Island); Population: 601,427 (est. 1913)

The northeastern quarter of New Guinea and the adjacent islands of Neu Pommern (New Britain), Neu Mecklenburg (New Ireland) and Bougainville. The districts on the New Guinea mainland were known as Kaiser-Wilhelmsland and the islands as the Bismarck Archipelago, the name the islands still bear. Although German traders and missionaries had been active earlier it was not until 1884 that New Guinea was annexed. The territory was administered in a haphazard fashion by the New Guinea Company until 1899 when the German Reich took it over. The German ambition to turn New Guinea into a prosperous plantation colony, another Java, never amounted to much in the face of an inhospitable climate, malaria, labor shortages and uprisings. Few Germans were willing to settle in such a remote colony.

In 1914, shortly after the outbreak of World War I, an Australian military and naval force, meeting only token resistance, occupied German New Guinea. The colony was renamed the Territory of New Guinea and given to Australia as a League of Nations mandate in 1920 and later as a United Nations Trust Territory. The Trust Territory of New Guinea was joined in an administrative union to the Australian dependency of Papua in 1949. The two together became known as Papua New Guinea and under that name independence was granted in 1975.

Kaiser's yacht Hohenzollern

Readings: *Encyclopedia of Papua and New Guinea*, 1972; Snow, 1989.

GERMAN SAMOA / NAVIGATOR'S ISLANDS

> If you wish to go there you will have no trouble about finding it if you follow the directions given by Robert Louis Stevenson. . . . "You go to America, cross the continent to San Francisco, and then it's the second turning on the left."
> — Mark Twain, 1897.

Area: 1,133 sq. miles (2,934 sq. km); Capital: Apia
Population: 37,791 (est. 1922)

A group of tropical islands in the south-central Pacific Ocean inhabited by Polynesians since 1000 B.C. British, German and American traders and missionaries began arriving in Samoa early in the 19th century. The missionaries were extraordinarily successful, converting virtually the entire population. Meanwhile the governments of Great Britain, Germany and the United States began an intense competition for dominance in Samoa that was way out of proportion to any strategic or economic gains that they could hope to make. The presence of outsiders worsened the already complex web of Samoan factional disputes. Things reached such a state that in March 1889 seven warships (American, German and British) were anchored in Apia harbor, their crews glaring at each other over their guns. When the ships were caught by a typhoon, which sank or beached six of them and killed 150 sailors, the three governments realized the error of their ways. A conference was held in Berlin that provided for Samoan neutrality under a tripartite protectorate. The condominium that was set up was clumsy and after a treaty with the ruler of Samoa in 1899, U.S. supremacy was recognized in eastern Samoa and German supremacy in the west. Great Britain withdrew from Samoa upon receiving exclusive rights in Tonga and the Solomon Islands as well as concessions in Africa. The Germans ran an efficient administration but were obliged to suppress a Samoan resistance movement in 1908. German Samoa was occupied by a New Zealand expeditionary force in 1914 and renamed Western Samoa. The islands were hard hit by the worldwide influenza epidemic after World War I. About 20 percent of the population died. New Zealand governed under League of Nations and later, United Nations auspices. Western Samoa became independent in 1962. The eastern portion of Samoa is the unincorporated territory of American Samoa.

Robert Louis Stevenson, author of *Treasure Island* and *Kidnapped*, spent the last five years of his life in Samoa, dying there in 1894.

Kaiser's yacht Hohenzollern

Readings: Craig, 1981; *Encyclopædia Britannica*, 1926.

GILBERT AND ELLICE ISLANDS

> The first experience can never be repeated. The first love, the first sun
> rise, the first South Sea Island, are memories apart, and touched a
> virginity of sense.
> — Robert Louis Stevenson, 1889.

Area: 375 sq. miles (971 sq. km); Capital: Bairiki
Population: 57,816 (est. 1973)

Two island groups straddling the equator in the central Pacific
Ocean. The first English navigator to sight the Gilberts was Captain
John Byron (grandfather of the poet) in 1765. The last of the islands
were not discovered until 1828. The islands became a British
protectorate in 1892 and, at the request of their inhabitants, a colony
in 1915. Additional islands were added to the colony as late as 1937.
In World War II the Japanese occupied the Gilbert and Ellice Islands
until driven out by American forces during 1942 and 1943. The island
of Tarawa was the site of a particularly fierce clash. The colony was
dissolved in 1975 when each island group became a colony.

Canoe crossing a reef
and King George VI

Readings: Craig, 1981; Grimble, 1952.

GILBERT ISLANDS

> A low island, except for coconuts, is just the same as a ship at sea
> . . . brackish water, no supplies and very little shelter . . . I pine for
> an island with a profile.
> — Robert Louis Stevenson, 1890.

Area: 365 sq. miles (945 sq. km); Capital: Tarawa
Population; 51,999 (est. 1973)

The Gilbert Islands became a British colony in 1975 when the Gilbert and Ellice Islands colony was split in two. The Gilbert Islands became self-governing in 1976 and independent in 1979. At that time the name was changed to the Republic of Kiribati. The islands, mostly low-lying coral atolls, are sprinkled over more than 2,000,000 square miles (5,000,000 sq. km) of ocean.

Readings: Craig, 1981; Grimble, 1952.

HAWAII

> In what other land save this one is the commonest form of greeting not
> "Good day," nor "How d'ye do," but "Love?" That greeting is Aloha
> — love, I love you, my love to you.
> — Jack London, 1916.

Area: 6,423 sq. miles (16,635 sq. km); Capital: Honolulu
Population: 150,000 (est. 1899)

A group of twenty islands in the Pacific Ocean about 2,000 miles (3,200 km) southwest of San Franciso. The major islands are Hawaii, Maui, Oahu, Kauai, Molokai, Lanai, Niihau and Kahoolawe. The archipelago was discovered by Captain James Cook in 1778 and named the Sandwich Islands after the First Lord of the Admiralty, the Earl of Sandwich. Cook was killed on the island of Hawaii the next year. King Kamehameha I, using European weapons and military advisors, unified the islands (1782-1795) and established the Kingdom of Hawaii. He and succeeding rulers made Hawaii prosperous and progressive, achieving international recognition as a sovereign country. Hawaii, under missionary influence, had a declaration of rights, and a written constitution and enjoyed a high rate of literacy. However, the introduction of unfamiliar diseases, heavy immigration, intermarriage and the steadily growing power of American settlers reduced the numbers of native Hawaiians and weakened the kingdom. In 1893, after reactionary forces attempted to set aside the liberal constitution, a provisional government sought American annexation. The Americans at first rejected the Hawaiian request and a republic was established in 1894. In 1898, at the request of its American-dominated legislature, Hawaii was finally annexed by the United States, becoming a territory in 1900. Hawaii has been an American state since 1959.

View of Honolulu

Readings: Craig, 1981; *New Encyclopædia Britannica*, 1991.

MARIANA ISLANDS (Marianen)

> The northern-most inhabitable island of the chain is named Maug, and is about the same latitude as Mexico City. It is interesting to note that the name Maug is Guam spelled backwards, but it is not known whether any significance is attached to this coincidence.
> — Russell L. Stevens, 1953.

Area: 184 sq. miles (477 sq. km); Capital: Garapan
Population: 6,500 (est. 1951)

A group of fifteen islands 1,500 miles (2,400 km) east of the Philippines. The islands were discovered by Magellan in 1521 and named the Ladrones, or Thieves Islands. Spanish occupation dated from 1668 when they were renamed in honor of Queen Mariana. Over the next three centuries the Spanish had to contend with numerous rebellions. During the Spanish-American War (1898) the American navy seized Guam, the southernmost and most important island. The

Spanish, deciding to rid themselves of their Pacific colonies, sold the rest of the Marianas to Germany in 1899. The new owners attached the islands administratively to German New Guinea. During World War I the Japanese replaced the Germans. Japan governed the Marianas under a League of Nations mandate until 1935 and then annexed them. In World War II Japanese forces captured Guam but after battles in Saipan, Tinian and Guam the Americans drove the Japanese out of the entire chain of islands. The Marianas, except for Guam, which remains an unincorporated American territory, became part of the U.S.-administered Trust Territory of the Pacific Islands in 1947. In 1978 the islands became the Commonwealth of the Northern Marianas, a sovereign state in free association with the United States.

Readings: Craig, 1981; Stevens, 1953.

NEW FRANCE (Nouvelle France) / FREE COLONY OF PORT BRETON

> Amongst his other extravagant flights of fancy for Port Breton, de Rays had planned a cathedral and for it the migrant ships carried 180,000 bricks, certain timbers, fittings and a beautiful altar [which became] the first cocktail bar in the Pacific Islands.
> — R.W. Robson, 1965.

An unauthorized French colony in eastern New Guinea and adjacent islands. Between 1880 and 1882 an eccentric French adventurer and speculator, the Marquis Charles de Rays (self-styled King Charles of New France), established a colony on the island of New Ireland. Rays had a far-fetched dream of re-creating the glories of aristocratic Catholic France in the far Pacific. After advertising for settlers, and promising them free land in a fertile country with a salubrious climate, Rays sent out four ships. Aboard was a motley collection of 570 French, German, Italian, Belgian and Swiss colonists. Unfortunately the reality was nothing like the advertising. Disease, death and lack of supplies crippled New France from the start. In 1882 the surviving settlers relocated to Australia. Rays, who never went to the colony, was imprisoned in France on a charge of criminal negligence. The brief existence of New France spurred the establishment of sanctioned colonies and protectorates in the region. What had been New France was incorporated into German New Guinea in 1884.

Readings: *Encyclopedia of Papua and New Guinea*, 1972; Robson, 1965.

NEW HEBRIDES (Nouvelles-Hébrides)

> They seemed most pleased with Marbled Paper & some of them immediately converted it, before our Eyes into a covering for the only part which is covered about them.
> — William Wales, 1774.

Area: 5,700 sq. miles (14,763 sq. km); Capital: Vila
Population: 112,596 (est. 1976)

An archipelago of thirteen large islands and about fifty smaller ones in the southwestern Pacific. Captain James Cook visited the islands in 1774 and named them for their supposed resemblance to the Hebrides of Scotland. The arrival of French and British traders and missionaries in the mid-19th century led to conflicting claims by the two powers. It was agreed in 1878 that the islands would be neutral and that their administration would be placed under a mixed group of British and French naval officers. Further pacts led to the creation of an unusual system of colonial rule — government by condominium. Beginning in 1906 Great Britain and France exercised joint rule over the New Hebrides but not territorial sovereignty. Each power had its own resident commissioner, and operated its own schools, courts and other institutions. Each power had exclusive authority over its own nationals and shared authority over the indigenous population. The Condominium of the New Hebrides became the independent Republic of Vanuatu, "Our own land," in 1980.

Prior to independence every government office displayed portraits of the president of France and the queen of England. Many of the islanders thought they were husband and wife.

In World War II the islands were spared Japanese occupation but became a major Allied staging area. As the result of a massive American military presence and the resulting flow of material goods, a bizarre cargo cult arose on the island of Tanna. The John Frum Cult, so named after its shadowy founder, used the U.S. flag, military uniforms and drill in its worship. Frum was seen as a beneficent spirit or king of America who would bring a peaceful work-free millennium with boundless "cargo" — Western material goods. The Condominium government suppressed the cult but was eventually obliged to recognize it as a religion.

Irirtki Island and Port Vila

Readings: Craig, 1981; *New Encyclopædia Britannica*, 1991.

NEW SOUTH WALES

> . . . it is the hospitable home of every species of culture and of every species of material enterprise, and there is a church at every man's door and a race-track over the way.
> — Mark Twain, 1897.

Area: 310,372 sq. miles (803,860 sq. km); Capital: Sydney
Population: 1,355,355 (est. 1901)

On the southeast coast of Australia, the continent's oldest and most populous colony. New South Wales was given its name by Captain James Cook and claimed for Great Britain in 1770. It became a British colony in 1788 with the establishment of a penal settlement on the site of Sydney. The American colonies, which had been the favored place to dump convicts, had become independent so a new penal colony was needed. There were also commercial and strategic advantages for Great Britain to have a colony in the south Pacific. Although emancipists (liberated convicts), free settlers and former prison guards began to outnumber prisoners in the 1820s the transportation of convicts to New South Wales did not end until 1840. It was the introduction of fine wool sheep that made New South Wales more than a penal colony and the need for additional pastures was the motive for expanding the colony into the western plains. New South Wales originally encompassed about half of Australia but was reduced in size by the establishment of Queensland, Victoria, South Australia and Tasmania. A partially elected council was created in New South Wales in 1843 and responsible government established in 1856. New South Wales federated with the other Australian colonies in 1901. An enclave in the southeast and a small area on the coast were ceded in 1911 and 1915, respectively, to create the Australian Capital Territory. Captain William Bligh, of mutiny on the Bounty fame, was governor of New South Wales between 1805 and 1808. He was not popular.

Seal of New South Wales

Readings: Docherty, 1992; Snow, 1989.

QUEENSLAND

> The subject of heat is one of extreme delicacy in Queensland. . . . One does not allude to heat in a host's house any more than to a bad bottle of wine or an ill-cooked joint of meat. . . . You may call an inn hot, or a court-house, but not a gentleman's paddock, or a lady's drawing-room. And you should never own to a musquito.
> — Anthony Trollope, 1873.

Area: 666,795 sq. miles (1,727,000 sq. km); Capital: Brisbane
Population: 498,129 (est. 1901)

In northeastern Australia, the second-largest colony on the continent of Australia. Queensland was originally part of New South Wales but was detached in 1859 when responsible government was conferred. Queen Victoria suggested the name and the new colony was named in her honor. The first European settlement, a penal colony, was started near Brisbane in 1823. The site was chosen because it was suitably distant from the "fleshpots" of Sydney and therefore more appropriate for hardened criminals. Free settlers began to arrive in Queensland about 1840 and the interior was occupied in the 1860s and 1870s. The Aborigines of Queensland put up a determined but hopeless resistance to European encroachment. Fighting, strongest in the north, cost ten to twenty thousand Aboriginal and one thousand European lives. In the 1890s Queenslanders were divided over federation with the other Australian colonies. Those in the north, distant as they were from the rest of Australia and close as they were to the potential threat of German New Guinea, were strongly in favor of federation. People in Brisbane and southern Queensland feared domination by New South Wales. Nevertheless, when a referendum was held on the issue, a majority chose to federate. On January 1, 1901, Queensland joined the other Australian colonies to form the Commonwealth of Australia.

Queen Victoria

Readings: Docherty 1992; Snow, 1989.

SOUTH AUSTRALIA

> Out on the wastes of the Never Never —
> That's where the dead men lie!
> There where the heat waves dance for ever —
> That's where the dead men lie!
> — Bancroft Henry Boake, 1913.

Area: 380,070 sq. miles (984,377 sq. km); Capital: Adelaide
Population: 358,456 (est. 1901)

In south-central Australia. In common with the other colonies in the eastern half of Australia, South Australia was originally part of New South Wales. It was created a separate British province in 1836. Unlike the other Australian colonies it was never a penal settlement. South Australia was a planned colony. It was developed according to the theory of "systematic colonization" propounded by Edward Gibbon Wakefield. According to this theory land would be sold at a "sufficient" price that would allow only a minority of settlers to purchase it. This would attract a small number of capitalists and a larger number of settlers working for wages. The profits from the sale of land would then be used to bring out additional settlers. The trouble was that the theory never really worked in practice and South Australia went bankrupt in 1840. The next year it became an ordinary crown colony. Over the next few decades the population of South Australia steadily increased as ex-gold miners from New South Wales and Victoria arrived to take up farming and sheep rearing. South Australia became an Australian state in 1901. Its capital, Adelaide, was the only 19th-century city in Australia to be planned.

Queen Victoria

Readings: Docherty, 1992; Snow, 1989.

TASMANIA / VAN DIEMEN'S LAND

> Now the Tasmanians declare themselves to be ruined. . . . When the stranger asks the reason of this ruin, he is told that all the public money has gone with the convicts, and that — the rabbits have eaten up all the grass.
> — Anthony Trollope, 1873.

Area: 26,383 sq. miles (68,331 sq. km); Capital: Hobart
Population: 172,475 (est. 1901)

An island colony about 175 miles (280 km) southeast of the Australian mainland. Discovered by Dutch navigator Abel Janszoon Tasman in 1642 the island was named Van Diemen's Land after a governor of the Dutch East Indies. The name was changed to Tasmania in 1856 when responsible government was established. Tasmania was largely forgotten after its discovery until the British established a prison settlement there in 1803. Tasmania, which was a dependency of New South Wales until 1825, became Australia's major convict destination. Between 1803 and 1850, when the practice came to an end, 62,300 convicts were transported to Tasmania, 43 percent of Australia's total.

When transportation to New South Wales was abolished in 1840
Tasmania took up the slack. As late as 1848 38 percent of Tasmania's
population were convicts. The Tasmanian Aborigines attempted to resist
the Europeans but by the 1820s they had almost been exterminated. The
last native Tasmanian died in 1876. Tasmania entered the
Commonwealth of Australia in 1901 as a state. The island is the home
of several indigenous animals including the Tasmanian wolf (possibly
extinct) and the Tasmanian devil.

Mount Wellington

Readings: Docherty, 1992; Snow, 1989.

TRUST TERRITORY OF THE PACIFIC ISLANDS

Yap, if I may use the expression, is "the genuine article," . . . my
information . . . was obtained from beachcombers of diverse
nationalities who, for various reasons have drifted into this easy state
of "living for the day."
— R.V.C. Bodley, 1933.

Area: 680 sq. miles (1,761 sq, km); Capital: Saipan
Population: 75,836 (est. 1962)

More than two thousand tiny islands sprinkled over 3,000,000 sq.
miles (7,770,000 sq. km) of the western Pacific Ocean. The major
island groups were the Carolines (including Yap), Marshalls, Marianas
and Palau. The Spanish discovered the islands in the 16th century but
did not exercise sovereignty over them until late in the 19th century. In
1899, following its defeat in the Spanish-American War, Spain sold the
islands to Germany, which in turn was supplanted by Japan in 1914.
The United States captured the islands in World War II and in 1947 the
American-administered United Nations Trust Territory of the Pacific

Islands was created. Following referenda in the 1970s Palau, the Northern Mariana Islands and the Marshalls split off from the Trust Territory and proceeded separately to associated statehood and independence. The remaining islands, mainly the Carolines, in association with the United States became the Federated States of Micronesia in 1979. Full independence came in 1991.

Outrigger canoe and flag of the Federated States of Micronesia

Readings: Craig, 1981; *New Encyclopædia Britannica*, 1991.

VICTORIA

Imagine a huge chessboard flung on to the earth, and you have what is the true and characteristic Melbourne.
— Francis Adams, 1893.

Area: 87,884 sq. miles (227,619 sq. km); Capital: Melbourne
Population: 1,201,070 (est. 1901)

In the extreme southeast of mainland Australia. At one time Victoria was part of New South Wales but was constituted a separate colony in 1851. In 1856 responsible government with a bicameral parliament and constitution was conferred. The coast of Victoria was explored in the 1790s and the interior in the 1820s. The earliest convict settlement was started in 1803, but it was not until after 1830 that the first permanent settlements were established, by farmers and herders from Tasmania in search of new pastures. Between 1838 and 1851 the population grew from 3,500 to 77,300 due to emigration from New South Wales and Britain. The Aboriginal population is believed to have declined by two-thirds during the same period. Between 1850 and 1860 the population grew even faster, due to a gold rush. Victoria federated with the five other Australian colonies in 1901. Melbourne, the second-

largest city in Australia, was the capital of the Commonwealth of
Australia from 1901 to 1927.

Queen Victoria

Readings: Docherty, 1992; Snow, 1989.

WESTERN AUSTRALIA

An ingenious, but sarcastic Yankee, when asked what he thought of
Western Australia, declared that it was the best country he had ever
seen to run through an hour-glass.
— Anthony Trollope, 1873.

Area: 975,096 sq. miles (2,525,500 sq. km); Capital: Perth
Population: 184,124 (est. 1901)

An arid colony that covered about one-third of Australia's
landmass. Captain George Vancouver took possession of Western
Australia for Great Britain in 1791 and the colony was officially
established in 1829. Development proceeded slowly. After a few years
of fighting, the coastal Aborigines were subdued, but conflict continued
as Europeans pushed inland. As the transportation of convicts ended in
the rest of Australia it was begun in Western Australia. As the colony
was remote it suffered from a labor shortage. When a pro-
transportation movement arose the British Government was only too
happy to send Western Australia all the convicts it wanted, about ten
thousand between 1850 and 1868. Despite the influx of involuntary
settlers Western Australia did not become a viable colony until a series
of gold rushes between 1888 and 1893. In the decade before 1901,
when it joined the Commonwealth of Australia as a state, the
population of Western Australia grew nearly fourfold.
    Western Australia complained that it was isolated and ignored by

the rest of Australia. It was not linked by telegraph to the rest of the country until 1877 or by rail until 1917. In 1906 the Parliament of Western Australia passed a motion of secession. In a 1933 referendum two-thirds of the electorate voted to secede from Australia. But when a state delegation traveled to London its case was rejected. Western Australia remains a state in Australia.

Swan

Readings: Docherty, 1992; Snow, 1989.

Bibliography

Aflalo, F.G., ed. *The Sportsman's Book for India*. London: Horace Marshall & Son, 1904.

The American Cyclopaedia. New York: D. Appleton, 1883.

Andrieux, Jean-Pierre. *St. Pierre and Miquelon*. Lincoln, Ont.: W.F. Rannie, 1983.

Anthony, John Duke. *Historical and Cultural Dictionary of the Sultanate of Oman and the Emirates of Eastern Arabia*. Metuchen, N.J.: Scarecrow, 1976.

Armstrong, William N. *Around the World with a King*. Rutland, Vt.: Charles E. Tuttle, 1977 (1903).

Arnold, Edwin. *India Revisited*. Boston: Roberts Brothers, 1886.

Barrows, David Prescott. *Berbers and Blacks: Impressions of Morocco, Timbuktu and the Western Sudan*. Westport, Conn.: Negro Universities Press, 1970 (1927).

Barth, Heinrich. *Travels and Discoveries in North and Central Africa*. London: Frank Cass, 1965 (1857).

Bartlett's Familiar Quotations. 15th ed. Boston: Little, Brown & Co., 1980.

Baudez, Claude, and Sydney Picasso. *Lost Cities of the Maya*. London: Thames and Hudson, 1992.

Bean, Walton, and James J. Rawls. *California*. New York: McGraw-Hill, 1968.

Bolger, Francis W.P. *Canada's Smallest Province.* Halifax, N.S.: Nimbus, 1991.

Bothwell, Robert. *A Short History of Ontario.* Edmonton: Hurtig, 1986.

Brassey, Lady. *In the Trades, the Tropics, & the Roaring Forties.* London: Longmans, Green, 1885.

Brebner, John Bartlet. *The Neutral Yankees of Nova Scotia.* Toronto: McClelland and Stewart, 1969.

Brockhaus Enzyklopädie. Wiesbaden: F.A. Brockhaus, 1967.

Brown, Mervyn. *Madagascar Rediscovered: A History from Early Times to Independence.* Hamden, Conn.: Archon Books, 1979.

Bulpin, T.V. *Lost Trails on the Low Veld.* London: Hodder & Stoughton, 1950.

Bumsted, J.M. *Land, Settlement and Politics on Eighteenth-Century Prince Edward Island.* Kingston, Ont.: McGill-Queen's University Press, 1987.

Burki, Shahid Javed. *Historical Dictionary of Pakistan.* Metuchen, N.J.: Scarecrow, 1991.

Burton, Sir Richard F. *A Mission to Gelele King of Dahome.* New York: Frederick A. Praeger, 1966 (1864).

—. *Personal Narrative of a Pilgrimage to Al-Madinah and Meccah.* London: Longmans, 1855.

Campbell, G.G. *The History of Nova Scotia.* Toronto: Ryerson, 1948.

The Canadian Encyclopedia. 2nd ed. Edmonton: Hurtig, 1988.

Canby, Courtlandt. *Encyclopedia of Historic Places.* New York: Facts on File, 1984.

Cannistraro, Philip V., ed. *Historical Dictionary of Fascist Italy.* Westport, Conn.: Greenwood, 1982.

Careless, J.M.S. *The Union of the Canadas.* Toronto: McClelland and Stewart, 1967.

Castagno, Margaret. *Historical Dictionary of Somalia.* Metuchen, NJ.: Scarecrow, 1975.

Chandler, Douglas. "Flying around the Baltic." *National Geographic* (June 1938): 777-784.

Charrière, Henri. *Papillon.* New York: William Morrow and Company, 1970.

Churchill, Randolph. *Men, Mines and Animals in South Africa.* London: Sampson Low, Marston & Co., 1893.

Cockerell, F.P. "Upper Silesia and the League." *Fortnightly Review* (October 1921): 685-696.

Collier's Encyclopedia. New York: P.F. Collier, 1994.

Connelly, Owen, ed. *Historical Dictionary of Napoleonic France, 1799-1815.* Westport, Conn.: Greenwood, 1985.

Coppa, Frank J., ed. *Dictionary of Modern Italian History.* Westport, Conn.: Greenwood, 1985.

Cowan, C.D. *Nineteenth-Century Malaya.* London: Oxford University Press, 1961.

Craig, G.M. *Upper Canada.* Toronto: McClelland and Stewart, 1968.

Craig, Robert D., and Frank P. King, eds. *Historical Dictionary of Oceania.* Westport, Conn.: Greenwood, 1981.

Curzon, George N. *Russia in Central Asia.* London: Longmans Green, 1889.

Cyclopaedia of India. Graz, Austria: Akademische Druck - u. Verlagsanstalt, 1967 (1885).

Davis, Robert H. *Historical Dictionary of Colombia.* Metuchen, N.J.: Scarecrow, 1977.

Decalo, Samuel. *Historical Dictionary of Chad.* Metuchen, N.J.: Scarecrow, 1977.

—. *Historical Dictionary of Dahomey.* Metuchen, N.J.: Scarecrow, 1976.

—. *Historical Dictionary of Togo.* Metuchen, N.J.: Scarecrow, 1976.

Delpar, Helen, ed. *Encyclopedia of Latin America.* New York: McGraw-Hill, 1974.

De Selincourt, E. *Journals of Dorothy Wordsworth.* London: Macmillan, 1952.

Dickinson, J.A. *A Short History of Quebec.* Toronto: Copp Clark Pitman, 1993.

Dillon, Michael. *Dictionary of Chinese History.* London: Frank Cass, 1979.

Docherty, James C. *Historical Dictionary of Australia.* Metuchen, N.J.: Scarecrow, 1992.

Donovan, Kenneth, ed.: *The Island.* Fredericton, N.B.: Acadiensis, 1990.

Eaton, Clement. *A History of the Old South.* New York: Macmillan, 1975.

Enciclopedia Italiana di Scienze, Lettere ed Arti. Rome: Istituto della Enciclopedia Italiana, 1949.

Enciclopedia Universal Ilustrada Europeo-Americana. Madrid: Espasa Calpe, 1958 (1908).

Encyclopædia Britannica. 13th ed. London: Encyclopædia Britannica, 1926.

Encyclopedia of Papua and New Guinea. Melbourne: Melbourne University Press, 1972.

England, George Allan. *Isles of Romance.* New York: The Century Co., 1929.

Ensor, F. Sidney. *Incidents on a Journey through Nubia to Darfoor.* London: W.H. Allen, 1881.

Farr, Kenneth R. *Historical Dictionary of Puerto Rico and the U.S. Virgin Islands.* Metuchen, N.J.: Scarecrow, 1978.

Fehrenbach, T.R. *Lone Star.* New York: Macmillan, 1988.

Fermor, Patrick Leigh. *A Time of Gifts.* London: John Murray, 1977.

Foray, Cyril P. *Historical Dictionary of Sierra Leone.* Metuchen, N.J.: Scarecrow, 1977.

Forbes, Rosita. *India of the Princes.* London: The Right Book Club, 1939.

Forsyth, Frederick. *The Biafra Story.* Harmondsworth: Penguin, 1969.

Forward, Charles N., ed. *Vancouver Island.* Victoria, B.C.: University of Victoria, 1979.

Furlong, Charles Wellington. *The Gateway to the Sahara: Observations and Experiences in Tripoli.* New York: Charles Scribner's Sons, 1909.

Galtier, Joseph. "A Visit to Fiume." *The Living Age* 301, no. 3907 (May 24, 1919): 449-454.

Gannon, Michael, ed. *The New History of Florida.* Gainesville: University Press of Florida, 1996.

Gastmann, Albert. *Historical Dictionary of the French and Netherlands Antilles.* Metuchen, N.J.: Scarecrow, 1978.

Graham, R.B. Cunninghame. *Mogreb-el-Acksa.* London: Century, 1988 (1898).

Grand Dictionnaire Universel du XIXe Siècle. Geneva: Slatkine, 1982 (1866-1879).

Grande Enciclopédia Portuguesa e Brasileira. Lisbon: Editorial Enciclopédia, 1935-1960.

La Grande Encyclopédie. Paris: Société Anonyme de la Grand Encyclopédie, 1886-1902.

Great Soviet Encyclopedia. 3rd ed. New York: Macmillan, 1975.

Greene, Graham. *The Lawless Roads.* New York: Penguin, 1979.

Grimble, Arthur. *A Pattern of Islands.* London: John Murray, 1969 (1952).

Grotpeter, John J. *Historical Dictionary of Zambia.* Metuchen, N.J.: Scarecrow, 1979.

Guinness Book of Records. New York: Bantam, 1992.

Hahn, Lorna. *Historical Dictionary of Libya.* Metuchen, N.J.: Scarecrow, 1981.

Haliburton, Gordon. *Historical Dictionary of Lesotho.* Metuchen, N.J.: Scarecrow, 1977.

Haliburton, Richard. *The Royal Road to Romance.* Garden City, N.Y.: Garden City Publishing Company, 1925.

Hallet, Jean-Pierre. *Congo Kitabu.* Greenwich, Conn.: Fawcett World Library, 1967.

Hamilton, Robert M., and Dorothy Shields. *The Dictionary of Canadian Quotations and Phrases.* Toronto: McClelland and Stewart, 1979.

Hannay, James. *History of New Brunswick.* St. John, N.B.: J.A. Bowes, 1909.

Harrer, Heinrich. *Seven Years in Tibet.* London: The Reprint Society, 1955.

Harris, John. *Much Sounding of Bugles.* London: Hutchinson, 1975.

Heath, Dwight B. *Historical Dictionary of Bolivia.* Metuchen, N.J.: Scarecrow, 1972.

Hedrick, Basil C., and Anne K. Hedrick. *Historical Dictionary of Panama.* Metuchen, N.J.: Scarecrow, 1970.

Heravi, Mehdi. *Concise Encyclopedia of the Middle East.* Washington, D.C.: Public Affairs Press, 1973.

Hodgskin, Thomas. *Travels in the North of Germany,* vol. 1. New York: Augustus M. Kelley, 1969 (1820).

Horgan, Paul. *Great River: The Rio Grande.* New York: Holt, Rinehart and Winston, 1968 (1954).

Hornsby, S.J. *Nineteenth-Century Cape Breton.* Montreal: McGill Queen's University Press, 1992.

Hosmer, Dorothy. "Rhodes; and Italy's Aegean Islands." *National Geographic* (April 1941): 449-480.

Howard, C., ed. *West African Explorers*. Oxford: Oxford University Press, 1955.

Imperato, Pascal James. *Historical Dictionary of Mali*. 2nd ed. Metuchen, N.J.: Scarecrow, 1986.

Imperial Gazetteer of India. Oxford: Clarendon Press, 1908-1909.

International Yearbook and Statesmen's Who's Who. London: Burke's Peerage, 1956-1994.

Jackson, George, and Robert Devlin, eds. *Dictionary of the Russian Revolution*. New York: Greenwood, 1989.

Jacquemont, Victor. *Letters from India 1829-1832*. London: Macmillan, 1936.

Johnston, H.J.M., ed. *The Pacific Province*. Vancouver: Douglas & McIntyre, 1996.

Kalck, Pierre. *Historical Dictionary of the Central African Republic*. Metuchen, N.J.: Scarecrow, 1980.

Kaul, H.K. *Travellers' India: An Anthology*. Delhi: Oxford University Press, 1979.

King, Joan Wucher. *Historical Dictionary of Egypt*. Metuchen, N.J.: Scarecrow, 1984.

Kingsley, Mary H. *Travels in West Africa*. London: Frank Cass, 1965 (1897).

Kipling, Rudyard. *From Sea to Sea: Letters of Travel*. New York: Doubleday, Page & Co., 1923 (1899).

Knoll, Arthur J. *Togo under Imperial Germany 1884-1914*. Stanford, Ca.: Hoover Institution Press, 1978.

Kodansha Encyclopedia of Japan. Tokyo: Kodansha, 1983.

Kubijovyc, Volodymyr. *Ukraine: A Concise Encyclopedia*. Toronto: University of Toronto Press, 1963.

Kurian, George Thomas. *Historical and Cultural Dictionary of India*. Metuchen, N.J.: Scarecrow, 1976.

Kurtz, Laura S. *Historical Dictionary of Tanzania*. Metuchen, N.J.: Scarecrow, 1978.

Lamar, Howard R. *The Reader's Encyclopedia of the American West*. New York: Thomas Y. Crowell, 1977.

Lannois, M. Philippe. *The Gulf Emirates*. Geneva: Nagel, 1976.

Larousse du XXe Siècle. Paris: Libraire Larousse, 1933.

Lavender, D.S. *California*. New York: Norton, 1976.

Leamington, C.W. "The French in Tonquin." *Nineteenth Century* 30 (1891): 285-291.

Le Vine, Victor T., and Roger P. Nye. *Historical Dictionary of Cameroon*. Metuchen, N.J.: Scarecrow, 1974.

Lewis, Ethelreda., ed. *Trader Horn*. New York: Simon and Schuster, 1927.

Lewis, Wyndham. *Filibusters in Barbary*. New York: Robert M. McBride, 1932.

Liniger-Goumaz, Max. *Historical Dictionary of Equatorial Guinea*. Metuchen, N.J.: Scarecrow, 1979.

Little, Henry W. *Madagascar: Its History and People*. Edinburgh: William Blackwood and Sons, 1884.

Livingstone, David, and Charles Livingstone. *Narrative of an Expedition to the Zambesi and Its Tributaries, 1858-1864*. New York: Johnson Reprint, 1971 (1865).

Lobban, Richard. *Historical Dictionary of the Republics of Guinea Bissau and Cape Verde*. Metuchen, N.J.: Scarecrow, 1979.

Lux, William. *Historical Dictionary of the British Caribbean*. Metuchen, N.J.: Scarecrow, 1975.

McCullagh, Francis. *Italy's War for a Desert*. Chicago: F.G. Browne, 1913.

MacEwan, Grant. *Cornerstone Colony*. Saskatoon, Sask.: Western Producers Prairie Books, 1977.

McFarland, Daniel Mills. *Historical Dictionary of Ghana*. Metuchen, N.J.: Scarecrow, 1985.

Mackenzie, John. *Ten Years North of the Orange River*. London: Frank Cass, 1971 (1871).

McKenzie, Kenneth. "East of the Adriatic." *National Geographic* (Dec. 1912): 1159-1187.

McLeod, Lyons. *Travels in Eastern Africa*. London: Frank Cass, 1971 (1860).

MacNutt, W. Stewart. *New Brunswick, a History*. Toronto: Macmillan, 1963.

McPherson, J.M. *Ordeal by Fire*. New York: Knopf, 1982.

Mansfield, Charlotte. *Via Rhodesia*. London: Stanley Paul, 1911.

Marcosson, Isaac F. *An African Adventure*. New York: John Lane, 1921.

Martin, Michael Rheta, and Gabriel H. Lovett. *Encyclopedia of Latin American History*. Indianapolis: Bobbs-Merrill, 1968.

Martin, Phyllis M. *Historical Dictionary of Angola*. Metuchen, N.J.: Scarecrow, 1980.

Mercer, Charles. *Legion of Strangers*. New York: Pyramid, 1965.

Mercer, John. *Spanish Sahara*. London: George Allen & Unwin, 1976.

Minkus New World-Wide Postage Stamp Catalog. New York: Minkus Publications, 1974.

Morris, James. *Pax Britannica: The Climax of an Empire*. Harmondsworth: Penguin, 1981 (1968).

Morrison, J.H. *Streams in the Desert: A Picture of Life in Livingstonia*. New York: Negro Universities Press, 1969 (1919).

Morton, H.V. *In Search of South Africa*. London: Methuen, 1948.

Morton, W.L. *The Critical Years*. Toronto: McClelland and Stewart, 1964.

Mundy, Captain. *Pen and Pencil Sketches Being the Journal of a Tour in India*. London: John Murray, 1833.

New Encyclopædia Britannica. 15th ed. Chicago: Encyclopædia Britannica, 1991.

New Grolier Electronic Encyclopedia. Danbury, Conn.: Grolier Electronic Publishing, 1991.

Newitt, Malyn. *The Comoro Islands: Struggle against Dependency in the Indian Ocean*. Boulder, Colo.: Westview Press, 1984.

Newman, Peter C. *The Company of Adventurers*. Markham, Ont.: Viking Canada, 1985.

Norman, Henry. *All the Russias*. Boston: Longwood, 1977 (1914).

Northcliffe, Alfred Viscount. *My Journey round the World*. Philadelphia: J.B. Lippincott, 1923.

Ogot, Bethwell A. *Historical Dictionary of Kenya*. Metuchen, N.J.: Scarecrow, 1981.

Olson, James S., ed. *Dictionary of the Vietnam War*. New York: Greenwood, 1988.

Ormsby, Margaret A. *British Columbia*. Toronto: Macmillan, 1958.

Osbourne, Christine. *The Gulf States and Oman*. London: Croom Helm, 1977.

Ossendowski, Ferdinand. *Beasts Men and Gods*. New York: E.P. Dutton, 1922.

Ouellet, Fernand. *Lower Canada, 1791-1840*. Toronto: McClelland and Stewart, 1979.

Owen, William Fitz William. *Narrative of Voyages to Explore the Shores of Africa, Arabia, and Madagascar*. London: R. Bentley, 1833.

Oyewole, A. *Historical Dictionary of Nigeria*. Metuchen, N.J.: Scarecrow, 1987.

Phillips, Henry Albert. *Meet the Germans*. Philadelphia: J.B. Lippincott, 1929.

Pottle, Frederick A., ed. *Boswell on the Grand Tour: Germany and Switzerland 1764*. London: William Heinemann, 1953.

Prouty, Chris, and Eugene Rosenfeld. *Historical Dictionary of Ethiopia*. Metuchen, N.J.: Scarecrow, 1981.

Raban, Jonathan. *Arabia: A Journey through the Labyrinth*. New York: Simon and Schuster, 1979.

Range, Peter Ross. "Oman." *National Geographic* (May 1995): 112-138.

Rannie, W.F. *Saint Pierre and Miquelon*. Lincoln, Ont.: Rannie, 1977.

Rasmussen, R. Kent. *Historical Dictionary of Rhodesia / Zimbabwe*. Metuchen, N.J.: Scarecrow, 1979.

Report on Portuguese Guinea and the Liberation Movement. Washington, D.C.: U.S. Government Printing Office, 1970.

Richardson, R.N. *Texas, the Lone Star State*. Englewood Cliffs, N.J.: Prentice Hall, 1981.

Rivière, Claude. *Guinea: The Mobilization of a People*. Ithaca: Cornell University Press, 1977.

Robson, R.W. *Queen Emma*. Sydney: Pacific Publications, 1965.

Rosenthal, Eric, ed. *Encyclopaedia of Southern Africa*. 2nd ed. London: Frederick Warne & Co., 1964.

Rossi, Ernest E., and Jack C. Plano. *Latin America: A Political Dictionary*. Santa Barbara, Calif.: ABC-CLIO, 1992.

Rowe, Frederick W. *A History of Newfoundland and Labrador*. Toronto: McGraw-Hill Ryerson, 1980.

Sadler, Thomas, ed. *Diary, Reminiscences and Correspondence of Henry Crabb Robinson*. London: Macmillan, 1869.

Sandeman, E.F. *Eight Months in an Ox-Waggon*. Johannesburg: Africana Book Society, 1975 (1880).

Saunders, Christopher. *Historical Dictionary of South Africa*. Metuchen, N.J.: Scarecrow, 1983.

Schweinfurth, Georg. *The Heart of Africa: Three Years' Travels and Adventures in the Unexplored Regions of Central Africa from 1868 to 1871.* Chicago: Afro-Am Press, 1969 (1874).

Scott Standard Postage Catalogue. New York: Scott Publishing Co., 1993.

Shor, Jean, and Franc Shor. "On the winds of the Dodecanese." *National Geographic* (March 1953): 351-390.

Shukman, Harold, ed. *Blackwell Encyclopedia of the Russian Revolution.* Oxford: Blackwell Reference, 1988.

Simpich, Frederick. "What Is the Saar?" *National Geographic* (February 1935): 241-264.

Skrine, Francis Henry, and Edward Denison Ross. *The Heart of Asia.* London: Methuen, 1899.

Smallwood, Joseph R., ed. *Encyclopedia of Newfoundland and Labrador.* St. John's: Newfoundland Book Publishers / Harry Cuff, 1981-1994.

Smith, Harold E. *Historical and Cultural Dictionary of Thailand.* Metuchen, N.J.: Scarecrow, 1976.

Snow, John, ed. *The Concise Encyclopedia of Australia.* Revised 2nd ed. Buderim, Queensland: David Bateman, 1989.

Spencer, William. *Historical Dictionary of Morocco.* Metuchen, N.J.: Scarecrow, 1980.

Standard Encyclopedia of Southern Africa. Cape Town: Nasou, 1971.

Statesman's Yearbook. London: Macmillan, 1873-1994.

Stayt, Hugh A. *The Bavenda.* London: Frank Cass, 1968 (1931).

Stephens, John L. *Incidents of Travel in Central America, Chiapas and Yucatan.* New York: Dover, 1969 (1841).

Stevens, Richard P. *Historical Dictionary of the Republic of Botswana.* Metuchen, N.J.: Scarecrow, 1975.

Stevens, Russell L. *Guam, U.S.A.: Birth of a Territory.* Honolulu: Tongg Publishing, 1953.

Stigand, C.H. *The Land of Zinj.* New York: Barnes & Noble, 1966 (1913).

Struk, Danylo Husar, ed. *Encyclopedia of Ukraine.* Toronto: University of Toronto Press, 1993.

Swire, J. *Albania: The Rise of a Kingdom.* New York: Arno Press, 1971 (1929).

Thesiger, Wilfred. *Arabian Sands.* London: Longmans Green, 1959.

Thomas, Thomas Morgan. *Eleven Years in Central Southern Africa.* London: Frank Cass, 1971 (1872).

Thompson, Virginia, and Richard Adloff. *Historical Dictionary of the People's Republic of the Congo.* 2nd. ed. Metuchen, N.J.: Scarecrow, 1984.

Traill, Walter. *In Rupert's Land.* Toronto: McClelland and Stewart, 1970.

Treat, Ida. "Sailing Forbidden Coasts." *National Geographic* (September 1931): 357-386.

Trollope, Anthony. *The West Indies and the Spanish Main.* London: Chapman & Hall, 1860.

Twain, Mark. *More Tramps Abroad.* London: Chatto & Windus, 1922 (1897).

—. *A Tramp Abroad.* New York: Harper & Row, 1977 (1880).

Vieuchange, Michel. *Smara the Forbidden City.* London: Methuen, 1933.

Voll, John Obert. *Historical Dictionary of the Sudan.* Metuchen, N.J.: Scarecrow, 1978.

Wallace, Alfred Russel. *The Malay Archipelago: The Land of the Orang-Utan and the Bird of Paradise.* New York: Dover, 1962 (1869).

Waterton, Charles. *Wanderings in South America.* London: J.M. Dent, 1925 (1825).

Weeks, William Earl. *John Quincy Adams and American Global Empire.* Lexington, Ky.: University Press of Kentucky, 1992.

Weinstein, Warren. *Historical Dictionary of Burundi.* Metuchen, N.J.: Scarecrow, 1976.

Wollaston, A.F.R. *Pygmies and Papuans: The Stone Age To-Day in Dutch New Guinea.* London: Smith, Elder & Co., 1912.

Wood, Junius B. "A Visit to Three Arab Kingdoms." *National Geographic* (May 1923): 535-568.

Wood, Louis Aubrey. *The Red River Colony.* Toronto: University of Toronto Press, 1964.

Worldmark Encyclopedia of the Nations. New York: John Wiley and Sons, 1976.

Yapp, Peter. *Travellers' Dictionary of Quotation.* London: Routledge, 1983.

Index

About the Author

Born in one dead country, Newfoundland, and raised in a second, Upper Canada (Ontario), Les Harding has had a varied employment history: steel worker, movie extra, consumer advocate, expeditor, book store clerk, child care worker, bibliographic editor, indexer, historical researcher, and freelance writer. More recently he has been a reference librarian at the University of Waterloo and a civil servant with the government of Newfoundland and Labrador. He has a B.A. in philosophy and religion from McMaster University and an M.L.S. from the University of Western Ontario.

Les Harding is the author of *Voyages of Lesser Men: Thumbnail Sketches in Canadian Exploration* (Escart, 1991); *Historic St. John's: City of Legends* (Jesperson, 1993); *A Book in Hand is Worth Two in the Library* (McFarland, 1994); *Journeys of Remarkable Women: Their Travels on the Canadian Frontier* (Escart, 1994); and with Gary Brannon, *Carto-Quotes: An Inspirational Companion for the Map-Maker and the Map-User* (Upney, 1996).

Mr. Harding is married, has two children, and resides in St. John's, Newfoundland.

CPSIA information can be obtained at www.ICGtesting.com
Printed in the USA
LVOW081511030513

332227LV00004B/46/P